24 HOURS AT AGINCOURT

Also in the series

24 Hours at Waterloo by Robert Kershaw
24 Hours at the Somme by Robert Kershaw

24 HOURS AT
AGINCOURT

MICHAEL JONES

1 3 5 7 9 10 8 6 4 2

WH Allen, an imprint of Ebury Publishing,
20 Vauxhall Bridge Road,
London SW1V 2SA

WH Allen is part of the Penguin Random House group of companies
whose addresses can be found at global.penguinrandomhouse.com

Penguin
Random House
UK

First published by WH Allen in 2015
This edition first published by WH Allen in 2016

www.eburypublishing.co.uk

A CIP catalogue record for this book is available from the British Library

ISBN 9780753555460

Printed and bound in Great Britain by Clays Ltd, St Ives PLC

Penguin Random House is committed to a
sustainable future for our business, our readers
and our planet. This book is made from Forest
Stewardship Council® certified paper.

Contents

Preface

It is a pleasure to write this book for the 600th anniversary of Agincourt. The sequence of 24 hours follows the English and French armies from the moment they first sighted each other, on the ridge northwest of Blangy-sur-Ternoise on the afternoon of 24 October 1415, to the culmination of the battle a day later. In the introduction and early chapters it also allows the reader to become acquainted with the qualities of Henry V's leadership and the story of the campaign as a whole. Without an understanding of these it is hard to make sense of the battle.

It is important also to mention the three 'Ts' – time, testimony and terrain. Agincourt is one of the first major battles for which the '24 hours' approach is appropriate: the mechanical clock had been invented in the fourteenth century, and by the early fifteenth most towns, abbeys and palaces had one prominently displayed. Portable timepieces also existed. So it was possible, by 25 October 1415, to tell the time reasonably accurately – if a clock was available and if one actually wished to do so.

This form of measurement was known as 'merchant time', because it was most frequently used in the medieval world of business. The older system, where the day was divided into the eight 'hours' of religious practice (that actually existed at roughly three hourly intervals – from 'prime', at around 6 am, onwards) was known as 'monastic time', and this form of timekeeping was more general than exact. And along with sundials and water clocks, and at night with candles marked at hourly or three-hourly intervals, people would simply look at the position of the sun or moon in the sky.

This distinction is important because in the fifteenth century people still believed that the outcome of battle lay in the hands of God, and while it might be appropriate to measure time accurately on the approach to combat, it would be unlucky or inappropriate to do so during the actual engagement. Hence, chroniclers and writers of the day largely used the monastic system of time and the position of the sun to delineate the unfolding of events on the battlefield – and, as the sources sometimes contradict each other, the timings given in the time-line and the sequence of chapters can only be approximate.

Testimony from a battle makes it come alive for us, and allows us to hear the 'voices' of the participants. At Waterloo, whose 200th anniversary was commemorated in June 2015, a wealth of first-hand accounts, diaries and letters can be drawn upon. But in the late Middle Ages, where letters and diaries were a rarity, and first-hand battle reminiscences infrequent and relatively brief, a tapestry of different sources needs to be stitched together. This book draws on the relatively few eyewitness accounts that survive, the broader battle memory preserved in the chronicles of the time and supporting documentary material – alongside the visual evidence of tomb memorials and illuminated manuscripts. The main 'voices' are introduced as the text unfolds, and can also be found – for reference – in a brief summary ('Voices from Agincourt').

Medieval chivalric society was acutely conscious of the progression of battles in the recent past, and spun its own martial narrative from a web of previous victories and defeats. Agincourt has therefore been placed firmly within the story of other fourteenth- and early fifteenth-century campaigns, to get closer to the participants' own perceptions and to place their experiences in a larger military context.

Alongside the morale and motivation of the combatants, battlefield terrain is crucial to understanding Agincourt's outcome. I suggest that the plan formulated by the English drew upon hunting ritual as well as military tactics, and the key points of that argument are set out in the text and also in a supporting Appendix.

Our understanding of Agincourt has advanced considerably in the last few years, and this book owes a considerable debt to the scholarship of others – whose work is set out in the Bibliography, Acknowledgements and Endnotes sections.

Above all, *24 Hours at Agincourt* is the story of a friendship. One of these friends, the king of England, Henry V, has become immortalised through the passage of history; the other, his mentor and fighting companion Edward, Duke of York, largely forgotten. Yet I believe the battle plan these two men created together lies at the heart of the Agincourt story.

York dedicated his hunting treatise, *The Master of Game* – the first book on hunting in the English language – to Henry, and I have used this source with a broader aim, to try to illuminate the spirit of the king, the magnate and the army in 1415.

In one section of *The Master of Game* York discarded the elaborate protocol of the French source he was translating from (and in the book the duke would make valuable additions of his own) on the killing and stripping of the carcass, with the comment that the English forest bowman was well aware what he needed to do. Implicit in this observation (and York was too courteous to make it explicit) was a sentiment

ix

that spoke, respectfully but firmly, not just for England's huntsmen, but her soldiers as well:

We know how to fight – and we don't need lessons from the French, or anybody else.

Agincourt would demonstrate the truth of that.

Agincourt Time-Line – 1415

13 AUGUST   Henry V invades France.

22 SEPTEMBER Harfleur surrenders to the besieging English army.

8 OCTOBER   Henry begins his march to Calais.

11 OCTOBER   The English army reaches Arques.

13 OCTOBER   The crossing at Blanchetaque is held by the French. It becomes clear that Marshal Boucicaut and Constable d'Albret are building up a second army near Abbeville in addition to the original force gathering at Rouen.

14 OCTOBER   Henry's soldiers reach Pont-Remy on the Somme, only to find the bridge broken. The morale of the English army plummets.

15 OCTOBER   The French hold Amiens in strength against the English, forcing Henry's army further upriver.

17 OCTOBER   A skirmish at Corbie lifts English spirits.

19 OCTOBER   The English manage to cross the Somme between Voyennes and Béthencourt. The French armies junction at Péronne – and in a council of war resolve to fight the English within a week.

20 OCTOBER   French heralds appear before Henry and summon him to fight.

21 OCTOBER   North of Péronne, English troops see thousands of hoofprints in the mud and realise the size of the force assembling against them. The Duke of Brittany leaves Rouen for Amiens.

23 OCTOBER	Henry swings north, on the road to Calais. The French army shadows him on his right flank and prepares to cut across his path. The Duke of Brabant leaves Brussels with a small riding retinue, with the intention of joining the French.
24 OCTOBER	The English and French armies come into view on the ridge northwest of Blangy-sur-Ternoise.
14.00	English scouts catch their first glimpse of the French army.
16.00	The English army draws up in full battle array on the ridge at Blangy. The French are about three-quarters of a mile distant, with a small valley between the two forces – but they do not engage.
18.00	Shortly after sunset the French army pulls back to a night-time camp across the Agincourt–Tramecourt road, blocking the English army's escape route to Calais.
20.00	Henry keeps his army drawn up in formation well into nightfall, and then pitches camp at Maisoncelles, about a mile and a half south of the French. It starts raining heavily.
21.00	A surprise night-time attack on the English war camp is made by Arthur, Count of Richemont. It is beaten off – and afterwards the English king orders his troops to maintain essential silence.
24.00	Henry sends a picked body of knights to explore the battlefield by moonlight. This thorough night-time reconnaissance will yield a number of advantages – the setting of a clever archer ambush to help offset his foe's numerical superiority, and the creation of a battle plan (on the advice of Edward, Duke of York and Sir Thomas Erpingham) to provoke the French forward across

the muddy terrain, which owes as much to hunting practice as military tactics.

25 OCTOBER

06.00   Henry begins his battle preparations before sunrise. He plans to dedicate the battle's outcome to the martyred saints of Soissons, Crispin and Crispinian. The French, now under the nominal command of Charles, Duke of Orléans rather than the experienced soldier, Marshal Boucicaut, jettison Boucicaut's original battle plan and relegate their missile-bearing troops to the rear of the army, along with all their squires and servants.

08.00   Henry motivates his troops to fight, drawing upon the encouragement of the ordinary soldier he has used throughout the campaign and powerful pre-battle ritual. The French have now determined to fight an 'honour' battle, with most of the leading aristocrats in the vanguard and no effective command or control of their army.

09.00   The English army moves up from Maisoncelles to its battle position at the narrow end of the Agincourt–Tramecourt woods. The land forms an escarpment, dropping away from both sides of the battlefield, creating a funnel effect. Henry's soldiers take position on a ridge of firm, unploughed land. The majority of the battlefield has been newly ploughed and is exceptionally muddy. The French take up position at the broad end of the funnel, about 1,000 yards from the English line. Neither side is willing to make the first move and for two hours the armies watch each other.

11.00   Henry starts the battle. A signal is given by Sir Thomas Erpingham – rendered by the chroniclers as 'Nestrocque', most plausibly interpreted as

xiii

'*menée* stroke', the hunting call or signal for driving deer into a killing ground. A squadron of archers, placed in front of the main English position, quickly runs forward and puts the main French line – now bereft of missile-bearing troops – under fire. The archer ambush does the same thing, opening fire on the French flank from a concealed meadow within the Tramecourt woods. The main English line slowly starts to move forward, taunting the French, making 'un grand hué', the vocal imitation of the hunting horn. The provocation works. French patience now snaps – they launch their cavalry assault on the main archer positions and their men-at-arms start moving forward across the muddy battlefield.

11.30   The French cavalry attacks fail. They are under-manned and English archers strike at the unprotected flanks of the horses. The few horse-men who do get through collide with the stake wall protecting the bowmen's position and are easily brought to the ground and killed. The main French force of dismounted men-at-arms, grouped in two formations, the vanguard and second divi-sion, slowly closes in on the English position. The French, in their heavy armour, struggle across the waterlogged battlefield, growing increasingly breathless. Their advance is disrupted by riderless horses from the failed cavalry assault charging across their path, and by the intensity of English archer fire from their flanks. Sustaining heavy casualties the French form into three columns and attempt to punch their way through the English line of men-at-arms.

12.00   Fierce fighting takes place in the mêlée, the clash between the dismounted men-at-arms. The Duke

xiv

of York and the Earl of Suffolk are killed and the English king fights over the wounded body of his brother, Humphrey, Duke of Gloucester. The English bowmen, having loosed all their arrows on the French, now join in the fight using hand weapons – swords, daggers and even mallets, taking advantage of their superior mobility and driving deep into the French line.

12.30   The French second division crashes into the disintegrating vanguard, and as the English archers keep pushing forward – and their men-at-arms hold firm – thousands of French soldiers are asphyxiated in the crush. Henry, seeing a battle-winning opportunity – orders his men-at-arms to advance, and his opponents' position collapses. The French troops are suffocated or surrender in droves.

13.00   The Duke of Brabant and his small retinue appear on the battlefield. Brabant and his followers are quickly overwhelmed but the battle springs uneasily back to life. The French third line – which contains many horsemen – appears to be preparing to charge the English position and an attack is made on Henry's baggage train. Fearing he may still lose the battle, the English king orders the execution of his French prisoners.

13.30–14.00   The French third line melts away and the killing order is rescinded. It is clear at last that the English have won the battle. French casualties run into thousands; the English lose at most just over one hundred men. Henry thanks his soldiers and asks that all credit for the victory be given to God.

26 OCTOBER   The English army leaves the vicinity of Agincourt and resumes its march on Calais.

29 OCTOBER   Henry V and his soldiers reach Calais.

16 NOVEMBER   The English army ships across the Channel to Dover.

23 NOVEMBER   The Agincourt victory pageant is held in London.

Agincourt – List of Maps

1 The Agincourt campaign – the route of Henry V's army from Harfleur to Agincourt and the French forces shadowing him.

2 The traditional view of the battle of Agincourt.

3 The alternative view – the English use a mix of hunting ritual and battle tactics to goad the French forward.

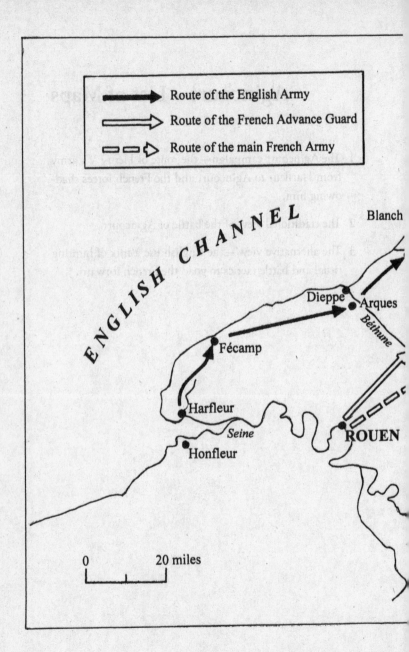

Route of the English Army

Route of the French Advance Guard

Route of the main French Army

ENGLISH CHANNEL

Blanch

Dieppe

Arques

Béthune

Fécamp

Harfleur

Seine

Honfleur

ROUEN

0   20 miles

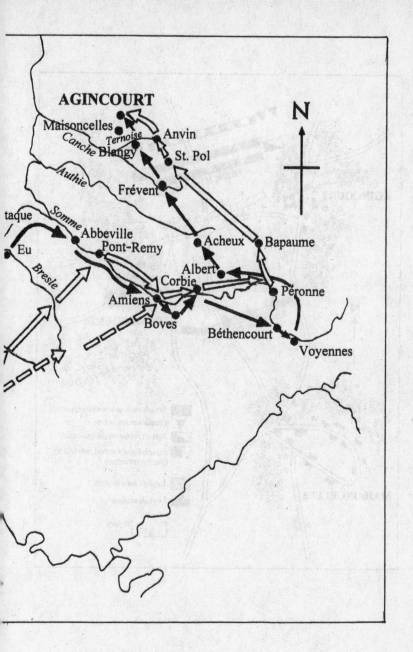

AGINCOURT

Maisoncelles

Canche

Ternoise Anvin

Blangy

St. Pol

Authie

Frévent

taque

Somme

Abbeville

Acheux

Bapaume

Eu

Pont-Remy

Bresle

Albert

Corbie

Péronne

Amiens

Boves

Béthencourt

Voyennes

N

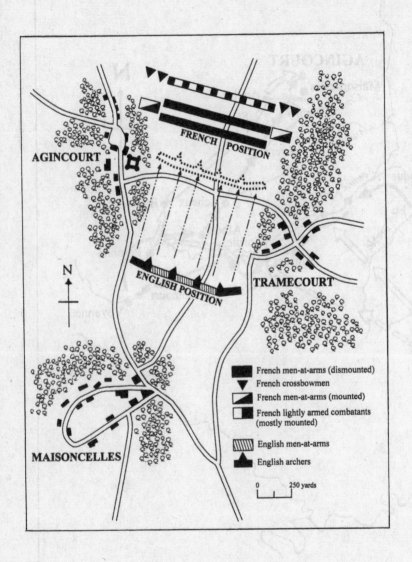

AGINCOURT

FRENCH POSITION

ENGLISH POSITION

TRAMECOURT

N

MAISONCELLES

■ French men-at-arms (dismounted)
▼ French crossbowmen
◨ French men-at-arms (mounted)
◨ French lightly armed combatants (mostly mounted)
▥ English men-at-arms
◣ English archers

0   250 yards

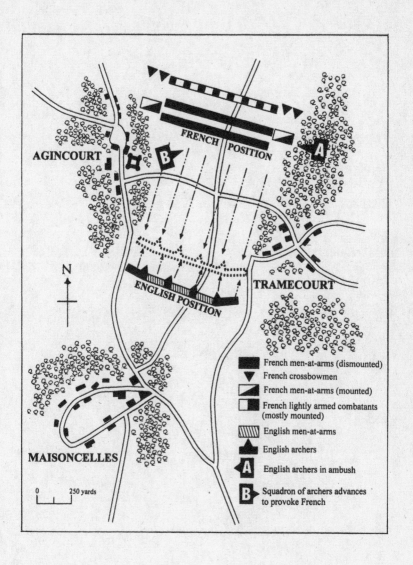

FRENCH POSITION

AGINCOURT

B

A

N

ENGLISH POSITION

TRAMECOURT

MAISONCELLES

0   250 yards

◼ French men-at-arms (dismounted)

▼ French crossbowmen

◢ French men-at-arms (mounted)

▯ French lightly armed combatants (mostly mounted)

▨ English men-at-arms

▲ English archers

A English archers in ambush

B Squadron of archers advances to provoke French

Introduction

O N 25 OCTOBER 1415 at Agincourt a small, bedraggled English army defeated a French force between four and six times its size. It was a stupendous victory – won at the cost of only a hundred or so casualties – that left thousands of French dead on the field of battle. The result was made even more powerful by the desperate condition of the English forces: riven with dysentery and without food or provisions – many soldiers had not eaten for over a week. The French by contrast were both well fed and well equipped. And yet they suffered an annihilating defeat. It was an astonishing triumph of the underdog, a meeting of David and Goliath, and this was how the battle was presented in celebratory pageants held across London in the aftermath of victory.

For the remarkable leader of this army, King Henry V, the battle secured eternal fame. His defeat of the French reverberated across Europe. The victory at Agincourt ensured the survival of his dynasty and allowed him fully to renew the Hundred Years War, returning to Normandy in 1417 generously bankrolled by the English Parliament, conquering the duchy two years later and in 1420 being recognised as successor to the throne of France by the Treaty of Troyes. His death at the relatively young age of 35, succumbing to dysentery after the siege of Meaux, left him at the pinnacle of his fame. He remains one of England's greatest warrior kings.

The strongest impact of all was made by the doughty warriors upon whom the king placed his trust: the English archers – and their formidable killing weapon, the longbow. The longbow had greater range than the crossbow and its arrows could be fired much more rapidly. Henry V deployed more than 5,000 archers on the field of Agincourt, and their massed fire – on French forces struggling through muddy and waterlogged ground – was devastating. The bowmen of England and Wales were recruited from the peasantry, and in an age acutely conscious of social standing this made their victory over the cream of the French aristocracy even more pleasing.

Agincourt quickly spawned its own folklore and mythology, never more powerfully than in Shakespeare's *Henry V*. Written some 180 years after the battle, the play nonetheless caught timeless truths about the bloody combat – and the extraordinary way that Henry cajoled and motivated his tired and demoralised soldiers. For the French the battle was a catastrophe: scarcely a family in the entire country was left unaffected by its outcome and the nation fell into a state of shock. The chronicler Pierre Cochon did not mince his words – for him it was 'the ugliest and most wretched event to befall France in the last thousand years'.

The broader story of Agincourt begins on 11 August 1415, when Henry V set sail for France with an invasion fleet of some 12,000 soldiers, sailors, craftsmen and members of the royal household. For the previous few weeks Henry had been assembling his army at Southampton. With a major campaign imminent, some of his soldiers hurriedly put their affairs in order. Five days earlier Richard de Vere, Earl of Oxford, waiting to sail with 29 men-at-arms and 79 archers, drew up his will. If he died on campaign, he wanted to be buried with his ancestors in the priory church of Earl's Colne in Essex. He left his goods and chattels to his wife. The arrangements were modest, and their lack of ceremony might suggest that Oxford, an experienced soldier, sensed the challenges he was likely to face on this great expedition.

Vere's enthusiasm for all things military was shown in the summer of 1405, when at the age of 19 he had served in a fleet raiding the northern French coast led by Henry IV's second son, Thomas, Duke of Clarence. A year later he accompanied the king on an expensive and ultimately fruitless expedition to Wales against the revolt of Owen Glendower. In 1412 he joined the force under Clarence sent to support the faction of Charles, Duke of Orléans in France. Vere was rarely at court and little interested in regional power – it was the soldier's career that fascinated him.

The Sussex knight Sir Thomas West, also about to set out with the royal army with a retinue of 14 men-at-arms and 40 archers, was similarly cautious in his own will. West had a distinguished martial pedigree: his grandfather had fought at Crécy in 1346; his father had served with distinction in the Calais garrison and also in Ireland in the reign of Richard II. In the event of his death during the forthcoming campaign, West requested that no more than £40 was to be spent on food, drink and candles on the day of his funeral, and that a further £24 be paid to two priests to celebrate divine service each day, to pray for his soul for a further two years.

The hustle and bustle of the preparations found its way into the records of the time. The household accounts of John Mowbray, Earl of Norfolk, the marshal of Henry's army, cast a fascinating light on how an English aristocrat prepared to go to war with his king. He had a large retinue of 55 men-at-arms and 147 archers. Through late July and early August Mowbray was busy equipping his men, buying bows, arrows and bowstrings from local fletchers and tradesmen. He also

3

spent the massive sum of over £70 (about £30,000 in today's money) on his own armour. It was Mowbray's first campaign, and he was keen to cut a fine figure.

One London armourer supplied him with steel plates to encase his upper body, another two helmets and a third protective plates for his arms and legs. Further pieces were provided for his hands and feet. Internal padding was supplied to prevent chafing. The earl also spent handsomely on heraldic garments to wear over this military equipment. An embroiderer was paid £40 (over £16,500 today) for a silk surcoat or tunic decorated with Mowbray's coat of arms. This lavish expenditure forced the earl to borrow money to meet his costs.

At the other end of the spectrum, more humble men-at-arms were also feeling the strain. John Cheney was a squire in the retinue of Sir John Cornwall, and he wrote anxiously to a friend, Sir John Pelham, in mid-July, in one of the rare private letters that have survived from this time:

> *Right worshipful and worthy Sir, I recommend myself to you with all my heart, thanking you for the great kindness and gentleness that you have shown me up to now, without fail, praying you might always be of good continuance, and that you will wish to know that the king and all the lords here are well blessed by God ... Furthermore, you will want to know that I am here, and have been at great costs and expense, wherefore I need to borrow a notable sum before I go and fare from my house ... having full hope and trust in your gracious and gentle person, to help and succour me at this time, in my great necessity, to lend me some notable sum of gold such as the bearer of this, my servant Thomas Garnetier, shall truly declare ... praying the Holy Trinity send you honour, prosperity and joy. Written in haste at Southampton.*

Cheney was from Drayton Beauchamp in Buckinghamshire. His family had been involved in rebellion and John had only just received a royal pardon. He had real potential as a soldier, described by one of his contemporaries as 'a man of exceptional strength', but was preoccupied by money worries and it was hard for him, in such circumstances, to see any bigger picture. Henry needed to inspire men like Cheney to have any hope of victory in France.

The majority of Henry's army were bowmen. Tough and self-reliant, they were recruited from the English and Welsh peasantry, skilled in archery and attracted by the wage of six-pence a day if they signed up for the campaign. On 4 August, Sir James Harrington's contingent passed through the city of Salisbury on its way to Southampton. An argument broke out between some of the townsmen and Harrington's bowmen.

The city's ledger book recorded:

> *On 4 August, the Sunday after St Peter in Chains, a crowd of the Duke of Lancaster's men lodged at Fisherton by Salisbury, whose leader was James Harrington, engaged to set out with the king overseas, and they attacked many of the city's men on Fisherton bridge, driving them off with arrows and swords and killing a number of them with arrows.*

In the ensuing clash five men were killed, four of them men of Salisbury. The archers were the least well armoured of Henry's troops – an old helmet, a leather doublet or chain mail tunic were luxuries for them – but they knew how to look after themselves in a fight.

As Henry V's army assembled, the king had a clear vision of its purpose – to renew the claim of his great-grandfather Edward III to the throne of France and enforce it by military might. Titus Livius, born Tito Livio dei Frulovisi, an Italian scholar who drew upon the remembrances of Henry's brother Humphrey, Duke of Gloucester in order to write an account of the English king's life, put it like this:

> Henry decided to win back the kingdom of France which belonged to him by birth-right. First, however, he sought advice in all the schools and universities from men learned in divine and human law whether he might justly, and without fear of wrong-doing, seek to regain the crown of France through force of arms. The king then sent out an embassy with instructions to present his claim to a council of the French and, if the French should refuse him justice, to announce to them that the king would come with an army to claim his rights.

These carefully orchestrated preliminaries were important. They followed the medieval notion of a 'just war' – establishing the case that Henry's claim was legally and morally justified – and communicating it to the expedition's participants. The message struck home. John Hardyng, who would fight on the campaign, expressed the ordinary soldier's understanding of it: the right of the English king to France 'by succession of blood' was clear.

To advance his claim to France, Henry had first to draw a line under the civil war of his father's reign and create a mood of reconciliation and hope for the future. The king had to be tough in rooting out conspiracy – and Henry admirably showed his mettle in dealing with the Southampton plot, a conspiracy of a small group of disaffected aristocrats, shortly before the expedition set sail – while giving the noblemen of families previously disloyal the chance to rally round the flag. Henry achieved this, typically, through powerful symbolic ritual.

Henry was well aware that his father had come to the throne through the deposition and likely murder of an anointed king, Richard II. He realised that this unresolved issue could hang spectre-like over the military enterprise he wished to conduct. As a medieval army lined up to fight, its combatants were faced with the possibility of a sudden, violent death. Many would try to make their peace with God in any way they could, and sometimes an improvised soldierly communion sprang up in the ranks, using whatever was to hand: for example, finding three-leafed clovers to represent the Trinity and putting up makeshift wooden crosses. As men prepared themselves for battle, they would inevitably wonder if their commander might be punished by God for a particular sin or fault.

It was a tribute to both Henry's martial and human instinct that he anticipated such a scenario and pre-empted it. At the beginning of his reign he reburied Richard II with full reverence in Westminster Abbey. His father, Henry IV, had disposed of the unfortunate king with scarcely any ceremony at all, and Henry was making a strong, visible statement to his realm – he wished to make peace with the past. The chronicler Thomas Walsingham related:

In this year [1413] the body of Richard, once king of England, buried in the church of the Dominicans at King's Langley was lifted from its tomb and taken to London and buried at Westminster, as a king should be.

As Walsingham put it, Henry venerated the deposed king as much as his own father and for that reason had him 'regally entombed at Westminster'. But Henry did more than that. He managed to transform Richard II from an omen of misfortune into a symbol of blessing. Stories were soon circulating at court – doubtless with the king's encouragement – that the deposed king had foretold a brilliant military future for him,

7

Richard believing that Henry's 'immense soldierly industry' would one day shine throughout the world. Whether founded in truth or not, this powerful legend could only help Henry's military cause.

Sir Simon Felbrigg had been Richard II's standard-bearer; he now joined Henry V's army for the Agincourt campaign. It was an auspicious moment for the new king, and one that would have reassured his men. And this king really cared about his soldiers. Henry had a strong interest in battlefield surgery, and in his preparations he drew up contracts for two surgeons, Thomas Morstede and William Bradwardine, who were to serve for the duration of the campaign. Morstede was a highly skilled practitioner, author of one of our first surgical treatises, and in his will he left a host of surgical instruments and also a suit of armour – a reminder that surgeons could fight as well as tend to the wounded. Significantly, Henry had stipulated that Morstede bring a team of surgeons with him, a most unusual step which would have attracted the notice of the gathering soldiers.

Morstede brought 12 additional surgeons, a horse and cart to carry their supplies, extra medicines and an escort of three archers. His colleague William Bradwardine brought another nine surgeons with him. They were there to minister to the entire army, not just the privileged few. The Agincourt expedition was the first English force to be accompanied by a full medical train.

Such provision of care from a military leader was exemplary. A fifteenth-century illuminated manuscript depicted Alexander the Great visiting his wounded soldiers. Alexander was esteemed as a warrior hero in the Middle Ages and his deeds held up as a model of leadership. By sharing his medical resources, Henry attained a similar standard and helped to forge a mood of unity within his army.

A mood of unity within an army, however, depends on something more durable – a structure to bind it together. Henry's choice would be a telling one – he would make the third-century Christian warrior St George a symbol for all his soldiers. Today we are accustomed to seeing the red cross of St George – the English flag – as a symbol of national identity. The powerful sense of patriotism is captured by Shakespeare at the end of Henry's rousing speech at Harfleur:

> ... *upon this charge*
> *Cry, 'God for Harry! England and Saint George!'*

The banner of St George is seen prominently in the Sir Laurence Olivier film *Henry V*, flying proudly above the English army. This patriotism is based on a real event – the deeply shared experience of all Henry's soldiers in 1415.

When Henry V came to the throne St George was increasingly, but not yet exclusively, associated with English fortunes. The army of Edward I which invaded Scotland carried a banner of the saint, and armbands displaying the red cross were given out to some of the troops. King Edward III took things further, making St George the patron of his new chivalric body, the Order of the Garter. Edward also encouraged the use of 'Saint George!' as a formidable war cry. In a remarkable feat of arms on the Crécy campaign of 1346, two English knights defiantly rode up to a well-defended river crossing and uttered a vigorous shout of 'Saint George for Edward!' The French were nonplussed. The knights then laid about them, killing two of the enemy and wounding many others before speeding off.

Henry V now chose to build on his illustrious predecessor's achievement, widening the saint's appeal to encompass the entire army – and indeed the whole nation. He achieved this by making St George accessible to everyone. Military ordinances drawn up by the king compelled his men to wear a large red St George's Cross on their front and back, at all times. This was for the purpose of recognition – Henry was providing a uniform for his army. Although the ordinances that survive were compiled after the battle, there is good reason to believe that the measures were first put into effect during the Agincourt campaign. Soldiers were then encouraged to appeal to the saint for his intercession. Henry's chaplain tells us that as the army marched along the River Somme, with morale faltering, the troops sought the protection of 'the blessed Saint George, to mediate for us between God and our poor people'.

We see this clearly in the memorial brass to Sir Simon Felbrigg in St Margaret's, Felbrigg, Norfolk. Sir Simon is shown with the cross of St George marked on the pieces of his armour fitted to protect his armpits. The red cross was intended not only for recognition in combat but also to invoke the protection of the saint in battle – and the brass, commemorating the last campaign in which Felbrigg fought, forms a time capsule of the Agincourt experience.

Henry made such sentiments concrete by ensuring that his soldiers not only wore the cross of St George, but saw actual depictions of the saint as often as possible. The household accounts of John Mowbray reveal what the king had in mind. As the army gathered at Southampton, Mowbray purchased 'a piece of cloth of gold, sufficient to make a cross, on a trapping bearing the image of Saint George'. On top of his tent, a huge metal weather vane had been fashioned, again depicting St George. Amid the army's banners and standards, Henry wanted his men always to be able to see the saint, wherever they looked – and thus feel St George was actually with them.

The focal point to all this ritual was the banner of St George. A medieval army depended on its banners and standards, not merely for recognition and display, but as rallying points during battle. Soldiers would look to the men grouped around them to see how well they were fighting. It was always a crisis if a banner went down and a sign of valour if a man recovered it. Henry's ordinances of war made clear the importance of the banner of St George within the army – and to carry it on campaign and during combat was an exceptional honour. As the expedition assembled, the king made a striking gesture, one that had a considerable impact on his men.

Thomas Strickland was a poor squire from Cumbria. He had little land or money and was constantly in debt. As great aristocrats arrived in Southampton with retinues of hundreds of men, Strickland could scrape together only two men-at-arms and six archers. He was a little-known soldier and Henry had many magnates in his army of proven reputation. Yet the king bestowed upon Strickland the highest martial honour – the right to bear the banner of St George for the duration of the campaign.

Here it is worth noting a perceptive comment made about Henry V by a Frenchman, the Monk of Saint-Denis: 'he knew how to exalt the lowly' – he could make the ordinary soldier feel special. Strickland himself never forgot the experience, proud to say that he was 'bearer of the banner of St George' at Harfleur and Agincourt; he would go on to serve on all Henry's later campaigns.

The penurious Cumbrian squire had fought for the royal army at Shrewsbury 12 years earlier, in 1403, a civil war battle that saw Henry's father, Henry IV, fighting for his very survival and that of the fledgeling Lancastrian dynasty. It was the battle in which Henry himself, then the 16-year-old Prince of Wales, had received his own initiation in the bloody

11

art of combat. Strickland had distinguished himself in that terrible clash of arms, for he was later rewarded for his 'good services'. Another grant, of two fine horses formerly belonging to Henry Percy, nicknamed 'Hotspur', Henry IV's opponent that day, suggest Strickland was fighting in the desperate mêlée around the royal standard when Hotspur launched a do-or-die attack that came close to winning the battle. In 1415, therefore, Henry's choice powerfully recalled and paid tribute to the bravery of the humble soldier. He also sent a strong message to his gathering army: on this campaign, it was courage that mattered, not just rank. This was the spirit by which the king hoped to bind his men on the challenging road ahead.

On 14 August 1415 Henry's army landed in Normandy, on the Seine estuary, close to the port of Harfleur. The king's first aim was to capture this strongly defended town and make it a base for any future operations. More than 2,000 English men-at-arms, and nearly 9,000 archers, along with several hundred masons, carpenters and labourers, were now deployed.

The subsequent siege prompted Shakespeare's celebrated soliloquy beginning 'Once more unto the breach, dear friends, once more', and his exhortation to 'imitate the action of the tiger' was, in August 1415, heeded by one Englishman in particular. The English landing was several miles north of Harfleur, at a place called Frileuse, and one soldier's testimony brought alive the moment the army first reached foreign soil.

In Shakespeare's *Henry V* we learn that the likeable ruffian Jack Falstaff has died broken-hearted after being banished by the new king. Henry V had to organise his military expedition with care and there was no place for Falstaff's antics. Although Falstaff was a fictional character, he has often been confused with a genuine historical figure, the medieval soldier John Fastolf. That the two could not have been more different gives the developing campaign story an ironic twist. In the play, Falstaff's death marked a rite of passage and the arrival of manhood and responsible and effective kingship for Henry V. In real life, it was the encounter between Henry and Fastolf which set the tone for the campaign in France.

Fastolf was an ambitious 35-year-old Norfolk squire. Brought up in an aristocratic household, as a 12-year-old he had gained an appetite for adventure when, as a humble page, he travelled across Europe in the retinue of Henry Bolingbroke – the future Henry IV – and ended up on a pilgrimage to Jerusalem. He had learned his soldierly trade in tough frontier fighting in Ireland, joined a sea expedition to Flanders and held a military captaincy in Gascony. Now, on 14 August 1415, with the great English ships anchoring off the French shore, he was first off the small boats, leaping into the water 'up to his sword belt', as he later proudly recalled. Henry was struck by Fastolf's enthusiasm and decided to draw his soldiers' attention to it. With the landing complete and the army assembled, the king promised Fastolf the first lands conquered in France. He kept his word. In January 1416 it was duly recorded that Fastolf had received the lordship of Frileuse – confiscated from its French owner.

The heavily defended town of Harfleur was a daunting sight to the English soldier and Henry's chaplain gives us a striking eyewitness account of it:

> The town is situated at the very end of a valley, on the banks of the River Seine, from which the sea flows in around the middle of the town, ebbing away to a distance of a mile or more. And the fresh-water river, which descends through the middle of the valley, fills the ditches to a good depth and breadth.

The chaplain was struck by the strength of Harfleur's fortifications:

> *The town was fortified with high and well-built towers and three gates. And in front of the entrance to every one of these gates, the enemy had constructed a strong defensive work, which we call a barbican.*

Harfleur certainly had substantial water defences, for the River Lézarde ran through the town from north to south – its entry and exit points protected by towers and gates – to join the Seine estuary. There were three town gates: the northeastern could be protected by flooding from the river valley; the southeastern was sheltered by the river. The most vulnerable was the Leure gate, but it was protected by a massive barbican which reached almost to the height of the surrounding walls. The garrison could gain access to it through a moveable bridge across the moat and then take shelter there and fire on attackers.

Harfleur was a considerable prize. The port dominated the Seine estuary and it would be an ideal base if the king wished to return to Normandy with an army of conquest. On the present campaign, its capture would allow Henry the military options of attacking along the Seine towards Rouen and Paris or towards the English garrison at Calais. Henry had to plan his next move. Harfleur's normal garrison strength was 50 men (35 men-at-arms and 15 crossbowmen) but 300 extra soldiers had just gained access to the town under the leadership of the talented young French nobleman Raoul de Gaucourt. The king needed to stop further reinforcements arriving and conclude matters swiftly before an opposing army could be gathered against him, so that his men would not be caught between an ongoing siege and a strong relief force.

Henry first completed the encirclement of the town. On 18 August his brother, the Duke of Clarence, took a force round to the eastern side of Harfleur and established a blockade. The soldiers set to work digging protective trenches around the English war camp, putting up outposts and keeping watch for any French counter-attack. Then the king began to position his cannon – the biggest of which were 12 feet long and two feet wide. To be really effective against such impressive fortifications, Henry needed to get them as close to the defences as possible. But pushing the cannon forward carried a real risk, putting them within range of the enemy's own artillery and making them vulnerable to a spoiling raid from the defending garrison.

Henry had recruited more than 30 skilled gunners for the campaign to spearhead his attack, supported by over a hundred labourers. Now the king showed astonishing energy, supervising the construction of gun emplacements, protective trenches and moveable wooden screens, to be raised for a volley of fire and lowered to protect these specialists from the enemy. He was seen urging his men on and advising them on the placement of the cannon. Before long, all was ready and a deafening bombardment ensued: 'Behold the ordnance on their carriages, / With fatal mouths gaping on girded Harfleur.'

In Olivier's *Henry V*, the first shot of the siege shows a large cannon being manhandled towards the town's walls. Contemporaries were fascinated and awe-struck by these monsters. The cast-iron guns could launch projectiles weighing up to a quarter of a ton. They gave the largest nicknames: 'London', 'The Messenger', 'The King's Daughter'. The Monk of Saint-Denis described the terrible firing of these 'enormous stones, enveloped in thick clouds of foul smoke', emitting a 'terrifying noise' as if 'vomited from the very jaws of hell'. Their barrage continued day and night. It was the focal point of the siege.

With his guns in action, Henry spread a brutally effective joke to lift the spirit of his troops. The good commander instinctively knows how to communicate with his men and can use simple, down-to-earth imagery to make his point. The particular image used by the king was immortalised by Shakespeare, for early in the play *Henry V* we learn that, mockingly, the French have sent a gift of tennis balls to disparage Henry's claim to the throne of France, suggesting instead that he occupy himself with a little light recreation. The king's reply is appropriately robust:

> *When we have matched our rackets to these balls*
> *We will, in France, by God's grace play a set.*

He then rounds on the Dauphin, the son of the French king Charles VI, who he believes is behind this flippancy:

> *Tell the pleasant Prince this mock of his*
> *Hath turned his balls to gun stones.*

The story is no mere dramatic invention for it is found in a number of contemporary sources. Thomas Elmham confirmed that tennis balls were sent to the king before his invasion of France, and John Strecche, canon at the Augustinian priory of St Mary's Kenilworth, close to Kenilworth Castle where the Dauphin's embassy was received, gave us Henry's forceful reply: 'I shall play with such balls in the Frenchman's own streets that they will stop joking, and for their mocking game win nothing but grief.'

In his youth Henry was no wastrel: he was a good soldier and administrator, but his reputation for wild living had a basis in historical fact. Chroniclers noted approvingly that once Henry became king he dismissed his drinking cronies and then developed the necessary seriousness and maturity to govern his people properly. As Thomas Walsingham put it, he had transformed into 'another man, zealous for honesty, modesty and gravity'. And this new self-discipline was vital to win the respect of his army. Nevertheless his earlier drinking companionship in the taverns of London – or, in Titus Livius's words, such pleasures as 'the licence of a soldier's life permits' – meant that he could talk to the ordinary soldier without affectation.

Henry V was the first English king to deliberately prefer the English language, or vernacular, to the language largely used by court, government and aristocracy, French. Henry regularly addressed his subjects in English, and when he sent newsletters to the major towns of his realm, informing them of the progress of his campaign, he wrote in English. In other words, he chose a language that everyone in his army – not just the nobility – could understand. And when he addressed his soldiers, the king's use of English was refreshingly direct and surprisingly modern, showing the down-to-earth way he spoke to his men.

Today we might call this effective man management, and in an age where rank, status and the social hierarchy counted for so much it was an unusual and important skill. As the Monk of Saint-Denis emphasised – with grudging yet very real respect – Henry 'made it a point of honour to treat everybody [in his army], of whatever rank or degree, with the utmost affability'. A London chronicler described him doing the rounds during the siege of Harfleur to encourage his men. His words seem to have been remembered almost verbatim: 'Fellows, be of good cheer! Save your energy, keep cool [be kele you well] and maintain your calm for, with the

17

love of God, we shall soon have good tidings.' On another occasion he called them 'Lads!' ('Loddys!') – one of the first instances the use of this word was recorded in a medieval chronicle.

The French clearly underestimated Henry, as both a warrior and as a king. And in devising a riposte, timing is everything. The king did not release the details of the episode with the tennis balls before the invasion, but waited until his men were already assembled outside Harfleur. Then Henry allowed the story to spread and the gist of it was soon circulating in popular ballads. This was a clever ploy, for now the slightest gesture of the French would anger the entire army. Henry's tough response would raise a laugh in the ranks and lift morale, with the firing from his big guns 'shattering the town itself and its walls', as the late medieval chronicler and historian Adam of Usk noted with grim satisfaction. This was a most effective rejoinder – and, as one popular chronicler made clear, Henry had visibly returned the compliment and his soldiers enjoyed seeing it: 'He played at tennis with his hard gun stones.'

These guns were supported by an array of wooden machines, which catapulted projectiles. Henry was concentrating his fire on the massive barbican protecting Harfleur's Leure gate. It was a tough target – but the king knew that if he could win the barbican and place his guns there, the intensity of fire would breach the walls and allow an assault on the town. The garrison performed heroically, blocking up gaps in the walls and repairing the defences. Henry's chaplain was moved to declare: 'I should not be altogether silent in praise of the enemy. They could not in the judgement of our men have resisted our attacks with greater determination and skill.'

However, the sheer weight of firepower began to tell. By 16 September the barbican was badly damaged and its masonry disintegrating. With commendable spirit, the garrison sallied out in a surprise attack and destroyed a couple of the English guns. Henry's response was immediate: he launched a counter-move, sending an assault party to storm the barbican. It was a dangerous assignment, because the soldiers had to fight their way in under fire from French troops manning the nearby town walls. A number of the king's companions expected the command to go to an experienced captain. They were surprised when Henry gave it to a relatively untested nobleman, Sir John Holland, described by the chaplain as 'brave and high spirited, though young'.

Holland proved to be an inspired choice. His father had lost his lands for supporting rebellion against Henry IV, but the new king was giving his son the chance to restore his family's reputation and regain their estates. Holland now led the assault with élan. He and his men first set fire to the barbican with a volley of flaming arrows and then ran forward and stuffed firebrands through the holes in its walls. Using a clever trick – perhaps suggested by Henry himself – they scattered an inflammable substance (possibly sulphur) to intensify the flames, then burst into the stronghold. The French retreated to their inner defences, but these were subjected to the same treatment and the triumphant Holland then raised his banner over the whole fortress to signal victory. The garrison was forced to retreat to the town walls, hastily blocking the Leure gate with timber, stone and earth. But their position was now highly vulnerable.

Onlookers were impressed by Holland's bravery. In giving him the chance to lead the attack, Henry showed astute judgement. And in allowing the young aristocrat a chance to win his spurs, so the king motivated his army.

Holland's success paved the way for Harfleur's surrender. Henry's chaplain surveyed the damage done to the town. Its fine towers had been 'rendered defenceless' and throughout Harfleur 'very fine buildings, even in the middle of the town, either lay altogether in ruins or were so shaken as to be exceedingly damaged'. On 18 September the French captain Raoul de Gaucourt opened negotiations. He felt the terms offered by Henry were too harsh – and the English in return prepared for an all-out assault. Proclamations were made throughout the army to ready men for the attack and a ferocious bombardment was unleashed. This prompted new negotiations, which led to a formal treaty of surrender being agreed on 22 September. The following day Henry entered Harfleur in triumph.

The king had faced determined resistance from Harfleur's defenders and this angered him. Though a superb military commander there was a darker side to Henry's personality – excessive severity. He could be needlessly cruel. Great leaders have to be ruthless, but this was Henry's Achilles heel. The chronicler Monstrelet caught the harshness of his response:

> *The greater part of the townsmen were made prisoner and forced to ransom themselves for large sums, then driven from the town with most of the women and children... It was a pitiful sight to see the misery of these people as they left their town and their belongings behind.*

We must be careful not to project our own modern sensibilities on to the tough realities of medieval warfare. If the besieger felt he had a right to a town, he would be under a moral obligation to protect its inhabitants only if the gates were freely opened to him at the outset. At the end of July Henry had written a last letter to the king of France from

Southampton. In it he had cited 'the law of Deuteronomy', making clear that 'whoever prepares to attack a town begins by offering it peace'. Since Harfleur had spurned his initial peace offer, it would have to face the consequences of its action.

Nevertheless, even within the conventions of the time observers felt that Henry's behaviour was vindictive. The Monk of Saint-Denis was struck by the peremptory expulsion of 'the sick, the poor and the elderly', and the Welsh commentator Adam of Usk, while appreciative of Henry's achievement, believed that the king's interpretation of laws of war went too far, describing how inhabitants were stripped naked and humiliated, 'with halters and nooses around their necks'. This was an excessive reaction – and clemency would have suited Henry's political purposes much better.

Yet winning Harfleur was a considerable success and Henry soon recovered his equanimity. He wrote a report of the siege to the city of London, expressing his delight at the force of the artillery bombardment and speaking movingly of his confidence in the 'fine power and good diligence' of his soldiers. But their achievement had come at a cost. Soon after the siege began, an alarming outbreak of dysentery had spread among the king's soldiers, striking down some of his leading followers. Strangely, it seems to have been more virulent among the aristocracy than the ordinary soldier. But soon it was decimating the army.

This was a most demoralising event, made conspicuous by the prominent figures in the army who fell victim. Michael de la Pole, Earl of Suffolk died, as did Richard Courtenay, Bishop of Norwich, a personal friend of the king's, who had been with him at the siege of Aberystwyth eight years earlier, when Henry had first demonstrated his interest in artillery. The death of this young clergyman was an ill omen – and the loss of Thomas FitzAlan, Earl of Arundel, an experienced warrior, who had fought against Glendower's rebellion and led a force on Henry's behalf in support of the Burgundians in 1411, was another. Arundel was carried back across the Channel, but died early in October. In his will he recalled a vow, made jointly with the king, that they would both make an offering each year to the shrine of St John of Bridlington, a saint revered within the Lancastrian court circle. His last thought was for his soldiers, directing his executors that 'all those who were with me at Harfleur in France be paid all the arrears of their wages'.

Another personal blow to Henry was the death of John Philip of Kidderminster. Philip was not a great aristocrat or promising prelate, but his memorial brass proudly proclaimed that he had been a friend of the king. Henry knew Philip as the nephew of one of his most trusted advisers, Sir Thomas Erpingham, and the friendship had come about through Philip's prowess as a soldier. He had distinguished himself in combat at Saint-Cloud when a small English force under the Earl of Arundel had supported the Burgundian side in the French civil war, an expedition Henry had sponsored. The memorial also recorded that Philip had fought with daring and bravery at the siege of Harfleur. The friendship of king and humble knight showed once again how Henry could cut across the divide of rank and status.

The wave of death and sickness hit the expedition hard. More than 1,500 men had to be invalided home in a convoy of boats. This was a very real crisis, as Adam of Usk made clear:

> Many died of dysentery during the siege; thousands of others returned home. The most prominent amongst them was one of the king's own brothers, Thomas, Duke of Clarence. Some went legitimately, having got permission to do so, while others were

invalided home because they were sick, but there were some
others who, disgraceful to relate, simply deserted the army.

Henry's chaplain estimated that the disease carried off a substantial body of troops, and 'directly afflicted or disabled the
remainder', so that the army's active strength – once a garrison had been installed at Harfleur – was left at a little under
6,000 men. Throughout this crisis the king showed his
mettle: his physician won fame through his efforts to heal the
sick and we find a record of that standard of care in the
household accounts of John Mowbray, the earl marshal.

Here was a man close to Henry, responsible for discipline
and regulation of the troops, with real concern for the suffering of his soldiers. The unfortunate Mowbray had been struck
down himself, and was soon purchasing medicines for 'the
sickness of the flux', and setting up his private toilet – a
freshly constructed seated latrine – as the ravages of dysentery set in. Yet he found the time and energy to tend his men
and try to prevent the disease, probably caused by infected
drinking water, from spreading. Mowbray's final contribution to the soldiers' wellbeing, before he was himself invalided
home, was to ensure that every man was issued with his own
drinking flask, regularly refilled, to protect them from passing
the infection on to one another.

To properly replenish his forces Henry had to take drastic
action. So those badly affected by disease were taken home in
a flotilla of boats and replacements found for many of them.
This was a complicated logistical operation that may have
brought the total strength of the English army back up to
around 7,000 men. But Henry's need for reinforcements
forced him to stay in Harfleur longer than he had anticipated.
He had to hold the port and await the arrival of fresh troops.
Henry needed to do something to lift their morale and his

response was masterly. On 26 September he sent a formal challenge to Louis de Guienne, the Dauphin of France, the 19-year-old son of Charles VI, inviting him to a duel.

By issuing his challenge from 'his town of Harfleur' Henry was throwing down the gauntlet to the French court and making clear his serious wish to give battle. He was also making a joke to cheer up his soldiers. This invitation to man-to-man combat was proclaimed to the English army with mock-theatrical ritual:

> We offer to place our quarrel, at the will of God, between our person and yours ... For it is better for us, cousin, to decide this war between our two persons than to suffer [allow] our quarrel to destroy Christianity ... We pray that you may have such an anxious desire for it.

Here the banter over tennis balls and gun stones was being resumed with a vengeance. Soldiers were being asked to imagine their lithe, athletic, 28-year-old king in armed combat with the slovenly 19-year-old dauphin, whose life-style had long been a cause for scandal. Here is Titus Livius on Henry's physical strength:

> He was marvellously fleet of foot, faster than any dog or arrow. Often he would run with two of his companions in pursuit of the swiftest of the deer and he himself would always be the one to catch the creature.

The dauphin's athletic regimen was rather different. Dissolute, fat and sluggish, he normally rose at 4 pm and spent the night in a series of drunken debauches. He was so physically unfit that a royal trip across Paris had to be abandoned because he was complaining of exhaustion at the Île de la

Cité. The epithet of one Paris citizen was simple and to the point: 'Wilful, but with little sense.'

The challenge caught the popular imagination. A monk of Westminster had the disparity between the two men in mind when he complimented Henry, declaring he was not 'fleshly or burdened with corpulence, but a handsome man, never weary, whether on horseback or on foot'. A more unlikely match could hardly be imagined. There was little danger of the challenge being taken up. But Henry's mock seriousness – the sending of the summons by herald, the number of days he would wait for a response – allowed his men a much-needed belly laugh.

Beneath the humour a serious point was being made. In the medieval world a nation's ruler not only headed the realm, but his physical condition was a symbol of the country's strength or weakness. The dauphin was heir to a ruler – Charles VI – who experienced periodic bouts of insanity during which he believed he was made of glass and had to be bound with leather, and then encased with hoops, in case he might break into pieces. The failure of either the unstable monarch or his portly offspring to exert authority had led to a terrible civil war between the aristocratic houses of Orléans and Burgundy. Henry was making clear to his soldiers that they had a king up to the task at hand, unlike their adversaries, and that the country they were invading was divided by feud and suspicion. Whatever hardships they had suffered, these circumstances still gave them a remarkable opportunity. Henry's message to his men – I am willing to risk my own person in battle, and submit to God's judgement, because my cause is right – showed his strength as a leader. Henry was reminding his men particularly of the disparity between the king of England and his French counterpart.

One archival detail bears this out poignantly. While Henry was leading the siege of Harfleur, setting out his great guns and bombarding his opponents, his rival, Charles VI, had arrived in Rouen. There, despite Harfleur's appeals for help, he stayed. But he did take one 'martial' action. A librarian from the Louvre travelled to the Norman capital and presented Charles with a book he had requested. It contained illustrations of guns and siege engines. While Henry encouraged his gunners, his rival perused drawings and sketches of the very weaponry that was destroying the town under his very nose – as if there was nothing else he could do. The striking contrast between the two kings was hammered home to the English army at every opportunity – it could not fail to lift their spirits.

Such clever and effective propaganda was all well and good, but the military situation was growing less and less advantageous for the English. For by the end of September French enthusiasm for the war – utterly lacking during the siege of Harfleur – was now growing. A pointer lay in the unfurling of the Oriflamme, the sacred banner used by kings of France at times of great danger to the nation. We should not expect Charles VI to do much banner waving but fortunately a proxy was at hand – Guillaume Martel, lord of Bacqueville – and on 10 September 1415 Martel reverently carried the banner from the abbey of Saint-Denis, north of Paris – the burial place of French kings – to Rouen, where it was unfurled a few days later.

The arrival of the Oriflamme, the red banner of war, offered the French an image of patriotism which could transcend the political intrigues and infighting and evoke the great triumphs of bygone days and the more recent success of Roosebeke in 1382 – a victory won before Charles VI lapsed into madness. As the Oriflamme was installed at the mustering point of the army, and news came through of the courageous if ultimately futile defence of Harfleur, the mood of the country began to change. Fresh recruits poured in, and the French army had soon grown larger than anyone had anticipated.

This force was originally intended to be 9,000 strong, but by the end of September one well-informed source, an anonymous chronicler at the court of Charles VI, believed that it now numbered more than 14,000 men and was increasing daily. And it was led by French aristocrats with proven military experience, the Marshal Boucicaut and the constable of France, Charles d'Albret. The French king and the dauphin might lack the capacity or will to fight the English, but the expanding army of Boucicaut and d'Albret now represented a real threat.

On 29 September and again on 5 October the English held councils of war to determine their next move. Henry proposed a plan to march on to Calais, and to fight the French if they blocked his route, but this was met with strong opposition. According to one chronicler, 'the majority of the councillors were of the opinion that a decision should be made not to march on', and it was only after the king vigorously intervened that it was concluded that they 'should pass from Harfleur to Calais following the overland route'.

Henry's chaplain provides valuable detail on what was actually discussed. The dysentery outbreak had not been contained, and although the English army had been reinforced, its numbers would continue to be depleted by illness as the campaign progressed. The chaplain related how most of the council of war believed it would be highly dangerous to send out an army 'daily growing smaller, against the multitude of French, which constantly growing larger, would surely enclose them on every side like sheep in folds'.

Henry had to assert his leadership. He still wanted to confront the enemy, and when the council of war re-assembled he was clear and decisive. Titus Livius caught the steely determination of the king's address to his captains:

> *I have the spirit of a very strong man more willing to enter all dangers rather than anyone should impugn the reputation of your king. We shall go with the judgement of God ... if they try to hinder us, we shall triumph as victors with great pride.*

Adam of Usk related how Henry, 'committing himself to God and the fortunes of the sword ... determined to set out bravely, like a lion'.

Ordinary soldiers approved of their king's resolve. John Hardyng, one of the assembled English army, commented that the king intended 'to go homeward through France like a man'. One factor remained in Henry's favour: the Burgundians had played no part in the French preparations. The English army would have to cross Burgundian lands in Picardy to reach Calais, and with Burgundy neutral the English still had a chance to gain their objective.

On 7 October, two days after the final council at war, Henry's lieutenant at Calais, William Bardolf, wrote that he was ready to help the king by leading 300 men into Picardy to draw any French troops away from the Somme crossing points, declaring:

> *We must make the most hard war that we can against the French, the enemies of our noble lord [Henry V], in order to prevent those on the frontier crossing or advancing to where he now is in person, to which purpose ... so please it God, I will carry things out, with all my power, diligence and strength.*

Bardolf realised that a major clash between the French and English was now almost inevitable, adding:

It has been reported to me, clearly and without any doubt, that the king our lord will have battle with his adversaries within the next fifteen days coming, at the very latest.

Bardolf was well aware of the risk, emphasising that from all the intelligence he had received the French force was growing by the thousand, with more and more noblemen joining its cause. The die was cast. On 8 October Henry V and his army marched out of Harfleur. The countdown to Agincourt had begun.

The English moved out of the town leaving much of their baggage behind and with such stores as were necessary carried on the backs of their horses. The experienced soldier Sir John Cornwall commanded the vanguard, the king and his brother Humphrey, Duke of Gloucester took the centre and Edward, Duke of York and Richard de Vere, Earl of Oxford the rearguard. They had food for eight days. The mood of the army remained good and its soldiers were up for the fight.

Thomas Hostell had been badly injured during the siege of Harfleur, 'there smitten by a springbolt [crossbow bolt] through the head, losing one eye and having [my] cheekbone broken' (as a later petition of his related). In this wretched state he was so inspired by Henry's leadership that he wanted to march with him. His wounds could scarcely have healed. Hostell must have believed that a momentous battle was about to take place and did not want to miss it – nothing else would justify someone in such a terrible condition accompanying the army.

The English moved northeast out of Harfleur, taking the coastal route and quickly passing the towns of Fécamp, Arques and Eu. By 13 October they were advancing towards the Somme and the ford at Blanchetaque, the famous crossing point used by Edward III on the Crécy campaign. Henry imagined that the French army at Rouen would follow them and offer battle before they reached the river. The chaplain related that the mood of excitement within the army was tangible as reports came in of a large force assembling in front of the Somme crossing. Some men wondered about the morale of those opposing them, and whether the prevailing suspicion of the Duke of Burgundy within the French camp might work to their advantage. All were readying themselves for combat.

Basset's Chronicle – a reliable source compiled from the testimony of English soldiers – described how the king halted and drew up his army to meet the French, knighting some of his followers. Jean de Waurin – from the French side – also reported that the English 'now arrayed themselves in order of battle on a fine plain'. But the anticipated challenge did not materialise. Instead, there was a most alarming and unexpected development. Blanchetaque was found heavily guarded by enemy soldiers. It was learned from the interrogation of a prisoner that the Burgundians had begun to support the French war effort and d'Albret and Boucicaut were recruiting a second army on the far side of the Somme. Crossing points over the river were now held in force against Henry's army.

An astonishing change was taking place in France, with a mood of reconciliation sweeping the country and old rivalries being laid aside. Few could have predicted it, but in an atmosphere of high emotion Burgundians had begun to rush to join what was fast becoming a national army of unity. Henry's force was now in terrible danger. It must have been an awful anti-climax for his troops when the anticipated clash failed to materialise and instead they encountered a resolutely applied scorched-earth policy. The chronicler Thomas Elmham described a fresh determination among the

French as they harried their opponents: 'Everywhere the bridges and causeways were broken by the enemy ... The French devastated farms, vineyards and food supplies.'

The English army was now forced to march upriver, and, as the expedition followed the course of the Somme past Amiens, continuing to find all crossing points held by the French, morale began to plummet. Food was running out – and Henry was beginning to lose control of his army. At the village of Boves, on 16 October, he had to reprimand his soldiers after some had uncovered a store of alcohol and gone on a drinking spree. A day later, some men who had stolen valuable objects from a church were hanged in front of the assembled troops. The soldiers watched in sullen silence.

Titus Livius reported brusquely:

The king ordered his host to halt ... Those who had committed the sacrilege were led out through the entire army and hanged on a high tree till dead. The host was then ordered to proceed.

It was sensible to maintain discipline on the march and to respect religious property, and one of Henry's military ordinances specifically prohibited the stealing of church goods and ornaments 'upon pain of death'. But it was a mistake to push the offence under the nose of the soldiers in such a harsh manner. A Roman military maxim set out by Vegetius, an author of the late fourth century, widely read in the late Middle Ages, put it well: 'Soldiers are corrected by fear and punishment in the camp; on campaign, hope and rewards make them feel better.'

One senses the king's inner turmoil – he had never anticipated such a situation, with the whole of France suddenly united again. His chaplain related how soldiers quite spontaneously flung themselves on their knees and implored God

31

for help, as the whole army plunged into despair. For an alarming couple of days it looked as if the expedition might disintegrate completely.

Yet, remarkably, Henry was able to retrieve the situation. A chance to turn things around came at the small Somme town of Corbie on 17 October. Sensing the despondency of their opponents, a force of French cavalry rode out and charged down a group of hapless archers. The sixteenth-century chronicler Raphael Holinshed preserved a remarkable vignette of what followed and, although this is a later source, the tone and feel of the military action he describes seems authentic. The marauding French horsemen had captured one of the English battle standards and were triumphantly carrying it back to the town. The king encouraged his men to go after it.

The Cheshire squire John Bromley, followed by a small group of soldiers, 'ran eagerly upon the French', hurled himself into their midst and grabbed it back. With Bromley waving the standard aloft, other English soldiers began to pitch in and the French were chased back inside the town. The king trusted his gut instinct, stopped persecuting his soldiers and started praising them again. Bromley was rewarded by Henry with a valuable cash annuity 'for his valiant recovery of the standard at the sharp and bloody skirmish of Corbie' and the mood of despair began to lift.

In battle psychology, the course of entire campaigns can depend on moments such as these. Henry's chaplain recalled a new sense of urgency and vigour in the English camp. Archers were instructed to cut wooden stakes, sharpen them and carry them as protection against sudden cavalry attack. Henry may have learned of the French plan through the interrogation of prisoners. The chaplain related that 'the enemy had appointed companies of horsemen to break the strength of our archers'. He added that this report was circulated throughout the army – with the instruction that the stakes were to be six feet long and arranged in formation in front of the archers' position. The sense that the king had good intelligence and was able to take counter-measures must have been an enormous boost to morale.

The army now raced to find an undefended crossing point of the river. On 19 October impromptu causeways were constructed between the small villages of Voyennes and Béthencourt and the English began to move across the Somme. To further lift his men's spirits the king selected a force of 200 bowmen to establish the bridgehead, supported by some 500 men-at-arms. The archers were leading the way – and all the units of the army were working together. Henry personally supervised the crossing, standing by one of the causeways to encourage his soldiers.

While Henry and his men had been crossing the river, a much larger French force had gathered at Péronne, west of the Somme. Their two armies had now joined together, and they were ahead of the English line of march to Calais. The new choice of muster point underlined an ominous reality of the developing campaign: the enemy army was now attracting considerable Burgundian support and would massively outnumber the English.

On 19 October the French commanders, the Marshal Boucicaut, the constable d'Albret, the Dukes of Bourbon and Alençon, held a council of war. They had been joined by the Duke of Burgundy's younger brother, Philip, Count of Nevers – another brother, Anthony, Duke of Brabant, had also been invited to join the rapidly swelling army. The younger brother of the Duke of Brittany, Arthur, Count of Richemont, had also arrived and the duke himself was on his way from Rouen. The Duke of Orléans was also expected shortly.

The French lords also had a battle plan, devised by Boucicaut, in consultation with d'Albret and Alençon, to neutralise the power of the English archers. Missile-bearing troops – particularly crossbowmen – would be used to wear down the English position, then carefully chosen cavalry squadrons would be launched against the archers. Then French dismounted men-at-arms would advance towards Henry's main position, and another force of cavalry would wheel round the English army and attack it from behind. Once all this was carried out, victory would be total.

The French resolved to formally challenge the English. Beneath such chivalric niceties, they knew they could impose battle on Henry V at a place and time of their choosing. Henry's troops had run out of provisions and were starving; the French could cut across their line of march, blockade the route to Calais and force them to fight whenever they wished.

On 20 October French heralds arrived at Henry's camp with a formal summons to battle. The king's army had recovered its sense of unity, even if some of the men were genuinely terrified of the vast force now shadowing their line of march. But their leader had regained his composure and self-belief and this was quickly transmitted to his soldiers. Henry would never have planned to fight in such circumstances – yet he was in these circumstances nonetheless and intended to conduct himself with honour.

Henry's captains knew that they were heavily outnumbered and in a desperate situation. Titus Livius described how the heralds first announced that all the great lords of the realm were assembling in their army and they then spoke directly to the English king: 'They will meet thee to fight ... and to be revenged of thy conduct.'

All eyes were now on Henry. What is striking in Livius's account – drawn from the testimony of Henry's brother,

Humphrey, Duke of Gloucester, who would have been standing beside him – is how every nuance of the king's reaction was scrutinised by his followers:

> *Henry, with courageous spirit, a firm look, without anger, and without changing colour, calmly replied, 'Be all things according to the will of God'.*

The king had made peace with himself, and God, and was now resolved to face whatever happened with dignity. Bravado would not work in this situation – the stakes were too high. The men around him were now looking for authentic leadership and this is what they got. Henry took command of the situation and spoke with real authority:

> *When the herald asked him what road he would take, he answered 'Straight to Calais, and if our enemies try to disturb us in that journey, it will not be without the utmost peril. We do not intend to seek them out, but neither shall we be in fear of them or move more slowly or quickly than we wish too'.*

The English army now moved north, with a much larger French force on their right flank. Between 21 and 23 October they kept up an impressive marching speed. Many in the army were frightened, but they knew there was no turning back.

Since the Somme crossing Henry had been wearing his heraldic surcoat – known as a *côte d'armes* – over his armour, and he encouraged others to do the same. On the evening of 23 October the king improvised a symbolic gesture out of pure fatigue. He mistakenly passed the village selected for his night's quarters, but he refused to turn back, telling those around him: 'God would not be pleased if I should turn back now, for I am wearing my côte d'armes.'

In the language of chivalry this made a simple statement. Once a true knight displayed his coat of arms he would never shirk from battle with his enemies: 'In that noble and perilous day, he cannot be disarmed without great dishonour, save in three cases: for victory, for being taken prisoner or for death.'

One can sense the power of this moment. As the 600th anniversary of this iconic battle approaches there are still important and fresh insights to be gained about Henry V's military skill and the blend of tactics, motivation and battle ritual that won him this exceptional victory. But we should not forget the sheer drama of the situation. As we follow the footsteps of these two armies, and hear the voices, the hopes and the fears of commanders, captains and ordinary combatants it is a chance to celebrate timeless qualities: inspirational leadership, triumph plucked from the jaws of defeat and the enduring courage of soldiers on both sides of the bloody field of combat.

There was not long now to wait. On the afternoon of 24 October 1415 the English army crossed the River Ternoise at Blangy and their scouts rode up to the ridge ahead. They galloped back, reporting a huge French force was now ahead of them, blocking the road to Calais. Battle was imminent.

CHAPTER I

The Ridge —•

The Rival Armies Come into View

14.00–16.00 (24 October 1415)

O N THE EARLY afternoon of 24 October 1415 a tired and bedraggled English army approached the village of Blangy-sur-Ternoise on the road north to Calais. Its strength was now a little under 7,000 men, a force whose small reserves of food had been exhausted almost a week ago and which was still suffering from an outbreak of dysentery. Shortly after 2 pm the first men crossed the small river that ran through the centre of Blangy. Above them was a ridge, running at an angle to the river, and the leaders of the English vanguard sent out scouts to quickly reach the high ground. They rode back in consternation. The French army was now ahead of them – and there were masses of enemy soldiers.

Titus Livius recaptured the moment:

And when the English army crossed the bridge over the Ternoise, the vanguard climbed to the top of the hill and sent out scouts, who quickly returned with news of the enemy. One, with worried face and anxious, gasping breath, announced that a countless multitude was approaching. Soon, others returned, and they confirmed this news.

The English king, Henry V, had put some of his most trustworthy men in the forefront of his army. These men represented the very best qualities of the force he had assembled – they were tough, brave and had an instinctive ingenuity in difficult situations. And that bravery and ingenuity was now desperately needed. With news that the enemy army was directly in front of them, the experienced soldier Sir John Cornwall, one of the commanders of the vanguard, now assessed the situation.

Cornwall already knew that the French were nearby – their forces had been shadowing the English army ever since it had crossed the River Somme five days earlier. He knew that their strength was rapidly growing – swollen by recruits from all over France, but particularly from the duchy of Burgundy. As one of the king's chief captains, Cornwall knew that Henry V had gambled on Burgundy – locked in a power struggle with the opposing Orléanist faction over the right to control France's weak king Charles VI – staying neutral if he invaded the country. Cornwall was resolutely loyal and he did not blame his master, but he knew that Henry had miscalculated and now the entire army was in peril.

Cornwall understood the complex political situation well. He had been one of the principal captains in an expedition sent in 1412 to assist the Duke of Orléans against the Burgundians. On another occasion he had visited the Burgundian court, and had personally met its duke. Cornwall knew the main players in the French game of thrones, knew their enmities and rivalries, but also their hopes and aspirations. To his surprise and dismay, these rivalries now seemed to have been buried, at least for the time being. For days Cornwall had realised the consequence of this – that soon the whole French host would swing across the road to Calais, blocking the English escape route and forcing them to fight.

When soldiers face a crisis a sense of comradeship with their fellow fighters is vital. Cornwall, a tough professional soldier, was encouraged by the quality of the men moving into Blangy behind him. One of the first was Sir Gilbert

Umfraville, described by the soldier John Hardyng, who accompanied him on the campaign, as 'a jewel for any king, wise in counsel and valiant in war'. 24-year-old Umfraville had been schooled in war from his mid-teens, on the Scottish border, where his family's estates lay. An energetic fighter, he had also distinguished himself in France, acquitting himself with honour at the Anglo-Burgundian victory at Saint-Cloud on 10 November 1411, an expedition planned by Prince Henry, with whom Sir Gilbert had already become closely associated.

Henry personally liked and admired Umfraville. A knight of the king's chamber, and also a Knight of the Garter, he had already acquired an impressive martial CV as the royal army assembled at Southampton and was remembered in Henry V's will of 1415 (drawn up before the king left for France) with the gift of a fine gold bowl. Umfraville was keen to distinguish himself on campaign, and he had brought a substantial retinue of 30 men-at-arms and 90 archers for that purpose. Some of these men had been sent home sick at Harfleur. The remainder were still ready to fight.

Henry V gave Cornwall and Umfraville tough assignments, knowing that they would acquit themselves well. Both were members of a special scouting party Henry had sent out just after landing in Normandy on 14 August 1415. Its purpose was to discover what resistance might be expected from the French – and to ascertain the best route to Harfleur. Once that siege had commenced, the two men also fought together in the attack on Harfleur's Leure gate on 16 September – the crucial assault that broke the will of the defenders and led to the town's surrender.

When Henry decided that the English army should march out from Harfleur and on to Calais ready to fight, on 8 October, he entrusted the joint command of the army's vanguard to the two of them. Cornwall and Umfraville repaid that trust – being first across the Somme 11 days later and standing shoulder to shoulder in defence of that crossing, allowing the rest of the army to reach the far side of the river.

Cornwall and Umfraville were natural commanders, but they relied on a close-knit group of soldiers to support them. The mettle of these men tells us much about Henry V's army. Sir John Gray was also a member of the scouting party sent out on 14 August after the expedition had landed. Gray was praised by one observer as 'a comely knight' – in other words, a natural soldier. The skill ran in his family. Gray's grandfather, Sir Thomas, was a long-standing fighter in the fourteenth-century wars with Scotland and the author of the *Scalacronica*, the first English chronicle to be written by a knight rather than a monk.

Gray's *Scalacronica* opened a vivid window on the life of a warrior on the Scottish border in the reign of Edward III. It extolled courage, the keeping of a cool head in dangerous situations and loyalty to one's fellow fighters – and it was an outlook Sir John sought to emulate. Always keen to seek out chivalric adventure, and also to maintain his readiness for combat, in June 1404 he and a fellow warrior, Richard Ledes, challenged two Scotsmen to a series of jousts on horseback at Carlisle. Gray subsequently fought with the young prince of Wales – the future Henry V – in the Welsh wars, where he was rewarded with an annuity of 20 marks by a grateful prince, and also took part in the expedition sent – on that same Prince's orders – to assist the Duke of Burgundy in the autumn of 1411. A king's knight through and through, he was looking to win renown on this campaign and was dependable in a crisis.

Another in that scouting party of 14 August – part of a crack squadron, who looked after each other, fought together

41

and led the way in any action – was Cornwall's 20-year-old stepson Sir John Holland, the man who had shown such bravery in the attack on the barbican at Harfleur. Sir John had been the first aristocrat to sign up for Henry's expedition – on 20 April 1415 – enlisting with a retinue of 20 men-at-arms and 60 archers. Holland was determined to prove his worth to the king and over time would become one of Henry V's most reliable commanders in France.

The fourth in this group was the Essex knight Sir William Bourchier. Bourchier was another experienced fighter, a diplomat and friend of Henry V, and the king held him in high regard. A man of great personal charm, he had made a clandestine marriage to the king's cousin Anne, Countess of Stafford and been fully pardoned for it – an amorous feat that Cornwall would also go on to emulate. Bourchier had fought with Prince Henry at the battle of Shrewsbury and on campaign in Wales and conducted a number of important diplomatic missions for him.

Bourchier, close enough to Henry V to send his own troupe of wrestlers to entertain him at Windsor, was now looking forward to doing some wrestling of his own against the French. Henry – who had put his own days of wild living behind him – nonetheless continued to trust Cornwall and Bourchier with important reconnaissance missions, perhaps taking the view that those adventurous in love were also enterprising in warfare.

Most telling in the group was the presence of William Porter, the final member of the scouting party and Cornwall's brother-in-arms. The two men had sworn a mutual oath to assist each other in war 'til death shall part us'. Porter was also high in Henry V's favour – both as a diplomat and a soldier, being sent on 'secret business' to Portugal in 1413 and on an embassy to Paris a year later – and was left a gold cup, a horse and six pounds in cash in the king's will. On campaign in 1415, the two men were inseparable – fighting together in a special barbican or fortification opposite Harfleur's Leure gate and both being sent by Henry as part of a special force to guard the Somme crossing the night before the full English army arrived.

During the course of the expedition these men became exceptionally close to each other. Time and time again, Henry would entrust to them actions requiring particular courage and skill. The soldier John Hardyng was in the Umfraville retinue and he was struck by how well they all worked together. Hardyng already had a fair amount of soldiering under his belt, fighting in numerous Scottish border campaigns, being present at the battles of Homildon Hill (1402) and Shrewsbury (1403) and serving as constable of Warkworth Castle, and he put some of his account to verse:

The king ... laid a siege to Harfleur mightily,
On every side, by land and water.
With bulwarks stout and bastions he began,
In which he put the Earl of Huntingdon [Sir John Holland],
Sir Gilbert Umfraville also, of great renown,
Which two, with others to them assigned,
Cromwell and Gray, Bourchier and Porter,
Full great assaults they made each day ...

This special group of fighters were now across the Ternoise at Blangy on the early afternoon of 24 October 1415, looking up at the ridge ahead of them and gauging how much time they had before battle commenced. They would have done this by the position of the sun, although the understanding of time had changed greatly in the last 50 years. For most of the Middle Ages the day had been divided into eight 'hours',

THE RIDGE

following the Benedictine rule of observance for monastic life. The medieval day for most ordinary people began at 'prime' – the first hour after sunrise, and assuming a summer day when 'prime' commenced at around 6 am, the day was then divided into three-hourly intervals, ending with 'compline' at around 9 pm, after sunset. The passage of time was recorded by sundials or water clocks. But in the latter part of the fourteenth century the mechanical clock had been invented – and then introduced to most towns and cities of medieval Europe.

For the first time it was possible to record time to the minute, which enabled an accurate natal horoscope to be drawn up for Henry V (according to an astrological source the king was born at Monmouth on 16 September 1386 at 11.22 am). Progressing this natal chart, in the month of October 1415 the placement of the planets was advantageous to him, with Mars, the god of war, in an auspicious house – but Henry was unaware of this, as he believed it was bad religious practice to consult astrologers before going on campaign. In his eyes, the outcome of battle should be left to the will of God.

In 1415 there were two parallel systems of measurement – 'merchant time', contractual, business time – the preserve of men – measured by the town clock, and 'monastic time' – the devotional day – apportioned around worship and religious observance, the preserve of God. Henry possessed a portable clock, but he would never have taken it on to the battlefield. The field of combat was governed by God's will, not man's.

But in practical terms from the position of the sun, partially visible in a cloudy sky, it was now a little short of 'none', between 2 and 3 pm. And that meant there were about three hours of daylight left. The later it got, the less likely a battle was – but nothing could be left to chance. The battle of Crécy had begun an hour after 'none', at around 4 pm – and continued into the twilight. The English would need to be ready for any eventuality.

The army was moving quickly, and the men-at-arms and archers of the vanguard soon joined Cornwall and his comrades. Henry had gathered a substantial body of bowmen for his army, and over 5,000 of them were marching with him to Calais. Never before had an English army contained such a high proportion of archers. They were recruited from the peasantry – but Cornwall was pleased to observe that the first contingents crossing the river still retained order and discipline on the march. And he well knew the lethal power of the weapon they carried. The longbow had greater range than the crossbow usually deployed by the French and a much more rapid rate of fire.

The archers were also carrying six-foot-long wooden stakes. The king had ordered these made as the army crossed the Somme five days earlier. Henry had learned that the French intended to use cavalry to overrun his bowmen and the stakes were intended to protect them from sudden attack. Cornwall was encouraged to see that the stakes were properly sharpened, and that each man was carrying one.

John Hardyng, present in the vanguard with Cornwall, recalled:

> After the king had passed the town of Corbie [17 October] he ordered that each archer should make for himself a stake or staff – either squared or rounded – six feet in length and sharpened at both ends, to be fixed in front of them into the ground at one end and with the other end set at an angle toward the enemy at time of battle.

However, the hardship the army was suffering was all too obvious to Cornwall, Umfraville and the men around them. Some soldiers were so weak with hunger that they walked unevenly, and as they marched in formation through Blangy easily stumbled. Others, following after them, were clearly still suffering from dysentery. The English force was wasting away in numbers and strength. Thomas Walsingham recorded the situation bluntly:

> *The king and his very small band were thin and weak from hunger, from the bloody flux [dysentery] and fever. When they made camp at night there was no more bread or meat to share out, and men made do with a few nuts scavenged during the day's march. For some two weeks the majority of our soldiers had to make do with nothing more than a little drinking water. With such delicacies were the athletes of the king of England nourished and fed. Exhausted from the constant marching, further weakened by the constant need to keep watch and debilitated by the cold nights, our men now learnt that they would soon be facing in battle an army of many, many thousands.*

And yet Cornwall was a natural optimist, a man who always trusted in his ability to manage challenging situations. Clapped in the Tower by Henry's father, Henry IV, after a clandestine marriage to this king's sister Elizabeth of Lancaster, he had taken a leaf out of Bourchier's book and quickly charmed his way out again, becoming an indispensable royal servant in the process. Although Elizabeth was considerably older than Cornwall, and already twice widowed, chroniclers believed the marriage was a love match, and that Elizabeth had fallen for Cornwall after watching him defeat a French knight at a joust in York several months earlier.

Cornwall was an innately skilful soldier who loved being in the thick of the action – he had fought in Scotland, Brittany and against Owen Glendower's revolt in Wales. Among the crack squadron of friends and fellow soldiers leading the way towards Agincourt, he was its foremost fighter – a widely respected chivalric figure, even though he was still only in his mid-thirties. In 1404 he had repulsed a French assault on Blackpool in Lancashire. Four years later he had commanded a force of English mercenaries fighting for the Duke of Burgundy at Othée. Unsurprisingly in 1409 he was elevated to the Order of the Garter – England's premier order of chivalry – in recognition of his martial prowess.

Sir John was a clever diplomat, employed on many English missions to France. He was also a highly regarded athlete whose jousting ability was renowned throughout Europe. In September 1406 he defeated a series of Scottish knights in jousts held in London. Thomas Walsingham said happily of that occasion: 'The English gave the Scots such a beating. It caused great dismay to the challengers and gave fame and honour to our men.' In 1409 he travelled abroad to Lille to face a challenge by Jehan Werchin, seneschal of Hainault, combat held over three days with all the weapons used in medieval warfare, 'which accomplishment is the greatest honour to which prowess and chivalry can aspire'. Cornwall so distinguished himself – fighting in turn with lance, sword, dagger and axe – that he was presented with a gold collar set in jewels by John the Fearless, Duke of Burgundy, who had presided over the whole event.

These were impressive achievements, which Cornwall carried off with seeming ease. Once, facing imprisonment in France, he had extricated himself by offering his captor a wager of a tennis match for his freedom. He won so convincingly that his opponent not only released him but rewarded him with 3,000 francs for winning with such skill.

Yet Cornwall was not romantic about war. He was a shrewd businessman, and as early as 1404 he had purchased a Norman knight and some other French prisoners, captured in a raid on Dartmouth, as an investment on their ransoms. In 1412 the hostages for the payment of 210,000 gold écus with which the Duke of Orléans had bought off the English army were placed in his hands, and a tenth of the entire sum allocated to him. It was typical that when the earl marshal John Mowbray was invalided home from Harfleur sick, Cornwall bought all his French prisoners – and at a knock-down price.

Cornwall's special relationship with William Porter, his 'brother-in-arms', was a warrior's contract. It meant that they would always assist each other at time of war and fight together whenever possible. Their arrangement showed an element of idealism, or at least considerable trust, but a healthy dose of realism, too, for it was primarily a business deal, one that protected both men from long imprisonment if captured (the other pledged to raise the first instalment of the ransom as quickly as possible) and their families from financial hardship if they were killed in battle (provision would be made for their dependants out of their shared war profits).

So Cornwall was not starry-eyed about medieval warfare or, indeed, about the warrior's life in general. He would live to see the death of his 17-year-old son and heir, his head blown off by a gun stone as he stood next to him during the siege of Meaux six years after Agincourt, an event that left him so profoundly shaken that he vowed 'never to wage war against fellow Christians again'. After making this resolution, Cornwall would shun active warfare and instead would go on to build a fine castle at Ampthill in Bedfordshire out of the profits of war ransoms. And in 1415, Cornwall, like all of Henry's war captains, had shared the ups and downs of a difficult campaign.

That summer Cornwall had brought a substantial retinue to Southampton. He had seen some of these men die during the siege of Harfleur, when his company was in the forefront of the action, manning a large bastion or siege fortress set up opposite the town's Leure gate. And from 8 October, as the army had marched out of Harfleur, heading towards the English-held town of Calais – still resolved to fight the French – Cornwall, in the vanguard, had seen others succumb to dysentery, too weak to march any further. Throughout all this, he had supported the king in his decision to seek out his foe, but as an experienced soldier he was well aware that they were taking a serious and mounting risk.

At first, this had seemed entirely justified. During the siege of Harfleur the enemy's resistance had been quiescent. Henry and Cornwall knew that there would be no royal commander to face them in the field of battle. And they were also well aware that France was in the throes of civil war, with two factions – Burgundian and Orléanist – vying for control of the government. During the siege of Harfleur these bitter internal tensions had created a state of paralysis.

Cornwall could make this pragmatic assessment easily enough. He had met the leaders of the rival parties and knew their ambitions and their fears. The Burgundians regarded the creation of a large army as an excuse to wrest control of parts of France under their own influence; the Orléanists feared that supporting such an army, whether in Normandy or Picardy, would allow the Burgundians to turn the tables on them, and seize Paris. So neither side had undertaken anything of substance, and the English had then captured Harfleur without a relief force being sent to its aid.

Dysentery or no dysentery, these factors gave grounds for a measure of optimism. Cornwall was aware that a small professional army was being raised to meet them, under France's best soldier Marshal Boucicaut, and as a fellow jouster of international repute he admired Boucicaut's skill. He also knew that the size of his force was not much greater than theirs and its morale was not high. It was being recruited in the Norman capital, Rouen, and when the English marched out of Harfleur on 8 October they had remained confident of bringing these troops to battle between the rivers Seine and Somme and roundly defeating them.

John Hardyng, accompanying Cornwall, caught this mood of resolution. Hardyng believed that the king's decision to march to Calais was 'full manly' – it was a brave and courageous thing to do – and 'bold'. He and Cornwall were aware of the unpredictability of war, but circumstances had then begun to change with a disconcerting rapidity. Where once there had been lethargy and inaction, now there was a new sense of patriotism and resolve. France's woes touched the hearts of those previously disillusioned by years of intrigue and the response was remarkable. Knights and lords from across the country vowed to bury their differences and unite to fight the English.

As Cornwall marched towards the Somme he began to hear rumours of this astonishing change. These rumours soon became tangible. Heading the army, he was the first to see that the crossing points of the river were now guarded by the Burgundians, Burgundians who Henry and his captains believed would stay neutral. They were now holding these places against the English by force, and as Cromwell and his vanguard sped further upriver they found that the bridges at Abbeville and Amiens could not be crossed either.

John Hardyng laconically reported the growing difficulties they faced:

> *The king approached close to the town of Abbeville, where he was not able to effect a crossing of the Somme because the bridges, fords and causeways had been broken. He made his way upstream of the Somme, with the city of Amiens on his left. Again, he could not find any crossing or ford. It was the same the following day …*

Hardyng, ever the professional soldier, was now gauging the distance to Calais against the meagre rations remaining to the army. The English troops – who had been travelling light, with only eight days' rations – were now forced further and further inland, away from their intended route. Reports were now reaching them that the French force at Rouen had already doubled in size, with more men joining daily, and would soon be following close behind them. To make matters worse, more troops were being assembled in Picardy. The numerical odds against the English were rising all the time – and it was alarmingly clear that the morale of the enemy was rising with them

To Sir John Cornwall's relief, a crossing point was at last found over the Somme between Voyennes and Béthencourt. Cornwall rode ahead with a party of chosen warriors to guard it for the king and on 19 October the entire army crossed the river. Hardyng, in the vanguard, recalled the moment:

> *The king … was informed that he could cross the River Somme in two places. On this account he sent Sir Gilbert Umfraville, William Porter, John Cornwall and William Bourchier with their standards to guard the crossing of the army over the river, which they did from mid-day to one hour before nightfall. The*

following day the king and his entire army crossed ... protected by these guards.

Henry's chaplain also recounted this morale-boosting operation:

And when the Somme was reached, we found two places where it could be crossed, the water at these fording points only rising as high as the belly of a horse. The approach was by two long, narrow causeways, partially broken up by the French, so that one could only reach the crossing riding single file. So Sir John Cornwall and Sir Gilbert Umfraville, banners fluttering in the breeze, and followed by a picked force of men-at-arms and archers, moved as quickly as they could, clattering along the causeway and then through the water, and establishing a small bridgehead on the other side.

Then the king ordered that the army's baggage be carried across one causeway, and our fighting men proceed along the other. And he and other captains positioned themselves at the entrance points, to ensure that the crossing was done in an orderly fashion, and not get jammed or choked with the press of men and belongings ...

Even so, before a hundred of our men had waded across, some enemy cavalry suddenly appeared, and rode up towards our position to see if it might be possible to drive our forces back.

Cornwall and Umfraville, sensing this new danger, rode out to engage them.

'Our mounted patrols immediately went out to meet them,' the chaplain continued,

... and the French, having underestimated our determination to fight, abandoned the place and vanished from our sight.

> *We had started our crossing about one o'clock in the after-*
> *noon, and it was only an hour short of nightfall before we were*
> *all across. It was a very cheerful night we spent in those hamlets*
> *nearby, having finally managed to cross the river.*

The English then swung north again towards Calais. But the French were rapidly closing in on them.

The following day Cornwall had witnessed the arrival of French heralds in the English war camp, delivering a formal summons to battle. They were jaunty, well aware they now held the advantage of numbers and that the English had run out of food. 'The heralds of the Dukes of Orléans and Bourbon came to the king, announcing that they were going to bring him to battle,' John Hardyng recalled bluntly. Cornwall and his fellow captains felt their king's quiet yet all-encompassing resolve, but they knew that many in his army remained frightened – as one of Henry's chaplains related, they could now all see masses of hoofprints on the muddy tracks ahead of them, clear proof of the size of force gathering to meet them.

But Cornwall's vanguard maintained an impressive march-ing speed. On the evening of 23 October Henry V mistakenly passed the village selected for his night's quarters but refused to turn back, aware that to do so would deliver the wrong message to his army.

Cornwall caught the underlying urgency of the king's gesture and well understood what was at stake. On the early afternoon of 24 October as he led the vanguard of the army across the Ternoise and sent his scouts to reconnoitre the ridge ahead, he sensed the presence of the enemy around him. His fears had been confirmed.

Ahead of him was a huge army, one so large his scouts were scarcely able even to guess at its numbers. French knights were still rushing pell-mell to join it. A large detachment under the Duke of Brittany was rumoured to be approaching. The youngest brother of the Duke of Burgundy, Philip, Count of Nevers, had also arrived and it was rumoured that another brother, Anthony, Duke of Brabant, was riding hard to join him. The French army was growing by the hour.

Within minutes, Cornwall's scouts returned from the ridge in a state of trepidation. The French army was now clearly visible in the valley below, they warned Cornwall, and they had never before seen such a vast assembly of men. It seemed as if the entire countryside was teeming with soldiers. The phrases used to describe the opposing French – relayed by the soldiers themselves and then repeated by the chroniclers who caught their words – are ominously revealing: 'an innumerable host of locusts', 'forests covering the whole of the country', as if a biblical plague or dark enchantment was about to be visited on the English army. We can feel the sheer terror of the occasion, but also the ordinary soldier's uncanny sense of wonder. The enemy had been sighted at last. The English were facing an army of overwhelming size and – as every scout on that ridge would have realised – one now powerfully motivated to fight.

The sun had now moved further west – passing the 'hour' of 'none' at 3 pm. There were less than three hours of daylight left. However, Cornwall instinctively guessed that there was unlikely to be an immediate attack. The French force was not moving from its position and if it did suddenly advance, it would have to negotiate a low valley that lay between the two armies. The ridge ahead of them commanded the surrounding countryside and there was enough space on it for the entire army to draw up. He instructed his scouts to keep watching the enemy – and waited for his king and commander to join him.

It was not long before Henry V reached Blangy and Cornwall quickly reported the situation to him. Sir John and his fellow fighters watched the king closely, curious to see how he would respond. Titus Livius remembered the scout who first saw the French now being brought to Henry in a state of shock, 'with worried face and anxious gasping breath'. The king remained calm:

> Without trembling or showing any anger he set spurs to his horse and rushed to see the approaching enemy. Once he had seen and obtained knowledge of their army – which was too large to be counted – he returned to his men, steady and unflinching.

The quality described here – that of restraint – was highly prized by the English. The chronicler Thomas Walsingham had praised King Edward III for similar attributes, his calmness in joy or adversity – 'at all times he was softly spoken and restrained'. Walsingham also noted this characteristic in Edward's greatest captains, men like Sir Hugh Calveley, 'a soldier of long experience in warfare, who in all places had won praise for his cool-headed feats of arms'.

Indeed, an English army had held this ground before: for three days, between 6 and 8 November 1355, Edward III had waited on the same spot to give battle to the French. On this earlier occasion in the Hundred Years War, they had not come. The enemy had now arrived in force, but would they offer battle on this site, or instead fall back, and choose another, more advantageous to them?

Cornwall, like all the captains around him, knew his history. The sense of destiny was palpable. Edward III had first claimed England's right to the throne of France through his mother, a claim that Henry V had revived. Edward III had first introduced archers en masse into an English army, a policy Henry had expanded upon. Edward III had powerfully introduced a sense of chivalry into his army – based upon devotion to St George – who became a talisman for his army; Henry used St George's red cross on a white background as a uniform for his troops. Both kings could reach out to and inspire the ordinary soldier.

Henry V now made what provisions he could. He took advice from Cornwall and his fellow fighters and chose a suitable deployment for his men. Titus Livius recalled the captains being properly briefed – the king drew up his men 'distributing to each leader the order and place of battle'. But the French did not repeat the tactics of Crécy – the great clash of arms fought on 26 August 1346, and a stirring victory for the army of Edward III – where they had launched a series of attacks on the English position in the early evening, and then fought on, even in the moonlight. Instead, they waited on the far side of the ridge, watching the English position.

It was now between the 'hours' of 'none' and 'vespers' – at around four o'clock in the afternoon. Sunset was two hours away.

French numbers were indeed growing. Their original force, recruited in Rouen by Marshal Boucicaut and his friend and fellow fighter the Gascon Charles d'Albret, constable of France, was always intended to be a small professional body – only a few thousand larger than the English opposing them. But now soldiers were joining it from all over the country. Others congregated on the eastern banks of the Somme. As they held the crossing points of the Somme against the English more and more were arriving – Bretons from the west, Orléanist supporters of Charles VI from the south, Burgundians from the east. There was a rendezvous for these troops at Péronne, and for the last few days they had shadowed the English soldiers. And now, on the early afternoon of 24 October, they cut across the English line of advance, confident that they could destroy their foe.

Among the French army gathering near Blangy, the Burgundian knight Ghillebert de Lannoy was contemplating his latest martial exploit. Lannoy was a younger son of an aristocratic family from Hainault, but while his older brother Hue had established himself at the Burgundian court as chamberlain to Duke John the Fearless, Ghillebert found it hard to settle into any fixed position. He would later tell the Burgundian duke with wry self-deprecation that no man should be appointed to a post on his governing council until he was at least 36 years old. 'For the first twenty-six years of a man's life he is a vagabond,' Lannoy mused, as if enlarging upon his own biography, 'and it will take another ten years after that to see how he turns out.' By his own reckoning, Lannoy was still engaged in a voyage of self-exploration, for at Agincourt he had only reached the age of 29. An almost hyperactive adventurer, his devotion to the chivalric ethos was only matched by his love of travel and a boundless appetite for new experiences.

In 1403, at the age of 17, Lannoy had signed up for his first expedition, one led by the Count of St Pol, which had raided the Isle of Wight. A year later, he enlisted with a force raised by Jacques de Bourbon that intended to aid the rebellion of Owen Glendower. Bourbon's men proceeded to sack the Cornish port of Falmouth, before the Channel winds turned against them, preventing the hoped-for landing in Wales and instead forcing them to seek shelter in Brest. While he waited in frustrated inactivity, Lannoy and his friend and mentor Jean de Werchin, seneschal of Hainault, whiled away their time by composing no fewer than 46 love ballads.

Lannoy chose not to pursue such poetic endeavours, concentrating instead on his travels, and his notes and jottings give us a vivid window on the life of a young knight adventurer. From them we learn that his next ten years were devoted to a non-stop round of travelling and fighting. In 1405–6 he went on a pilgrimage to Jerusalem. In 1407 and 1410 he jousted and crusaded in Spain. When a truce was proclaimed there he immediately obtained a safe conduct so that he could see the Moorish city of Granada, spending the next ten days sightseeing like any modern tourist among its palaces and gardens, and reporting with satisfaction that 'there were beautiful and marvellous things to see'.

Copenhagen was next on Lannoy's itinerary, where he enjoyed its fair and bought himself four fine new horses. He then joined up with the Teutonic Knights, being received by the head of that military order at the great castle of Marienburg and riding out with them against the Poles and Lithuanians. Dubbed a knight in the Baltic, he then took time off from campaigning, and went on an even more intriguing adventure, an impromptu excursion to the Russian city of Novgorod – the great trading post on the northern reaches of the Volga, then at its peak of power and importance – disguised as a merchant.

Lannoy travelled by sledge through the snow and bitter cold, undaunted by the hardship of his journey and entranced by the whole experience. His naturally observant eye prompted a series of comments on a winter so unlike that of Western Europe. Lannoy was fascinated by the sounds of trees cracking in the forest, by the freezing of his eyelashes and beard in the winter night, the way his metal drinking cup froze to his fingers. Novgorod impressed him – he was astonished by the number of its churches, although with a keen military instinct he observed its walls were not very sturdy. He was appalled by the vigorous slave market, which produced a rare critical remark: 'We French Christians would never do that, on our life.'

Lannoy returned home early in 1414, making a long land journey by way of Poland, Bohemia and Austria. In all these places he was received by the local king or duke, feasted, given presents and taken to see places of interest. His descriptions of his activities, while brief and factual, show acuteness of observation and the unflagging interest with which he explored all these new and different places.

With scarcely a pause Ghillebert de Lannoy then set off to Ireland, but was captured en route and only released after a cash payment of 3,000 francs from the Duke of Burgundy. Lannoy commented with frustration that his brief captivity had forced him to miss out on an important military occasion, the siege of Arras (in August 1414, when the rival factions of Orléanists and Burgundians first clashed and then agreed terms of peace), when 'everyone of note was there'. On 24 October 1415 he was determined not to miss the forthcoming clash with the English. Lannoy would fight among the retinue of the Duke of Burgundy's brother, Philip, Count of Nevers.

Another young knight, a younger brother of John the Fearless, Anthony Duke of Brabant, was still in transit. Brabant, a close friend of Lannoy, and one of those who had contributed to his ransom in 1414, had resolved not to miss the battle in any circumstances. His race towards the probable battle site was conducted at a breathless pace. For the medieval knight, a normal riding speed was around 20–30 miles a day. With teams of horses waiting in relays, 40–50 miles was possible. Brabant's headlong gallop towards Agincourt far surpassed this; indeed it exceeded anything seen before and the distances covered were recorded in amazement by the duke's secretary Edmond de Dynter.

On 19 October Brabant, in his castle of Louvain, had received letters from Boucicaut, d'Albret, and the Dukes of

Alençon and Bourbon. They had just held a council of war at Péronne. Edmond de Dynter took up the story:

> *The Duke of Brabant was informed that he should immediately set out in person, because the following week those assembled lords [at Péronne] intended to fight the English.*

Although Duke Anthony received the news at 9 pm (Dynter was careful to record the time), he immediately sprang into action.

> *The duke straight away had all his secretaries come before him and ordered that that very night they should write letters to all his nobles and officers in his duchy of Brabant commanding them that without any delay they should follow him with as many men-at-arms and archers as they could find, and make their way towards Cambrai, where they would receive fresh instructions from him, so that they might go and fight the English – the ancient enemies of the realm.*

Reeling from this sudden upsurge of work, Dynter then remembered that on 22 October the duke rode off suddenly to Cambrai and then Brussels, requesting that these towns also supply him with troops.

> *These towns agreed to his request and made hurried preparations to have their men arm and equip themselves, in large number.*

But before any of these contingents had time to assemble, the duke lost patience, and, fearing that he might miss the battle, rode off without them – leaving instructions that they should follow him as soon as they were able. Without a proper military retinue, Brabant nevertheless left Brussels with a small riding household of 40 men on the afternoon of 23 October. They kept moving, clattering through Mons just after midnight, and reaching Valenciennes by mid-morning on 24 October. At this point Brabant and his men had covered a remarkable 65 miles. But after changing horses and a brief stop for food and refreshment the company was off again, now heading towards Lens. By 4 pm Brabant's tally had risen further; he had now covered an astounding 85 miles and was still riding in all haste towards the French army.

Brabant's helter-skelter progress was carried out with a complete disregard for his own safety. He was hurtling towards a major battle with a tiny group of men and little military equipment. His own armour, weaponry and full retinue was being left further and further behind. And he was becoming utterly exhausted in the process. The ideal – to participate in the forthcoming battle at any cost – had superseded all reality. While for Ghillebert de Lannoy such conduct was wholly admirable, Sir John Cornwall and his fellows must have regarded it with utter bemusement.

Other breathless recent arrivals in the French army included the 22-year-old Arthur de Richemont, the younger brother of the Duke of Brittany, who had abandoned the siege of Parthenay on the urgent summons of the Dauphin and ridden hard eastwards with a force of 500 men. Richemont – ambitious, energetic and violent – had already shown himself to be a natural soldier. The most distinguished newcomer was the prince of the royal blood, the young Charles, Duke of Orléans, already a gifted poet, alert to the vivid if transient beauty of his surroundings and a lover of the tournament and joust.

Orléans was intoxicated by chivalric display, the rich trappings and decorations borne by the aristocracy, and had the wealth to equip himself with the finest available. In 1414 the duke had splashed out the sum of £276 for 960 pearls, which were to be sewn on to the sleeve of his doublet in the form of the words and music of a line from a love ballad he had just composed. Orléans was entranced by such showy, impulsive gestures. Now reunited with his baggage train after his own rapid journey from the Loire to the gathering army on the Somme, he typified a mood of exhilaration sweeping the French combatants. In the words of the chronicler Thomas Walsingham, Orléans 'thought himself unbeatable'.

Men such as Sir John Cornwall and Ghillebert de Lannoy were now regarding each other across the sweeping country-side north of Blangy. And Cornwall and Lannoy, although in rival armies, had much in common. They were both natural adventurers who revelled in the cult of chivalry, a cult that embodied the attraction of warfare to the knightly classes of England and France. Brave and experienced fighters, they were also charismatic and resolute in all matters of war. They differed in one important respect – a difference that caught a larger contrast prevalent among the opposing forces.

We glimpse this in, of all places, the Christian names of the soldiers facing each other at Blangy. On the English side was a solid array of Johns, Williams, Roberts, Thomases, Henrys and Nicholases (forming the majority of names listed in the king's retinue). Among the French was a body of names of heroes from chivalric romances – a flowery host of Lancelots, Hectors, Yvains and Floridases, Gawains, Percevals, Palamedes, Tristans and Arthurs. The popularity of such names among the French nobility showed a devotion to Arthurian romance and its courtly aspirations, from a nation that regarded itself as the birthplace of chivalry.

The Englishmen of Cornwall's generation had not experi-enced any great martial endeavours, unlike their fathers and grandfathers at the great battles of Crécy, Poitiers and Najera. And Cornwall, like many in the English army, was at heart a pragmatist. He understood the code of chivalry and admired some of its precepts, but his outlook remained down to earth and practical. On the afternoon of 24 October his main concern was simply to survive.

Sir John Cornwall and Sir Gilbert Umfraville were essentially military professionals. They understood the science of war and saw chivalry as its by-product. John Hardyng related how Umfraville, on a later campaign in France, was critical of a decision by the king's brother, Thomas, Duke of Clarence, to rush into battle before proper reconnaissance had been carried out and the army fully prepared. Umfraville considered Clarence's decision neither brave nor admirable, but foolhardy. He would have viewed the Duke of Brabant's headlong charge in much the same light.

In contrast, Lannoy and his fellows in the French army subscribed to a lofty idealism. He was aware that money could be made out of war, and sometimes considerable amounts, but it was beneath his dignity to pursue this objective. He wrote to his son, in rather detached fashion:

> *In the effort of war, it may happen to a wise, courageous and virtuous man that he takes a prisoner of such great wealth in land and lordship that he will become, and remain, rich for the rest of his own life and those of his heirs.*

Lannoy's son must have read this with mixed feelings. There would be no 'great wealth' handed down from this particular 'virtuous man' – Lannoy's ransom account was substantially on the debit side. To him it didn't really matter. His overarching objective was the pursuit of renown at any cost. And on 24 October this now seemed within his grasp. Lannoy fully believed that the divisive civil war in France would be healed by a great military exploit. Great honour was now to be won – by annihilating the English in battle.

CHAPTER 2

No Way Out →

The Rival Commanders

16.00–20.00 (24 October 1415)

O N THE RIDGE north of Blangy the two armies were lined up opposite each other, about three-quarters of a mile apart. The English had adopted a defensive formation, making use of the natural protection the high ground offered, with their archers grouped on the army's flanks and their men-at-arms holding the centre of the line – and were looking for the French to make the first move. But the French were content to wait.

Henry's chaplain, like everyone else in the army, was watching the opposing army:

> We had crossed the river [Ternoise] as quickly as possible, and as we reached the top of the hill, on the other side, we saw emerging from higher up the valley – a little more than half a mile away from us – the grim-looking ranks of the French. The enemy, in a compact mass of marching divisions and columns, his numerical strength vastly superior to ours, at length took up a position facing us, rather more than half a mile away, filling a very broad field like a swarm of locusts, and leaving only a narrow valley between us and them.

It was now between 'none' and 'vespers', shortly after 4 pm. The sky was overcast and soon the light would start to fade. The English army was drawn up in formation, with Henry riding along the ridge, encouraging his troops. The chaplain continued: 'Our king, very calmly and without fear of the danger we were all in, exhorted his soldiers and readied them for combat.'

Priests were moving along the battle line, receiving men's confessions, and the chaplain was one of them.

'Henry had drawn up his soldiers in one main division – with archers massed on the flanks,' Thomas Elmham recounted. 'And in comparison to the French army – drawn up in three large divisions – our forces seemed so very small. All our soldiers made their confessions to God, and as there was a shortage of priests, many confessed to each other.'

It was unusual for most of an army to want to take confession before a battle – and Jean Le Fèvre, a herald present with the English soldiers (he would remain with them throughout the battle), was struck by this:

Seeing the French before him, the king of England had all his men dismount and put them in battle formation. And you could see the English, thinking that battle was to be joined that very afternoon, paying their devotions, all kneeling with their hands towards the heavens, asking God to keep them in his protection.

And then Le Fèvre added, for emphasis: 'This is true – I was with them, and saw with my own eyes what I have just described.'

The two armies watching each other could not have more different. 'The French were well-provisioned and well-supplied,' Thomas Walsingham remarked ruefully, 'whilst we were weak and tired because of the desperate shortage of food.'

Much would now depend on leadership. King Henry was 29 years old. In appearance he had a long face, straight nose and broad forehead; thick brown hair, cut short at the sides and back. He was above average height, slim and athletic; he loved hunting and was a good shot with the crossbow. He was conscious of his bearing – in his household were several mirrors, as well as golden musk bulls to hold perfume – and unlike most of his royal predecessors he was clean-shaven. Such personal care had nothing to do with ostentation. Henry was never frivolous, he chose his words carefully and yet he could also be spontaneous and pleasingly direct, and humorous. He was tough and resilient, and could endure hardship as well as the ordinary soldier. And, above all else, he could sense the mood and emotions of those around him

From the age of seven he had a military tutor, and was skilled in jousting, horsemanship and wielding a sword. He was devoted to English saints, St George, St John of Bridlington and St John of Beverley, under whose banner English kings had often marched to battle against the Scots. As king, he had reopened the war with France and personally supervised the organisation of the expedition in 1415. He had upheld justice and order within his realm, and ruthlessly suppressed an attempted rebellion – the Southampton plot – as his army gathered under his banner. John Hardyng believed the way Henry stamped his authority upon England had built the foundation for his war abroad:

> Above all things, he kept the law and peace,
> Throughout all England, that no insurrection
> Nor any riots were not made to cease ...
> Complaints of wrongs always in general
> Reformed were under his justice equal.
> The peace at home and law so well maintained
> Were root and head of all his great conquest.

The situation Henry V faced in 1415 was more complex than Hardyng would admit, yet it is clear that the king brought energy and vision to his reign – and this was evident in his decision to claim the throne of France, and enforce that claim with an army behind him. Adam of Usk related how Henry:

> ... *sent a solemn embassy to France to demand from him those hereditary lands of his which were situated within his kingdom, and to ask for his daughter in marriage so that a proper peace might be had; but they were treated with derision; and returned to England without achieving any progress, whereupon the king, and the heroes of the realm, in their fury, began to direct their wrath towards the French.*

The French writer Jean Juvenal des Ursins related that when the two armies came into view, on the afternoon of 24 October, Henry reminded his captains that:

> ... *from time immemorial his predecessors had maintained their right to the kingdom of France, and that in good and just title it had fallen to him to conquer it, and that he wished greatly to conquer all that belonged to him ... For this reason he said to them that he had true hope of God of winning the battle, because his enemies were full of sin, and did not fear their maker at all.*

If Henry did talk to his men, he would need to gather his principal followers around him, speak simply and effectively, and then let them pass his message on to the rank-and-file troops. With the vast French army in full view, the king certainly wanted to reach out to his soldiers. In his formative years he had shown a remarkable aptitude for command, and this was also shown on the Agincourt campaign. But the king, along with everyone else, was only too aware that things had gone badly wrong and he would need all his skill in the battle ahead. It seemed as if Fortune had turned against the English – and as they lined up on the ridge, tired, hungry and heavily outnumbered, it was obvious that they were now in a desperate position.

Henry's military education had been forged in exceptionally tough circumstances. At Shrewsbury, on 21 July 1403, the 16-year-old – as Prince of Wales – received an initiation into the bloody art of war. 'It was the prince's first taste of fighting,' Thomas Walsingham said. He was catapulted into a vicious civil war battle that pitched Englishmen against Englishmen – with the longbow a killing weapon used by both sides. The Earl of Northumberland's charismatic son Henry 'Hotspur' Percy was in rebellion against the new Lancastrian dynasty and had taken the fight to Prince Henry's own father, King Henry IV. At a crucial stage of the battle, the future Henry V was badly wounded by an arrow in the face, but, fearing the consequences of leaving the field, and determined not to, snapped off the arrow shaft and continued the fight. The young Henry believed in leading from the front, and displayed great courage in doing so – behaviour he intended to repeat in the battle ahead.

There followed a dangerous operation to retrieve the arrow head, conducted by the surgeon John Bradmore. When Bradmore was called to the prince he found, according to his own account, that Henry had been: '... struck by an arrow next to his nose, on the left side ...'

So Bradmore cut through the Prince's face to the depth of the wound and then applied surgical tongs:

I put these tongs in at an angle ... Then, by moving it to and fro, little by little (with the help of God), I extracted the arrowhead. Many gentlemen and servants of the Prince were standing by and all gave great thanks to God.

The pain that Henry endured, both from his horrible injury and the dramatic surgery which saved him, can scarcely be imagined. Bradmore then spent days cleansing the wound and applying ointment to regenerate the flesh around it. He had saved the prince's life, and the surgical procedure he devised was regarded with wonderment.

Henry V's personal surgeon, Thomas Morstede, present on the Agincourt campaign, had assisted Bradmore during the course of the operation, which he described in his own work, *The Fair Book of Surgery*. Morstede, dynamic and able, would initiate a project to found the first English college of medicine, and later created the guild of surgeons.

Morstede's presence on the campaign was a reminder to the king and his captains of the operation that had saved Henry's life. Henry V's face would have been left badly scarred on one side. We are used to imagining him from the royal portrait now hanging in the National Portrait Gallery, London, which shows us the king's face unmarked. This picture was copied many years after the event and presents an idealised version. Aristocrats and ordinary soldiers, anxiously watching their commander, would have immediately been struck by his battle scars. They communicated far more powerfully than words that this was a man of outstanding courage, willing to take risks and lead from the front and, above all, that he was favoured by God. For his friends and supporters, it was a miracle that he had survived at all. Henry's scarred face would have acted as a talisman to his troops.

Over the next few years, Prince Henry fought against the rebellion of Owen Glendower. Hampered by difficult terrain and a shortage of money, the scrappy fighting and occasional battles in Wales shaped his outlook. From this came a sense of personal destiny, an abiding loyalty to his fellow soldiers and a strong awareness of the importance of raising the morale in difficult circumstances.

In putting down this revolt, he could at times be ruthless. On one occasion he reported to his father how he had destroyed Owen's main estates:

'We took our forces and marched to the place of the said Owen, well-built, which was his principal mansion, called Sycharth. On our arrival, we found nobody; and therefore caused the whole place to be burnt, and several houses nearby, belonging to his tenants.'

On 11 March 1405 Henry wrote another revealing letter to his father. He described how a large rebel army had assembled under one of Glendower's lieutenants and had raided the town of Grosmont in Monmouthshire. Henry dispatched a small force to the town's assistance and, although heavily outnumbered, it had taken battle to the enemy and won a resounding victory. He made a telling observation: 'But very true it is, that victory is not in a multitude of people but in the power of God, and this was well proved there.'

Medieval commanders would often surrender the outcome of battle to the will of God – but this was a striking comment.

In the summer of 1407 Prince Henry brought up cannon for the siege of Aberystwyth Castle – and put the fortress under sustained bombardment. It was the first time in the country that artillery had been used on such a scale. The bombardment brought the garrison close to surrender – although the stronghold was not finally captured until the following year.

Henry would retain a strong interest in military technology, recruiting 26 master-gunners and a further 52 assistant gunners in 1415 for the siege of Harfleur. The majority of these specialists were Dutch or German. The king's artillery – and the experts who manned it – had been left in Harfleur along with a substantial garrison when Henry marched out of the town.

On 24 October 1415, Henry knew that his army was small and had been weakened by disease and hunger. Much would now depend on its discipline and morale. The French had assembled a mighty force to oppose the English and the sheer size of the enemy army, clearly in view, was a terrifying prospect for many of Henry's soldiers. It was vital that the English king showed his men a resolve to fight and win – and then inspire his soldiers with that same determination.

Henry did not have to clutch at straws or put on an act that no one really believed. There were glimmerings of hope amid the gloom. The king and his senior commanders were aware that if French numbers continued to swell the sheer size of their army might work against them. For the medieval military theorist size was not everything; indeed, battle commentators recognised there were dangers in deploying an overly large army. Just a few years before Agincourt, the French writer Christine de Pizan brought out a military manual, *The Deeds of Arms and Chivalry*. She argued against the view that victory automatically belonged to the side with the most men. On the contrary, she emphasised that once an army became large and unwieldy it was far more difficult to maintain its cohesion and good order:

Therein lies the difficulty, for the larger army cannot easily move forward, but so many men will rather get in the way of each other, and in battle formation they lunge forward so hastily that they mingle needlessly with the enemy, and are exterminated.

Here Christine de Pizan was recalling a Roman military maxim: 'A greater multitude is subject to more mishaps.' One needs to be careful with such sayings. In most circumstances larger numbers, as one would expect, did indeed confer the greater advantage. Thomas Walsingham, describing a late fourteenth-century clash at La Réole (1377), where the English commander Sir Thomas Felton had been defeated, portrayed it as 'an engagement that brought sorrow to the whole of England'. Felton, the governor of English-held Gascony, 'very rashly attacked a larger French force with a small band of men, and was overwhelmed and captured *by their great numbers*' (my emphasis). Felton's defeat was a disaster not only for his small army, but also those remaining Gascon nobility who supported the English cause. There were many other such hopeless clashes at the end of the fourteenth-century phase of the Hundred Years War. Yet Pizan's warning that, if an army was too big, its men would simply get in the way of each other was remarkably prescient.

The qualities praised by Pizan – organisation and intelligence in military operations – would form the bedrock of Henry's approach to the fight ahead. But much work was required for such aspirations to become reality. The larger size of an army could become a liability if its command structure was not unified and became disjointed. On his side, the English king needed once again to stamp his authority on his soldiers. Above all, Henry needed to demonstrate to his men a willingness to stand and fight with what he had.

This particular stage in the lead-up to the battle was picked up by Shakespeare in *Henry V*, although he placed it on the morning of the battle itself. Amid a gathering of dispirited Englishmen, 'cousin Westmorland' bemoaned the number of the enemy compared with the meagre English army. Amid such pessimism, what was the king to do? If he ignored Westmorland's doubts, he would show himself out of touch with reality. If he confirmed them, he would admit to the

74

apparent hopelessness of the English position. In an inspired and inspiring rejoinder, Henry turned the situation around with one of the most famous speeches of the play:

> *No my fair cousin,*
> *If we are marked to die, we are enough*
> *To do our country loss; and if to live,*
> *The fewer men, the greater share of honour.*
> *God's will, I pray thee wish not one man more.*

He then built powerfully upon his theme:

> *We few, we happy few, we band of brothers,*
> *For he today that sheds his blood with me*
> *Shall be my brother, be he ne'er so vile,*
> *This day shall gentle his condition.*

No longer were the English hapless underdog; rather, they were a select band of brothers, chosen by God to take on the might of the French. It was a remarkable moment, and, with his words, Shakespeare instinctively caught the mood of Henry's army and was also true to the sources he drew upon. The eyewitness account of Henry's chaplain reveals that this incident really did take place (although on the afternoon before the battle), on the ridge at Blangy. In his contemporary account the chaplain remembered that it was Sir Walter Hungerford who had spoken up. 'A certain knight,' the chaplain related, 'Sir Walter Hungerford, expressed a desire to the king's face that he might have, in addition to the small company assembled around him, ten thousand more of the best archers of England.' The king rebuked him, saying that those who were with him were specially chosen:

Thou speakest foolishly, for by the God of Heaven, on whose grace I have relied, I would not, even if I could, increase my number by one. For those whom I have are the people of God, whom He thinks are worthy to have at this time. Dost thou not believe that the Almighty, with these His humble few, is able to conquer the haughty opposition of the French?

Thomas Elmham was struck by the power of Henry's rejoinder: 'I do not wish for one man more. Victory will not be won on the basis of numbers. God is all-powerful – my cause is firmly put in his hands.' Titus Livius, drawing on the testimony of the king's brother, Humphrey, Duke of Gloucester, also recalled this moment:

It is related that a certain man was heard to say, disclosing his prayer to others: 'If only our gracious God would grant, in his mercy, that all those knights who are in England might instead be with us in this battle.' To which our courageous king replied: 'Indeed, I do not wish a single man to be added to my army. We are small in number compared with the enemy. If God in his mercy favours my army with justice, which we hope, there is not one man amongst us who may attribute such a victory over so many of our foes to our own strength, but only to the help of God ... Be strong of heart and fight with all your might. May God and the justice of our cause defend us. May he render into our hands, and into our power, all that multitude of an exceedingly arrogant enemy, which you can all see before us.'

On the surface, this incident appears to show the English leader reprimanding a faint-hearted follower, but there was far more to it than that. Hungerford was a loyal supporter of the house of Lancaster, articulate and a quick thinker. Educated at Oxford, he was fluent in Latin as well as English and

76

French, and owned a Latin Bible and a number of theological works alongside a chivalric text, *The Siege of Troy*. He was no stranger to difficult situations. Shortly after Henry's father Henry IV came to the throne the Earls of Salisbury and Kent had plotted an uprising to put the previous king, Richard II, back in power. They had kidnapped Hungerford, robbed him of his Lancastrian livery collar (worth £20) and forced him to accompany them to Cirencester. While appearing to play along with their schemes, Sir Walter found a way of secretly warning the town officials, alerting them to what was going on and advising them to arrest the rebels. His advice was taken – and the townsmen went further: the following day Salisbury and Kent were lynched by an angry mob.

Afterwards, Hungerford became prominent in royal service (acting as chamberlain to Prince Henry's sister Philippa) and no one ever doubted his courage. In 1406 he was granted 100 marks in consideration of his expenses at Calais, 'where he had upheld the honour of England in arms against a certain knight of France'. In 1414 he had been elected Speaker at Henry V's first parliament, and had impressed his royal master enough to be sent on an important diplomatic mission shortly afterwards, travelling to Koblenz in an attempt to negotiate an alliance with the Emperor Sigismund. Hungerford had only returned from this in May 1415 and immediately set about recruiting a retinue of 20 men-at-arms and 60 archers to accompany the king to France. Hungerford would prosper in royal service before and after Agincourt – Henry clearly respected him and did not have a problem with him speaking his mind.

Nevertheless, on this occasion Henry chose to remind Hungerford of the example of Judas Maccabeus, who had been promised God's support in battle but complained about his small numbers nonetheless. Surely, Maccabeus asked

God, it would be better to wait for more troops? God told him to get on with it. Maccabeus did, and won.

Medieval writers sometimes made up speeches and put them into the mouths of commanders, but the detail recalled by the chaplain is plausible and convincing. Through his account we hear the voice of King Henry himself, captured and conveyed through time over six centuries.

It is difficult for a modern audience to appreciate the power these words would have had in medieval times. As men's morale faltered, a reference to what for us may be an obscure Old Testament character would for them be relevant and stirring. Judas Maccabeus was one of the nine worthies – one of the pantheon of warriors admired by medieval society – and thus instantly recognisable to Henry's audience.

It is likely that the English king saw, in the example of Maccabeus, a way to communicate to his soldiers and a reminder of the effectiveness of proper spiritual preparation as battle approached. The Dominican friar John Bromyard wrote in the 1390s that God's help could be sought before combat, adding: 'Judas Maccabeus fasted and prayed before battle – and thus he overcame his enemies.' Henry knew of Bromyard's writings and they strongly shaped his martial outlook.

The chaplain's account – through which we hear Henry's own voice – was not some propaganda device but a genuine recollection, and his testimony carries conviction because of his honesty about the dire straits the English found themselves in.

These terrible events would have been in everybody's minds as they watched the French army. Over the previous two weeks, as we have learned, Henry's army had been through a great deal. Their faith in God and their commander had already been tested to the limit – and the chaplain well knew this. He had witnessed how, unable to cross the Somme where they intended and instead being forced to march inland, food had begun to run out and the spirit of the army fell. Seeing the bridge at Pont-Remy broken, and realising that thousands of French were gathering, and that the head of the river – which they desperately needed to cross – was more than 60 miles away, morale plummeted, as the chaplain honestly recorded. Men were struggling to believe that God was still with them:

> *At that time we thought of nothing else but that, after the eight days assigned for the march had expired and our provisions had run out, the enemy, who had craftily hastened on ahead and were laying waste the countryside in advance, would force us – who were already hungry – to suffer a really dire need of food. And at the head of the river, if God did not provide otherwise, they would, with their great and countless host and engines of war and devices available to them, overwhelm us, for we were few in number, fainting with a great weariness, and weak from a lack of food.*
>
> *I, the author of this, and many other in the army, looked up in bitterness to Heaven, seeking the clemency of Providence, and called upon the Glorious Virgin and St George, under whose protection the most invincible crown of England has flourished from of old, to intercede between God and his people, that the Supreme Judge, who foresees all things, might take pity on the grief all England would feel at the price we would pay with our blood, and in His infinite mercy, deliver from the swords of the French our King and us his people … and bring us to the honour and glory of His name, in triumph to Calais. Without any other hope than this, we hastened on from there [Pont-Remy] in the direction of the head of the river …*

On 19 October the English had finally managed to cross the river. They now swung northwards again. But a large French force was now ahead of them. At Péronne the English troops had seen direct evidence of the growing mass of enemy soldiers. Again, the chaplain caught the mood of emotional and spiritual despair:

> We found the roads remarkably churned up by the French army, as if it had preceded us by the thousand. And the rest of our troops – to say nothing of our commanders – fearing that battle was imminent, raised our eyes and hearts to heaven, crying out with voices of deepest earnestness, that God would have pity on us and in His infinite goodness, turn away from us the power of the French.

This grim backdrop makes a build-up of fear before the battle all too believable. And for the English army to be effective in battle, Henry would have to address these doubts head on. Thomas Elmham was struck by how he turned these factors around, saying to Hungerford and the other captains:

> God has tested our faith by afflicting our army with disease. Being merciful, he will not now let us be killed by such enemies. Let our heartfelt prayers be offered to him.

It was a tribute to Henry's leadership that he was prepared to listen to others and let people speak their mind. He had brought on his expedition a veteran campaigner, Sir Thomas Erpingham. Erpingham was 60 years old and the king trusted him and held his experience and counsel in high regard. Sir Thomas was from established East Anglian gentry. He had chosen a military career from an early age. In September 1368, just 18 years old, he had accompanied his father to Aquitaine in the service of Edward Prince of Wales – the 'Black Prince'. Erpingham was knighted in 1372, and that year he served on naval and land expeditions to France. By 1379 he had become a servant of Henry's grandfather, John of Gaunt, receiving a generous annuity (an annual cash payment) of £20 in peace and 50 marks (£33 6s 8d) in war. He was with Gaunt on his campaign in Scotland in 1385 and accompanied him to Castile in the following year.

Soon afterwards, Erpingham was attached to the household of Gaunt's eldest son, Henry, Earl of Derby (Henry V's father) and he accompanied the future Henry IV on his crusading expedition to Prussia and Lithuania between 1390 and 1391, and on his pilgrimage to Palestine in 1392–3. When Henry was forced to flee abroad Erpingham went into exile with his master and remained with him until his landing in England with a small army in the summer of 1399. Sir Thomas played an important role in Henry's usurpation of the throne, which saw the reigning king Richard II first deposed and imprisoned, and then almost certainly murdered on Henry's orders.

Immediately after Henry's army landed at Ravenspur in Yorkshire in July 1399 Erpingham was dispatched to raise money, returning to the expedition in time to accompany Henry Percy, Earl of Northumberland to the crucial interview with Richard II at Conwy, which saw Richard taken into custody. He played a prominent part in the formal proceedings that led to that king's deposition, carrying Henry's sword before him as he processed into Westminster Hall and, 'on behalf of all the knights and commons of this land', renounced allegiance to Richard.

The new king, Henry IV, quickly rewarded Sir Thomas's loyalty, appointing him constable of Dover Castle and warden of the Cinque Ports – a strategically vital military command

– as early as August 1399. In January 1400 Erpingham commanded a division in the royal army that put down the 'Epiphany rising' (an attempt to release Richard II and restore him to the throne – the failure of which almost certainly led to Henry's decision to murder the deposed king) and, in the summer, served on the king's expedition against the Scots. He was appointed Knight of the Garter later that year.

Sir Thomas's closeness to Henry IV was noticed by contemporaries. The citizens of Norwich paid him 20 marks, 'for bearing his good word to the king for the honour of the city'. By October 1404 Erpingham became acting marshal of England, and his services to king and kingdom were specifically commended in Parliament. Sir Thomas was a soldier through and through. He disliked administrative business and attended the royal council only occasionally. By the end of 1404, now almost 50, he withdrew from any active involvement in court life – and his subsequent employment was chiefly diplomatic. In February 1409 he surrendered the constableship of Dover to Henry Prince of Wales in return for an annuity of £100. But when Henry came to the throne in 1413 he immediately appointed Sir Thomas to the post of steward of the royal household, and encouraged this seasoned veteran to join him on the Agincourt campaign, with a retinue of 20 men-at-arms and 60 archers.

Henry prized Erpingham's military experience, his outstanding record of service to his father and grandfather and his reliability in a crisis. The presence of Erpingham in the English army made a powerful symbolic link with the achievements of the Black Prince, and that was most important, for the Prince was England's great medieval warrior hero, the victor at Poitiers and Najera. Thomas Walsingham wrote a moving tribute on the Black Prince's death, in 1376, making clear the effect he had had on the English people:

As long as he survived, they feared no enemy invasion; and while he was in the field, no shock of war. While he was present, we never suffered the disgrace of a campaign that had been badly fought or abandoned. He attacked no nation that he did not conquer; no city that he did not capture.

In his choice of Erpingham, Henry gave the army a wise and pragmatic counsellor. The king was not worried by Sir Thomas's age; rather, he valued his wisdom and sought a place for it, appointing Erpingham one of the chief negotiators in the surrender of Harfleur.

Remarkably, Sir Thomas was not the oldest captain in Henry V's army. Thomas Lord Camoys, of Trotton in Sussex, was 65 years old, another veteran who had fought in Henry IV's wars against the Scots, Welsh and French – and now accompanied the expedition of 1415 with a retinue of 25 men-at-arms and 70 archers. Very much like Erpingham, Camoys had all but retired from public life by 1406, only to be invited by the new king to the council meeting that planned the invasion of France. Again Henry V valued his experience and reliability, giving him command of the army's rearguard as the English drew up in formation to face the French.

Henry Lord FitzHugh was another seasoned soldier, 53 years old at the time of the Agincourt expedition and a loyal servant of Henry's father, Henry IV. FitzHugh had participated in the defeat of the Scots at Homildon Hill in 1402 and was prominent in diplomatic embassies to Scotland and the government of the north. Henry V strongly identified with FitzHugh's devoutness, which ran parallel with his public service. When he went on an embassy to Denmark in 1406, for the marriage of Henry IV's daughter Philippa to King Erik, he became acquainted with the Bridgettine order of nuns and religious men, and subsequently endeavoured to create a Bridgettine community in England, promising his manor of Cherry Hinton in Cambridgeshire as an endowment. In 1408 FitzHugh went on crusade to Prussia, and shortly afterwards went on pilgrimage to the Levant and then fought for the Knights of St John at Rhodes.

Henry V admired Lord FitzHugh's dedication to the crusading ideal and the piety that underpinned it. After the king's accession FitzHugh became a close associate, acting as constable during the coronation and being appointed chamberlain of the royal household. In March 1415 he and Henry jointly endowed a Bridgettine house at Twickenham (later moved to Syon) – the one English foundation of that religious order to be established. In 1415 another northern aristocrat, Henry Lord Scrope, left FitzHugh a copy of *The Fire of Love* by the hermit and mystic Richard Rolle. The presence of FitzHugh, who jointly acted as negotiator for the surrender of Harfleur with Sir Thomas Erpingham, provided the English king with good counsel as well as religious solace.

Hungerford, Erpingham, Camoys and FitzHugh were men whom the king trusted completely. Their loyalty was absolute and Henry was comfortable enough with his own authority, and the clearly unified system of command within his army, to let them speak frankly. His remarkable conversation with Hungerford arose out of the latter's acceptance of his leadership rather than a wish to undermine it. But no one was under any illusion about the danger they were facing as the enemy massed before them.

In the French camp, the mood was upbeat. Once the English army had left Harfleur, Henry's principal adversary, Jean le Meingre, Marshal Boucicaut, had conducted the campaign with considerable skill. At 49, Boucicaut had the most distinguished military pedigree in Europe. His résumé was dazzling. He had first participated on a campaign (as a page) at the age of 12; he had then been knighted at 16, joined his first crusade at 18, become a Holy Land pilgrim at the age of 22 and marshal of France at 26. He had married well above his station, been entertained by kings, emperors and popes and showered with praise by the leading female writer of the age, Christine de Pizan. He had organised and fought in the most famous jousts of the fourteenth century.

By the age of 16, Boucicaut had gained a reputation for physical prowess. In a book of Boucicaut's chivalric deeds – composed during his lifetime and opening a remarkable window on his martial career – his training regimen was laid out:

> *Now, cased in armour, he would leap onto the back of a horse; to further build up his endurance he would walk or run long distances, again in full armour, and strike numerous blows – delivered at full force – with a battle-axe. He would turn somersaults while clad in a complete suit of mail, with the exception of the helmet, or would dance vigorously in a breastplate of steel; he would place one hand on the saddle of his warhorse, the other on the neck, and vault over him. He was able to climb up two walls, some four to five feet apart, using only the applied pressure of his arms and legs, and he would not rest during ascent or descent. When he was at home he would practise continually with other young esquires at lance-throwing and other warlike exercises.*

Boucicaut did not stay at home for long. At the age of 18, he undertook his first journey to Prussia in support of the Teutonic Knights. Two years later he was fighting against the Moors in Spain. He took some time off to make a pilgrimage to the Holy Land, where he penned the *Book of a Hundred Ballads*, exceeding Ghillebert de Lannoy's tally of 48 poems, and replacing its motifs of love and eroticism with a defence of the chaste knight, a central figure of chivalric literature.

Back in France, in 1390 he took part in a great tournament at Saint-Inglevert, where he defeated some of the most renowned English soldiers in single combat. The following year he was once more fighting in Prussia – and on his return was made marshal of France by Charles VI. Boucicaut's life was a round of non-stop combat. In 1396 he took part in the joint French-Hungarian crusade against the Turks, which was defeated at the battle of Nicopolis.

Captured and then ransomed, Boucicaut was undaunted by his experience, in 1399 founding his own chivalric order, one dedicated to the theme of courtly love, wondrously titled the Order of the White Lady on the Green Shield, together with his friend and fellow fighter Charles d'Albret, Constable of France, and then sailing with a small expedition the following year to assist the Byzantine Emperor Manuel II against the Turks. In 1401 he was appointed French governor of Genoa, beating off an attack by the King of Cyprus, and residing there until the city regained its independence in 1409. Three years later he was given wide-ranging powers to wage war in Gascony on behalf of Charles VI.

On 28 July 1415, after the French court had received news of the English army gathering at Southampton, Boucicaut was appointed king's lieutenant and captain general, with particular responsibility for the defence of Normandy. In the circumstances it was a natural appointment, but the man Boucicaut replaced, Jean, Duke of Alençon, an aristocrat of superior rank and a very brave fighter, but possessing little innate military ability, immediately resented it.

Alençon's *amour propre* was caught by Perceval de Cagny, a member of the duke's own household, who then claimed, somewhat implausibly:

> ... *when the king of England left Harfleur, wishing to cross the Somme at Blanchetaque, the Duke of Alençon knew immediately what had to be done, and by his diligence managed to reach the town of Abbeville before the English could make their crossing, and cut off their route, so that they were forced to march upriver* ...

De Cagny attributed to Alençon the delaying tactics that so effectively deprived Henry's army of food and sustenance on its march, 'so that they experienced a great lack of victuals ... which gave the English much trouble and anxiety'.

All other French accounts give Boucicaut and d'Albret the credit for this, and it is hard to imagine the duke acting with such prudence and restraint. Alençon's great-grandfather Charles – who led the French line at Crécy – was famous for his dangerously foolhardy courage. At Crécy he had refused to brook any delay in attacking the English, riding over the Genoese crossbowmen, in the vanguard of the French army, and launching a series of impetuous assaults even before his own sovereign and commander, Philip VI, had arrived at the battlefield. His descendant was cast in much the same mould.

Enguerrand de Monstrelet gave the more likely scenario:

> *At that time, the Lord d'Albret, Constable of France, the Marshal Boucicaut, the Count of Vendôme, the Duke of Alençon and the Count of Richemont were in Abbeville, already with a substantial body of men. On hearing news of the route the king of England was following, they went with their troops to Corbie,*

to continue to guard all the crossing points of the Somme against the English.

At this stage of the campaign there was a clear French command structure, headed by Boucicaut and d'Albret. As Henry's army was forced further and further upriver, Boucicaut devised a plan of battle for when the English were finally forced to fight. Its tone was clear, direct and forceful. Jean Juvenal des Ursins described how it came into being, at a French council of war – probably held at Péronne on around 19 October:

> *The lords and captains were assembled to decide what to do. They had already summoned the Duke of Orléans, the Duke of Brabant and the Count of Nevers to join them. There were diverse opinions and thoughts. Some said that they should let the English pass without offering battle – because battle was always a risky undertaking. But many said that the army they had assembled was now large and powerful, and its men well-armed and equipped. And that the English forces were in a bad state, their armour in poor condition and the leather jackets of the archers old and tattered. And being away from their homes and in danger, many of the latter would probably run away rather than stay the course of the fight and do their duty.*
>
> *The opposing argument was once again put – that the course of a battle was often risky and perilous, and there was a danger – once the English archers had engaged the French men-at-arms, who, because of their heavy armour would move much more slowly and ponderously – that things could go badly wrong. If they let the English go they could instead besiege Harfleur, and recover it easily enough. And if they decided to fight, they should summon the town levies, who might well prove useful in*

a battle. It was said that the Marshal Boucicaut and the Constable d'Albret, and several other knights who had much experience in warfare, were of this opinion.

The Dukes of Alençon and Bourbon and many others strongly opposed this, saying that the English were already badly demoralised and would not offer much resistance – and that there was no need to summon the town levies, they had plenty of troops as it was.

The Duke of Alençon taunted Boucicaut, saying that he was afraid; the marshal replied robustly that his war record spoke for itself. Finally, a compromise was agreed upon:

It was eventually decided that they would fight – but with the provision that a strong cavalry force – comprising men renowned for their courage and experience in warfare – would be set up, to charge the English archers and disrupt their arrow fire.

On 20 October a great council of French magnates was held at Rouen. The decision to fight the English was confirmed, and, according to Enguerrand de Monstrelet:

After this it was decreed throughout the whole of France that all nobles accustomed to bear arms and wishing to acquire honour should go by night and day in order to join the constable, wherever he might be found.

Boucicaut's battle plan was devised with considerable care and was testimony to his military experience. He recognised the risks, even in such an apparently advantageous position, and took steps to counter any possible danger. Firstly, he set out the dispositions of his troops:

This is how it seems to the lord marshal [Boucicaut], and to the lords who are with him, the Duke of Alençon, the Count of Richemont and the lord constable [d'Albret] …

At this stage Boucicaut remained in charge of the army and, while consulting with the others, took overall responsibility for it, stating:

First, in the name of God … it is advised that there should be a large division, which will form the vanguard. In this will be the constable and the marshal [d'Albret and Boucicaut] with all their men.

Also in this division, the banners of the constable and marshal shall be placed together. That of the constable shall be on the right and that of the marshal on the left. And on the right the troops should be all men of the constable – and on the left, men of the marshal.

It was considered a great honour to lead the vanguard, and Boucicaut and d'Albret were claiming this right, intending to fight together with their soldiers on either side. The Duke of Alençon, the Count of Eu, and any other great lords who joined the army, would follow up behind them.

More dismounted men-at-arms were placed on the flanks of these two forces. It was envisaged that the Bretons, Arthur, Count of Richemont and Jean, Lord of Combour, would command one of these formations, the leading members of the royal household, Louis, Count of Vendôme and Guichard Dauphin, the other.

In front of all these groups was a screen of crossbowmen and archers, and slightly to one side was placed an elite cavalry force: 'a division of heavy horse shall be formed, of good men, up to the number of a thousand at least'. It would be commanded by an experienced soldier – David, Lord of Rambures. A smaller cavalry force was placed in the rear of the army.

In making these dispositions Marshal Boucicaut envisaged a sequenced attack, one intended to utterly destroy Henry's army. The crossbowmen would open the fight, and through their fire weaken the English line. Then the heavy cavalry would charge the archers, and at that point, 'when the body of horsemen moves off, all the foot soldiers will advance together', after which the men-at-arms of both sides would then clash, the superior numbers of the French giving them the advantage. As the dismounted troops were fighting each other, and the heavy cavalry had eliminated the archers, the final French cavalry force would move off, swing round behind the English position, crash through their baggage train and then strike their main force from behind.

This was the plan of an experienced military professional. It did not underestimate the English, even in the desperate position they were now in. It recognised the danger posed by their bowmen, allocating an elite cavalry force to neutralise them, saying bluntly 'this division will attack the archers, and do the utmost to break them'. It set out a clear order of battle, emphasising how the French attack would be co-ordinated.

However, at this stage the plan was all theoretical. As the fifteenth-century French writer Philippe de Commynes observed, 'things in the field [of battle] seldom turn out as they have been planned indoors'. Commynes vividly recalled the chaos of a clash between French and Burgundians at Montlhéry, when the agreed battle plan was jettisoned. Commynes, riding with the young and impetuous Burgundian commander Charles, Count of Charolais, told how, through a series of cavalry charges, Charolais became separated from the main contingent of his army. His small force chased after a body of enemy foot soldiers. One of the fleeing men suddenly turned and struck Charolais in the stomach with a pike with such force that the mark remained clearly visible for days afterwards. The isolated opponent was quickly overpowered but it had been a dangerous moment.

Minutes later, as Charolais returned from a reconnaissance of an enemy position, he was dramatically surrounded by a body of horsemen. His escort was overwhelmed and his standard-bearer cut down. Charolais himself was wounded in several places. As the count attempted to hack his way out, he suffered a blow to the throat that left him scarred for life. Inches from death, he was suddenly saved by a large, rather fat knight, who quite by chance rode between him and his opponents.

Thus Commynes witnessed the terrifying chaos of a medieval battle at close quarters. His ride with Charolais left him so fuelled with adrenalin that he forgot to be afraid. Instead, he captured a series of intense, almost surreal vignettes.

The most memorable saw Charolais return to his command post in the middle of the battlefield. The banners and standards that served as rallying points for his troops had been torn to shreds. The count was so bloody as to be almost unrecognisable. Amid fields of flattened wheat, a huge dust storm had been kicked up, obscuring friend and foe. The small group of 30 or 40 men waited anxiously in the semi-darkness as clutches of horsemen appeared and disappeared in the gloom. They knew that if the enemy arrived in force they would be wiped out or captured, yet there was nothing to do but stand their ground, hoping that some of their own men would return.

Commynes's experience transmits important truths of medieval combat. In his view, events had developed a momentum of their own, and at such speed it was impossible to carry fresh orders to all parts of the army. Entire companies of men were left unsure what to do; indeed, unable to see clearly what was happening or where to go. Others, who had received orders, were simply too frightened to carry them out and fled from the battlefield.

For his own plan to be carried through, Boucicaut needed to remain in command of the army. Already the Dukes of Alençon and Bourbon (who on 1 January 1415 had founded his chivalric order of the prisoner's shackle – one in which its members vowed never to retreat before the English) had chafed at the marshal's authority. The French council meeting at Rouen, which had approved the plan to give battle to the English, now named Charles, Duke of Orléans as the army's overall commander. As Orléans took up his post, it remained to be seen whether he would support Boucicaut or not.

Henry may have come to learn of this plan, or he may instinctively have anticipated it – but he was under no illusion about the threat it posed to his army's very survival. The French, after watching the English for around an hour, began to pull back. As Henry's chaplain related:

And after a short while, the enemy – who had been watching us, taking our measure, and fully realising how small our numbers were – withdrew towards the Calais road, placing their forces in an area of open countryside, with a wood on one of their flanks. And our king, seeing the threat of their forces circling round this wood, and making a surprise attack on our army, or that others might move round the ridge we were occupying and completely surround us, began to move his soldiers forward, still in battle array, always making sure that our lines faced the enemy.

And when it was almost sunset, the French, realising that the fight would not be taking place that day, pulled back to the nearby villages and set up their camp for the night.

It was 'vespers' – 6 pm. But the English king was taking no chances. He kept his army in formation through the twilight and dusk, until only a sliver of moonlight lit the night sky. Then, as Henry and his army followed their foe in the gathering darkness, the germ of an idea was forming in the king's mind: that the overweening confidence of the French, their fine armour, the size of their army, the impressive turnout of well-provisioned and well-fed aristocrats in all their finery, might be turned into a weakness rather than a strength in the fight to come.

Henry had been occupying the ground where another great warrior, Edward III, had also once drawn up his soldiers. That war, with its great victories at Crécy and Poitiers, had then gone badly wrong, the masterful campaigns of Edward's heyday being replaced by the bungled military fiascos of the late 1370s and 1380s.

Thomas Walsingham caught this mood of sadness and disillusionment, describing a French raid on the south coast, near Lewes, in 1377, one of the worst that had been seen in 40 years. A small force had gathered under the local knight Sir John Fawley. An experienced soldier, Fawley had fought under the Black Prince, and at the battle of Najera (1367) had captured the constable of France, Bertrand du Guesclin. Ten years later, it was all so different. There were simply not enough defenders and Fawley and his men were overwhelmed by the enemy.

Walsingham recalled the glory days of the English war effort:

> Our men rode in circles over the whole of France, looting and laying waste the country, burning towns and estates. And the French became so terror-stricken that they chose to hide rather than confront our army ... Nor was it out of arrogance or vanity

that our troops tried to subjugate the kingdom, but in trusting
the just rights of their king.

The country's military decline in the late fourteenth century
was painful to witness. Walsingham continued:

All began to be afraid, not only the common people, but also the
knights themselves, who had once been brave, trained soldiers
full of spirit who were now timid and cowardly. And they began
to talk not about resistance, but about escape and surrender.

It is so awful. The land that once bore men who were respected
by their countrymen and feared by the enemy, now spews forth
weaklings who are laughed at by our foes and the subject of
gossip amongst our own people.

At the end of the fourteenth century friar John Bromyard wrote
about the war from a religious standpoint and offered his own
explanation for England's military decline. Bromyard praised
Edward III for going on pilgrimage before undertaking a war
– and for taking the advice of those learned in God. He could
not help but contrast this king's spiritual preparation with the
lax attitude of his successors. 'Yet nowadays, alas, princes and
knights and soldiers go to war in a different spirit.'

Henry was familiar with Bromyard's work and strongly
influenced by it. In 1408 the Oxford academic Richard
Ullerston dedicated a book to him on the moral and spiritual
requirements of being a knight, praising his 'desire for spiritual study' and commending him for his knowledge of the
scriptures. Indeed, from boyhood Henry had acquired a reputation for serious reading – in English, French and Latin.

John Bromyard's message for the warrior was simple yet
powerful: with the right preparation, and by seeking the help
of God in prayer, anything was possible. Bromyard's writings

emphasised one key idea, one that was also found in the example of Judas Maccabeus, Henry's letter to his father after the victory at Grosmont in 1405 and his rejoinder to Hungerford on the ridge earlier that afternoon. Bromyard expressed it simply yet powerfully: 'For victory in a clash of arms is not achieved by the size of one's army, but by the help of God.'

This spiritual promise offered Henry a ray of hope as he moved his army forward in the twilight. It was now between 'vespers' and 'compline' – at around 8 pm. Battle would now be joined the following morning.

CHAPTER 3

The Mud Bath —•

The Armies

20.00–24.00 (24 October 1415)

IT WAS AN hour or so before 'compline' – around 8 pm.
Dusk had fallen. The moon was in its last quarter and the
night sky overcast, allowing little light, as the French army
pulled back to the more open countryside north of the villages of Agincourt and Tramecourt. Marshal Boucicaut and
the Constable d'Albret were content to play a waiting game,
knowing that every hour brought more reinforcements and
left their foe increasingly tired and hungry. Confident that
their superior numbers would deter any attack from the
English, they broke ranks and sought quarters for the night.

Jean de Waurin was with these forces as they set up camp:

> Banners and pennons were furled around the lances, armour
> taken off, and baggage unpacked – and the lords sent their ser-
> vants to nearby villages to find straw to put under their feet, for
> the ground was much churned up by the trampling of our horses.
> There was a great deal of noise from our pages and servants ...

Boucicaut and d'Albret did not want to rush heedlessly into
battle against the English. Whatever the plight of their opponents, they did not underestimate them as fighters. They had
watched Henry's army as it sought to cross the Somme, and
knew that it remained determined and resourceful. 'For
it has often been noted that a small number of desperate
men can conquer a large and powerful army,' Christine de
Pizan had warned, 'because they would rather die fighting

98

than fall into the cruel hands of the enemy, so there is a real risk in fighting people in such straits, as their strength is doubled.' Instead she advised that a wise commander would delay battle until he could find out as much as possible about the state of his opponents.

The English army moved forward to the village of Maisoncelles, the troops stumbling forward in the darkness. As they began to set up camp in the surrounding fields, it started to rain. They knew that the French were still ahead of them, for they had lit huge bonfires around their banners, both to keep warm and to serve as rallying points for the troops still joining their army.

Henry now took the remarkable step of freeing all his French prisoners. Manpower was so short that he did not wish to waste soldiers on guarding duties who might be better employed fighting. Jean Le Fèvre described what happened:

> *The king had ordered all his troops to lodge at Maisoncelles. But before he arrived at his lodgings, he gave all the French prisoners in his army – nobles and others – permission to leave, and in return they promised that if the day of battle turned out in his favour, and God gave him victory, they would return to him and their captors, if they still lived. But if he lost the battle they would be quit of their promises.*

It was now the 'hour' of 'compline' – 9 pm.

War was a tough trade and one experienced soldier of the late Middle Ages, Geoffrey de Charny – warned prospective warriors of its harsh realities:

> *You will have to put up with great labour before you achieve honour from this employ: heat, cold, fasting, hard work, little sleep and long watches and exhaustion.*

99

And then the English received a shock. French cavalry was sent out to probe the English position. Monstrelet related that:

> *Arthur, Count of Richemont had gathered some 2,000 mounted men-at-arms, and got right up to where the English were encamped. For a moment it seemed as if this force might break into the war camp, but the English drew up soldiers and began firing on them. After this sortie, the French returned to their billets.*

And now Henry, fearing another attempt by the enemy, imposed silence upon his army. His chaplain recalled the order:

> *And at last the light failed and darkness fell between us and the French, and we, standing our ground in the fields about us, heard the enemy taking up their quarters, each one of them – as is usual in such a situation – calling out for a friend, servant or comrade, who perhaps had become separated from one another. And our men had begun to do the same, until the king ordered silence throughout the entire army, imposing strict penalties if this order was disobeyed. A gentleman who breached this instruction would lose his horse and equipment; a yeoman would have his right ear struck off. And so it was in silence that the army now set up its camp around the hamlet [of Maisoncelles] where there were just a few houses and the shelter of trees in nearby orchards for our men to rest. And the rain grew heavier …*

This was a remarkable – and necessary – imposition of discipline. 'Never did anyone make so little noise,' Jean Le Fèvre recalled. 'It was hard to hear even your neighbour – men spoke so low.'

This self-control, and the professionalism of the army that applied it, impressed even the French. The Monk of Saint-Denis was moved to comment:

> *Credible witnesses that I have talked to about the condition of the English at that time have assured me that they had little to be cheerful about and that they had great difficulty getting hold of any food, and yet they considered it a crime to have prostitutes in their war camp, showed more regard for the well-being of the local inhabitants than we did and strictly observed all rules of military conduct and scrupulously obeyed their king.*

The Monk of Saint-Denis – known by this epithet as a mark of respect throughout the centuries – was a 65-year-old historian from one of the greatest abbeys of medieval France. His real name was Michel Pintouin – and he was commonly regarded as the best informed and most perceptive chronicler at the court of Charles VI. As a biographer of the king, Pintouin had access to official documents and could gather valuable witness testimony. He had witnessed many battles, but advancing age meant that he would sit this one out in the monastic library. His curiosity and intelligence remained undimmed, and subsequently he was able to speak to a number of the French who had assembled for the fight.

Pintouin believed in strong ethical government. He was not taken in by the showy extravagance of chivalry, its 'intoxicated pride in its plate armour and plumed helmets', as he commented rather gruffly, but cared greatly about wise counsel and sensible, clear-headed decisions. He was impressed by the discipline of the English troops and the fact that they treated French inhabitants with respect. For Pintouin that was admirable in itself, but also the hallmark of a well-honed fighting force. To his experienced eye, an army that conducted itself well on campaign would fight well in battle.

Henry V had stamped such discipline on his troops from the moment they landed in France. His chaplain remarked that within days of leaving his ships, on 17 August 1415, Henry was already drafting military ordinances:

> The king had prudently issued, among other most worthy decrees, a command to the army that under pain of death there should be no more setting fire to places, as there had been to begin with, and that churches and sacred buildings, along with their property, should be preserved intact, and that no one should lay hands on a woman or a priest or any other servant of the church unless they happened to be armed, behaving violently and attacking someone.

The chaplain recalled that, as the army set out from Harfleur on 8 October, and began its northward march to Calais:

> Among other most pious and worthy ordinances, the king commanded that, under pain of death, no man should burn and lay waste, or take anything save only food and what was necessary for the march, or capture any rebels save only those he might happen to find offering resistance.

Titus Livius added that these commands covered even the smallest items of church property, 'that no one should dare take from the altar sacred vessels, books or anything which is necessary for the celebration of the divine office'. According to Thomas Elmham, these statutes were drawn up 'to the honour of God and the preservation of the army'. They were proclaimed to every soldier in it. Elmham emphasised how the king had also decreed: 'No one should renew ancient discords or suits, or seek vengeance in any matter that might cause disturbance to the army.'

Cohesion and unity were Henry's abiding priorities. He wanted God on his side, and God's favour in the battle ahead. And he wanted his troops always to behave responsibly. That to him was far more important than numbers. The king wished to recall England's glory days at the height of the Hundred Years War and create a new mood of self-belief within his army.

At the beginning of the fourteenth century, the chronicler Jean le Bel derided the English army as the laughing stock of Europe. But within a generation it had shown its mettle in the campaigns of Edward III and had achieved famous victories against the French at Crécy and Poitiers.

The English had employed a highly effective weapon, the longbow. The bow required years of training to use properly. The English kings of the twelfth and thirteenth centuries had relied heavily on Welsh archers to supply the majority of their bowmen, but by the late Middle Ages its use was widespread among English troops. Its speed of employment and range made it a much feared weapon. It was the highest compliment to English archers that by the early fifteenth century the Grand Master of the Teutonic Knights, the toughest chivalric order in Europe, began to recruit substantial numbers of English bowmen to fight in their own campaigns.

Henry's own battle experience at Shrewsbury in 1403 demonstrated to him the terrible effectiveness of the English longbow, and it is likely that on the Agincourt campaign he wished to forge these bowmen into a formidable fighting force, united under his command.

The possibility of the humble archer winning battles went against the grain of the class-based society of the late Middle Ages. It saw warfare as an aristocratic pursuit and chivalry, the code of conduct which governed it, as the preserve of the nobleman. In short, medieval warfare was something of an exclusive, members-only club and riff-raff were not welcome. This was certainly the French viewpoint. Jean Juvenal des Ursins recalled how, during the siege of Harfleur, the French king, Charles VI, in a rare moment of lucidity, wanted to introduce archery practice throughout his realm, in an attempt to match the power of the English longbow. His noblemen were aghast at the prospect of peasants joining their army and threatened to depose him if he tried to put the measure into effect. Henry V, in contrast, not only saw the military value of the longbow, but wanted the ordinary archer to feel welcome within his own face.

Henry was building on the style of leadership of his great-grandfather, Edward III, a man who not only showed skill in the way he deployed archers within his army, but would also speak to them directly, in order to motivate them to fight better. In one memorable incident, near Calais in 1350, King Edward and a small English force was suddenly confronted by a much larger body of French men-at-arms. The king immediately identified himself to his bowmen, who until then had been unaware he was in their midst. The chronicler Geoffrey le Bel told of the powerful effect of Edward's action: 'He encouraged his men and spoke to them courteously, saying "Do your best, archers – I am Edward of Windsor".'

The archers were galvanised by this, and with the king watching wanted to make every arrow count. Edward addressed his soldiers 'courteously' – he did not patronise or condescend to them – and he reaped the benefit, as his opponents were quickly put to flight.

Thomas Walsingham said of Edward III: 'He was not puffed up or proud – and he treated his inferiors, in rank and status, as equals.' And if Henry V chose to imitate King Edward's style of leadership, he also was influenced by his tactical deployment of the longbow. For archers played an important role in Edward's armies, and those of the great captains who followed him, as the chronicler Jean Froissart remarked pointedly after Crécy: 'I tell you that day the English archers gave great support to their side, for many said that by their shooting the affair was won.'

Walsingham gave a graphic description of the impact of an arrow storm at the battle of Gravelines (1383) – the last engagement of the great English war captain Sir Hugh Calveley:

> *Our bowmen sent a rain of arrows upon the enemy, which left few of our foes still standing on their feet. Such was the density of the onslaught that the sky grew dark, as if from a black cloud, and such was the frequency with which they were loosed that their men dared not lift up their faces. Anybody who tried to look up would in a moment be lamenting a lost eye or suffering a pierced head.*

There was now, within England, a growing awareness of the value of the longbow. Chroniclers began taking note of when the ordinary soldier had done well and to draw people's attention to it. In the English defeat of the Scots at Homildon Hill, in 1402, Thomas Walsingham emphatically stated:

> *Victory was not won by the hands of nobles or lords, but by the means of poor men and servants. No lord, knight or esquire took a step until the archers had defeated the enemy.*

The ferocity of the arrow storm at Shrewsbury, in 1403, drew much comment:

The archers began to draw so fast that it seemed to beholders like a thick cloud, for the sun, which at that time was bright and clear, then lost its brightness so thick were the arrows.

The following year, it was noted approvingly that the 'common folk' had defeated a French force attacking Dartmouth.

Thus far, the change in social attitudes, though striking, was limited by the English crown. Rewards were given by Henry IV in appreciation of the royal bowmen at Shrewsbury, but only to their captains, the knights and esquires who commanded their retinues. A memorial brass to Matthew Swetenham at Blakesley (Northants), for example, honoured the squire, giving him the epithet of 'bow bearer' to Henry IV. Swetenham was of gentry stock, holding a hunting office in the royal household and able to afford his own armour.

Nevertheless, for some at least remarkable opportunities had opened up. In 1407 Thomas Walsingham wrote a powerful tribute to the war captain Sir Robert Knolles, who had died that summer. 'That unconquered soldier,' Walsingham began, 'dreaded by the kingdom of France for his deadly might in war, feared by Brittany and Spain ...'

Knolles was one of a handful of professional soldiers who had secured substantial wealth, political and social status through success on the battlefield. And, crucially, he had begun his career as a humble archer. He was subsequently knighted, in 1351, and took an increasingly prominent role in following campaigns. He captured Bertrand du Guesclin, constable of France, in 1359 and served with the Black Prince in Spain in 1367. Three years later he led his own expedition to France. Knolles's lowly origins were resented by some of the English aristocracy, but his career was an outstanding achievement.

With the example of men like Knolles in mind, Henry V, in an unusual and significant act, gave greater recognition and status to the vast majority of ordinary archers. Whereas Edward III had used a roughly equal proportion of men-at-arms and archers in his armies, on Henry V's Agincourt expedition the archers formed at least three quarters of the whole force. His use of so many archers had more than just a tactical justification: the king could meet these men on their own level, and make them feel part of his enterprise.

The army Henry had recruited was based on a system known as 'indenture and retaining'. This was an innovation of Edward III's, which replaced the earlier practice of raising troops through feudal obligation. Edward had realised that the feudal levy, which limited active service to 40 days and sometimes produced poorly equipped troops, was unsuitable for more active campaigning in France. The indenture was the document which listed the names of knights and ordinary soldiers brought in by retinue – fighting men who were retained or supported by their lord. It had become standard practice for all foreign expeditions recruited by the English crown from 1369 onwards. Drawn up in duplicate between the king and the captain promising to bring troops, it followed a standard form in terms of content, giving the name of the indentee, the numbers and types of soldiers he had agreed to provide, the arrangement for payment of wages, for division of spoils of war and the overall length of service required.

The majority of indentures for the Agincourt campaign were drawn up on 29 April 1415. Henry stated that if the expedition was to sail to northern France, the men-at-arms would receive daily wages of a shilling a day and the archers sixpence. Noblemen received higher rates of pay, based upon their rank. The retinue's leader was given a quarter of a year's payment in advance, half of the sum to be handed over on the signing of the indenture, the other half after his troops had been mustered, with surety for all future wages secured on the delivery of royal jewels. The indentures also clarified the sharing of spoils of war. If a notable French aristocrat were captured, he would be transferred to the custody of the king, in return for a suitable reward to the captor. Henry was also entitled to a third of the gains of the retinue leader.

These documents were the building blocks of the late medieval English army. It was a much more professional arrangement, for the indenture, which specified the number of men-at-arms and archers to be raised in return for a daily rate of payment, was legally binding. It ensured that military contingents were up to scratch.

This documentary material provided an Agincourt 'voice' in its own right – as extracts from an indenture between the king and the Lancashire knight Sir Thomas Tunstall – who built a fine castle at Thurland in the Lune valley in the reign of Henry's father – show:

> *This indenture made between the king our sovereign lord on the one hand, and Sir Thomas Tunstall on the other, bears witness that the said Thomas is bound towards our lord the king to serve him on the expedition which he will make, God willing, in his own person ... into his kingdom of France. The muster of the men of his retinue to a place which will be informed to him within the month of May next by the king ... Thomas shall have with him six men-at-arms, himself included, and eighteen mounted archers ... In the event that Thomas goes with the company of the king into the kingdom of France he shall take as wages for each of the men-at-arms 12d a day, and for each of the archers 6d a day ...*
>
> *For surety of payment of the second quarter, the lord king will have delivered to the said Thomas on 1 June next, as pledge,*

jewels which, by agreement with Thomas, are worth as much as the value of the wages for that quarter ...

Thomas shall be obliged to be ready at the sea coast with his men well mounted, armed and arrayed as appropriate for their rank, to make muster on 1 July next, and later, after their arrival overseas, Thomas will be obliged to muster the men of his retinue before such person or persons as it may please the lord king to appoint and assign, and as often as Thomas shall be reasonably required to do so. Thomas shall have shipping for himself and his retinue, their horses, harness and provisions, at the expense of the king, and also the return shipping ...

If it happens that the adversary of France [Charles VI], or any of his sons, nephews, uncles or cousins, shall be captured in the expedition by Thomas or by any of his retinue, the lord king shall have the adversary or other person of the ranks mentioned above who are captured, and shall make reasonable composition with Thomas or with the person who has effected the capture. With reference to other profits or gains of war the lord king shall have the third part of the gains of Thomas ...

In witness of these matters, Thomas has affixed his seal on the half of the indenture remaining with the king ...

Individual retinues could vary enormously in size. Whereas the king's brother, Humphrey, Duke of Gloucester, was retained to provide 200 men-at-arms and 600 archers, a lowly squire might bring in just three archers, as did the wonderfully named Baldwin Bugge. Many of the barons contracted to bring 30 men-at-arms and 90 archers; knights often contracted for 20 men-at-arms and 60 archers. In all, the English exchequer recorded 320 men indenting to serve on campaign – from the great and the good to those bringing modest or small companies: at least 122 men contracted to serve with fewer than ten men. This was a far more sophisticated system than that used by the French, who still relied upon feudal service, and Henry V supplemented it by recruiting specialist groups of archers from Wales, Lancashire and Cheshire.

The Cheshire archers were raised from each of the hundreds of the county and paid by the chamberlain of the county palatine, William Troutbeck. His accounts show 247 archers serving on the campaign. From Lancashire, 500 archers were raised, grouped into companies of 50, each under the command of a local knight or squire. A further 500 archers were recruited from South Wales, from the counties of Carmarthen, Cardigan and Brecon.

Once a retinue had gathered it was mustered by the king's officials and then mustered again, usually at monthly intervals. These documents not only show the composition of a retinue but provide a snapshot of the campaign as a whole. The muster of the retinue of Thomas Lord Camoys – who would lead the English rearguard at Agincourt – was made on 8 July 1415, listing the barons, knights, men-at-arms and archers in his service. Men would serve with a captain for a variety of different reasons. Some were attracted simply by the pay; others by the reputation and status of the captain. Some were connected personally to the captain, perhaps in his household or on his estates. Simon Brocas, who served as one of Camoys's men-at-arms, might well have been one of these. He was from a gentry family resident in Hampshire, and was probably known to the Camoys family, who held estates in the same area.

Simon Brocas was emulating the military career of his father, John, who had served in the Calais garrison, though he hoped for a happier outcome. John Brocas had subsequently perished in a clash with a landing French force at Rottingdean in 1377. According to Thomas Walsingham, this Brocas 'fought with such bravery and courage in this skirmish against the enemy that in the end his entrails were left hanging down to his feet and – a terrible thing to tell – in his charges against the Frenchmen he at first dragged his entrails after him for a considerable distance, and finally he left them behind altogether'.

At the other end of the spectrum were individuals like Geronnet du Bayon, probably a professional soldier from English-held Gascony, recruited because of his military expertise. The document was annotated as further musters took place, showing those who died or fell ill at Harfleur, and had to be invalided home, and those who went on to fight at Agincourt. Sadly, Simon Brocas did not survive to reach Agincourt – a note against his name on the retinue list stated that he 'died at Harfleur'. But the majority of Camoys's company went on to fight at the battle.

The muster of the retinue of Sir Thomas Erpingham showed greater losses. Two of his men-at-arms, Thomas Geney and John Calthorp, were knighted on Henry's landing in Normandy, but were invalided home from Harfleur and died in England. Two archers, Henry Prom and Robert Beccles, died during the siege of Harfleur, and another, John de Boterie, was invalided home. Another archer, Richard Chapman, died on the march from Harfleur to Agincourt.

The dysentery outbreak seriously weakened Henry's army, even after replacements had been brought in. Thomas Walsingham believed that the force that set out from Harfleur was less than 8,000 strong, and more and more men were being lost to illness every day. But, in the circumstances, it was remarkable that the system worked as well as it did.

The system of indenture and retaining was thoroughly professional and gave men a sense of continuity and camaraderie. Within it, stronger bonds of friendship could flourish. Sir John Popham was 20 at the time of the battle. A younger son of a Hampshire gentry family, his father had been constable of Southampton Castle. Popham served as a man-at-arms in the retinue of Edward, Duke of York. Despite the gap in age and status between the two men, York left to Popham in his will (drawn up outside Harfleur on 17 August 1415) some of his armour, a helmet and a horse and also a life rent from one of his manors. The two were clearly friends, and the 42-year-old duke, an able soldier and passionate huntsman, did not stand on ceremony. Describing himself in his will as 'of all the sinners the most wretched and guilty', it was humility and modesty that enabled him to take Popham under his wing. Popham in return gave the duke his unswerving loyalty.

These were rough, tough soldiers assembling at the war camp on the night of 24 October and now conducting their affairs in eerie silence.

Sir Thomas Rokesby of Mortham in Yorkshire had crossed to France in the retinue of John Mowbray, earl marshal, and after Mowbray fell ill had then marched under the king's own banner. An able soldier and administrator, he had served as sheriff of Northumberland under Henry's father and in 1408 had organised a small army to defeat the rebel Earl of Northumberland and Lord Bardolph when they invaded the county from Scotland. Rokesby had raised the local levies, blocked the passage of the River Nidd at Knaresborough, brought the rebels to battle at Bramham Moor on 20 February and roundly defeated them. Northumberland was killed and Bardolph mortally wounded – and Sir Thomas had been rewarded with the earl's rich manor of Spofforth.

The chronicler Thomas Walsingham was struck by Rokesby's resourcefulness. The rebels had deliberately invaded northern England in atrocious winter conditions. The battle itself was 'a very hard fight' as Walsingham related, but

Rokesby organised his men well. At the height of the clash, he had 'unfurled the banner of St George' next to a pennon of his own coat of arms. Rokesby doubtless felt at home in Henry V's army.

Sir William Trussell of Elmesthorpe in Leicestershire was a man of a rather different stamp. He had enlisted to fight under the king's brother, Humphrey, Duke of Gloucester, with a small force of five men-at-arms and 13 archers. He had fallen sick at Harfleur but was determined not to miss the battle. Leader of a notorious gang of ruffians, of 'such might and power' that they were deemed beyond the reaches of the law, early in the reign of Henry V Trussell had taken a dislike to a neighbour, John Mortimer, and early one morning rode over to his house at the head of 'many evildoers', carried the hapless Mortimer off – clothed only in his doublet – assaulted him and humiliated him. Trussell took great delight in shaving off Mortimer's beard and then, as his cohorts landed a cascade of blows upon his victim, chanted: 'Slay him, slay him!' and 'Hamstring him!' Mortimer escaped any punishment for this episode; perhaps it was felt more prudent to find an outlet for his violence by turning him loose upon the French.

These were colourful times. Thomas Walsingham could on the one hand discuss in sober fashion parliamentary business, the state of the church, trade and military affairs, and, on the other, share lurid rumours about prophecy, plague and magic. In his accounts, a simple military event – the burning of Saint-Omer – was intertwined with bizarre reports that John the Fearless, Duke of Burgundy, was preparing to bombard English-held Calais with canisters containing 'snakes, scorpions, toads and other poisonous creatures', whose compressed remains would emit terrible fumes, leaving 'even armed men its victims when they came into contact with its deadly power'.

Walsingham set out in cogent detail the surrender terms Prince Henry offered the garrison of Aberystwyth during Glendower's revolt, and then speculated that another expedition had been forced to retreat by the sinister use of spells and dark magic. And soldiers' reactions could be similarly complex. The fourteenth-century English mercenary Sir John Hawkwood consulted the latest scientific treatises on war, but also had his horoscope cast before he went on campaign.

Sir Thomas Chaworth of Alfreton in Derbyshire had indented to serve in Henry's expedition with eight men-at-arms and 24 archers. He had served on campaigns against the Scots and Welsh in Henry IVs reign, being rewarded for his good services with a grant of 100 marks and the promise of timber to enclose his deer park at Alfreton. He also was rarely out of trouble in his locality. When he suspected Lord Darcy of trespassing on his property, he retaliated by raiding one of Darcy's manors, 'carrying off a chest of muniments, diverse goods and 100 pounds in cash'. He then became embroiled in a violent feud with another local landowner, Walter Tailboys, one that nearly led to Sir Thomas being murdered in Lincoln. Thrown into prison at the beginning of Henry V's reign, Chaworth had signed up for the 1415 campaign as a way of getting back into royal favour.

Yet Chaworth was also a pious and reflective man, who possessed a large number of devotional works (some of them in English), and a 'litell portose [breviary] that he toke with hym always when he rode'. Rather like the English soldier poets of the First World War, Sir Thomas fought during the day and at night pondered the consequences of his actions. A man inured to violence and mayhem, he nonetheless commissioned a lavishly decorated Antiphonal, a book of sacred music following the pattern of the daily services of the English church.

This was the English army about to go into battle, and, while the military professionals Boucicaut and d'Albret respected it, the majority of the French aristocrats assembling to fight did not. They underestimated the effectiveness of its system of recruitment and disparaged the morale and motivation of the men who enlisted for it.

To some extent this was understandable. In the recent past the English had seemed to think that they were fighting under an unlucky star – and the French took them at their own estimation. 'After the Black Prince died, all hope of the English died with him,' Thomas Walsingham said despondently. English forces had struggled for years against the Welsh rebels of Owen Glendower, prompting Walsingham to complain of one expedition, 'these knights and esquires appeared more to be followers of Venus than Mars, and Laverna [the goddess of thieves] rather than Pallas Athene [the goddess of war]'.

English foreign policy seemed muddled and poorly thought out. In 1412 Walsingham remarked of Henry IV's latest intervention in France:

> The king, with a decree from his council, decided to provide help for the Duke of Orléans, and sent the Duke of Clarence, his second son, Edward, Duke of York and many powerful men ... to support Orléans against the Duke of Burgundy ... although those who had previously crossed the sea with the Earl of Arundel, to support the Duke of Burgundy against Orléans, had not yet returned home. We cannot have our cake and eat it.

The terrible suffering of the English army on its march from Harfleur only served to confirm their prejudice – and on the night of 24 October, as more and more French dukes and counts assembled in their war camp, they chafed against Marshal Boucicaut's caution.

The Monk of Saint-Denis, Michel Pintouin, reported:

> *The French dukes now took charge of the plan of battle, showing a complete disdain for the small force opposing them, and impetuously ignoring the advice of older and wiser military professionals ... They persuaded themselves that the sight of so many Princes would strike terror into the hearts of the enemy, and cause them to lose their courage, as if all they had to do was simply turn up on the battlefield ... When it came to putting the army into battle formation each of these new leaders claimed for himself the honour of leading the vanguard. This led to considerable debate, and so there could be some agreement, they came to the rather unfortunate conclusion that they all should place themselves in the front line.*

Henry V's strong leadership and the discipline and unity of his army should have warned them that things were now very different in the English camp – but, preoccupied with their own quest for glory, they were unable to see this.

The Monk of Saint-Denis had chronicled the sad decline in quality of French government after the king's illness, which left physicians bewildered and the country in a state of chaos. Charles VI had experienced a first attack in Amiens in March 1392. He was 24 years old and had once been robust and healthy. The king had rested – and seemed to recover. Later that year, on campaign against the Duke of Brittany, 'the king began making silly sounds and odd hand gestures', Pintouin recorded. Startled by a sudden noise, 'he panicked, lashed out with his sword and killed several of his own men. After he was finally subdued his eyes kept rolling from side to side and he failed to recognise members of his own entourage.'

On 28 January 1393 the Monk of Saint-Denis vividly chronicled one lurid event – the *Bal des Ardents* (the Ball of the

Burning Men) that became symbolic of Charles's inability to rule, and the descent of his court into hedonism and corruption. A masquerade ball was organised in Paris by Charles's wife, Isabeau of Bavaria, to celebrate the remarriage of one of her ladies-in-waiting. The dancers – who included Charles himself and four other noblemen – were disguised as wildmen, and fitted with elaborate costumes. Proceedings were interrupted by the sudden arrival of the king's brother, Louis, Duke of Orléans, completely drunk, who held a burning torch over one of the dancers and set fire to the whole ensemble. The Monk recorded: 'Four men were burned alive, their flaming genitals dropping to the floor, releasing a stream of blood …' Charles survived by clambering under the Duchess of Berry's skirt.

The event caused a public uproar. One chronicler's illumination caught the scene: the dancers tore away at their burning costumes, one plunged into a wine vat, Charles VI cowered under the duchess of Berry's voluminous skirts and above them all, in the minstrel's gallery, the stunned musicians carried on playing. The entire court was forced to do public penance and these unseemly goings on were long remembered, in England as well as in France.

The Monk of Saint-Denis carefully noted the coming and going of Charles's symptoms over the following years and the failure to provide any effective form of treatment. He listed over 40 episodes of derangement. The king's mental faculties progressively weakened, he could not even recognise members of his own family and 'he complained of severe pains, as if he had been stabbed by a thousand spikes'. By 1415 all swords and sharp weaponry had to be removed from his presence in case they provoked another attack, 'which would leave him running through his palace until he was physically exhausted, only contained through him being bound up in a chair with leather straps'.

With the king unable to rule, the realm descended into faction fighting. And yet Pintouin retained his belief in the importance of good government. When the English king Richard II was deposed, Pintouin commented that he had not been open or honest with his advisers and 'had often failed to keep his word'. He had suffered the consequences of his own political failings.

However, the consequence of the political discord in France would be more serious in military terms, leading to the failure to develop a professional standing army to replace the feudal levy. The need for this had already been recognised. Bertrand du Guesclin said in a council of war in Paris in September 1373 that 'these English victories have greatly damaged our realm' – and that the answer was to raise a standing army on the English model. This proposal was approved by the French king Charles V in an ordinance of 13 July 1374, but, facing an increasing financial crisis, he was unable to fully put it into effect.

There was even an attempt to encourage archery practice. The French king urged his subjects to practise with the bow, shooting ranges were created, and in 1371 the accounts of the paymaster of Paris, Simon Gaucher, referred to the repair of two archery butts on the Île de Notre-Dame. Jean Juvenal des Ursins believed that fear of a peasant insurrection stopped efforts to create a large number of bow-armed infantry and the incapacity of Charles VI further stalled the process. By 1415 a variety of military components existed – troops mustered and paid for by the crown, retinues recruited by the aristocracy and militias provided by the towns – but there was no unified whole.

The records of the French treasury in 1415 are fragmentary, and the military response – on the evidence that exists – was initially disjointed. Some troops were recruited under the Duke of Alençon in July, more under Boucicaut and d'Albret in August. Surviving musters showed some companies solely consisted of men-at-arms; others a majority of men-at-arms and the remainder crossbowmen or bowmen. There were not enough troops to break Henry V's siege of Harfleur. But on 20 September a summons was issued for all noblemen to join the French army in Rouen and by 8 October over 230 paid companies had been assembled.

The skilled professional soldier David, Lord of Rambures was now strengthening French defences in Picardy. The 52-year-old Rambures had fought in Germany, Gascony and on the Calais frontier. He held the honorary post of Master of the Crossbowmen and in 1412 had begun building a fine new brick castle at Rambures.

And on 10 October Philip, Count of Charolais, son of the Duke of Burgundy, wrote a letter to the treasury at Lille informing them that his father 'will advance with all his power against the English'. In the event, John the Fearless chose not to get involved, but Burgundian troops were allowed to join the rapidly growing French forces. By 12 October Charles d'Albret, the constable of France, was at Amiens co-ordinating these efforts.

The gathering French armies at Rouen and Amiens, which would junction at Péronne on 19 October, were now primarily composed of aristocratic retinues. Their forces were numerically large but lacking unity and cohesion. And missile-bearing troops were being sent away – a company of crossbowmen from Tournai, informed that their services would no longer be required, returned to the city without having fired a shot.

Boucicaut, d'Albret and Rambures were able military professionals, but the glue which held this French army together was not professionalism but an exalted chivalric concept of honour. The book of deeds of Marshal Boucicaut – perhaps recognising this – extolled his performance in the joust as much as his skill in battle. In May 1390 at Saint-Inglevert three French champions – Boucicaut, Reginald du Roye and Jean de Sempy – faced 39 English challengers over four days, running 137 mounted jousts without being unhorsed. It was a striking achievement – and one, according to Boucicaut's book, that brought honour to the realm of France.

The evidence of pardons (*lettres de rémission*) issued by the French crown showed that by the late fourteenth century a verbal disparagement of one's reputation was seen as justification for a knight using physical force or violence in reply. In one example of this, in 1370 the Gascon knight Bertrand de Camourt was accused of insulting the honour of Bretons and challenged to a duel watched by 400 people. He was killed in the fight.

Ghillebert de Lannoy was struck by the importance of preserving one's good standing among one's peers. He wrote to his son warning of the power of words to destroy a knight's reputation. Lannoy compared insulting words to the unloosing of arrows – and the only remedy to a stain on one's honour, in his view, was to seek out the slanderer in a trial by combat.

Charles, Duke of Orléans was orchestrating a trial by combat of his own. He was fascinated by the joust, organising a series of them in 1414 – and seemingly believed that any battle should follow the protocol of the tournament book. He was much exercised in the composition of a knightly challenge to arms, to be delivered to the English king near Péronne. But the ever astute Monk of Saint-Denis regarded the appointment of Orléans as commander of the French army with dismay. He felt it would lead to 'much arrogant boasting, a failure to follow wise counsel and an ill-considered and disorderly rush into battle'.

The French were now to fight for the honour of destroying the English army – as if they had gathered in the lists as champions of the realm, in front of an adoring public. Everyone would wear their finest plate armour and best heraldic trappings. The carefully thought-out plan of Boucicaut would be discarded. There would be no place for archers, crossbowmen, squires and servants in the battle dispositions. The chronicler Pierre Cochon commented ruefully:

> *The French thought that they would carry the day because of their great numbers, and in their arrogance proclaimed that only those who were noble would go into battle. All those of lower rank would now be sent to the rear.*

For the French aristocracy the battle would be less about military tactics and more about celebrating the superiority of their social class. All they had to do, it seemed, was to stop the English soldiers fleeing the battlefield – before processing to victory the following morning with all the pomp of an elaborate pageant.

It was still raining and the ground was becoming increasingly waterlogged. It was now midnight.

CHAPTER 4

Well Met by Moonlight —●

Battle Tactics

24.00–06.00 (25 October 1415)

THE ENGLISH ARMY was at last enjoying some shelter. 'In a nearby hamlet,' the chaplain remembered, 'there were some houses – although few in number – along with gardens and groves for our respite, and there was rain in abundance for almost the whole night.'

It was all a far cry from Henry V's royal palaces or castles – Kenilworth, with its little pavilion, built for the king on the far side of the lake, or the splendour of Westminster. 'By chance a certain little house was available to the king that night for his lodgings,' Titus Livius remarked, drawing upon the recollections of the king's brother Humphrey, Duke of Gloucester. 'No sound was heard from the English around him.'

This would be Henry's headquarters as he planned his approach to the forthcoming battle. In the distance he could hear the noise of the French moving about in their large war camp – their shouts, laughter, drinking and merriment. The enemy was supremely confident.

A striking echo was found in the battle that first unleashed the power of the longbow upon an unsuspecting enemy. On 12 August 1332 a small English army had faced a much larger Scottish one at Dupplin Moor. The Scots were also supremely confident. The wars against the English had gone well for them, and their opponent did not seem to have an answer to their massed pike formation (the *schiltron*). The night before battle they gave little respect to their foe. 'To them, the small number of English troops were insignificant,' the canon of Bridlington wrote in his chronicle, 'and the night before battle the Scots army drank and caroused, sending to Perth for wine and ale.' But in the morning the English employed an entirely new formation – of dismounted men-at-arms with archers on their flanks – and won an impressive victory. 'A wise man dreads his enemy,' wrote the Scottish chronicler Andrew Wyntoun. 'For underrating him gives rise to over-confidence, and that often leads to defeat.'

For Henry V, there was much to attend to. But first, his chaplain said, 'he withdrew into silence' – he took a few moments of peace and quiet.

We have three eyewitnesses from the English army at Agincourt, a soldier (John Hardyng), a herald (Jean Le Fèvre) and a priest (referred to throughout as Henry's chaplain), who wrote an account of his experience (*The Deeds of Henry V*) within two years of his return to England, between late November 1416 and July 1417. We do not know this priest's name – although a plausible candidate is John Stevens, an Oxford graduate who served as royal chaplain and was familiar with official documents relating to diplomacy with the French. He provided us with a powerful account of campaign and battle – vivid, direct and written in the first person.

The chaplain was well informed about broader matters. He was often in attendance on the king, being with Henry V on the very day of Sir John Oldcastle's abortive Lollard uprising in January 1414 (when his narrative started), and on a number of occasions during the Agincourt expedition. He was not impartial, and to some extent his work was an officially approved account, shot through with propaganda objectives. The chaplain's purpose in writing up his experience, he related colourfully, was to encourage support for:

The king's unbreakable resolve to go overseas in order to subdue the stubborn and obdurate French, which neither the tender milk of goats, the consummate wine of vengeance nor the most thorough-going of negotiations could soften.

The chaplain saw Henry as a profoundly Christian prince whose cause was blessed with the support of God from the moment of his accession. The king's rigorous suppression of the Lollards was proof of this. The sect, based on the radical teachings of John Wycliffe, had challenged the authority of the church and thus was heretical. Henry's enthusiastic backing for delegates at the council of Constance – a European assembly trying to heal the split or schism within the papacy, that had led to two and sometimes three rival popes – underlined the point.

The chaplain believed Henry was God's instrument, a man of 'great humility and trust in prayer', a ruler of vision and ability, at the centre of events and able to fashion a sense of destiny out of them – yet also subjected to a series of trials which would test his faith and constancy. And the chaplain was remarkably candid about what those trials had consisted of, with the king's army in a state of near despair on its march to Agincourt. It is this honesty which makes his story so compelling.

Much of his account was based on what he observed, or discovered through conversation with others. He made jottings on campaign: his story of Sir Walter Hungerford wanting more troops was prefaced by 'amongst other things which I noted at the time'. The march to Agincourt is brought alive through his testimony. And yet, unsurprisingly, he did not possess an eye for military detail, struggled to understand battle formations and during the actual clash took shelter with the baggage train.

To gain a fuller understanding of Henry and his army we also need the reminiscences of soldiers who fought in it. John Hardyng was one such man. A tough northern soldier, interested in the history of the Anglo-Scottish border, his recollections, whether in verse or prose, are frustratingly brief. Thomas Walsingham, a monk at the Benedictine abbey of St Albans, certainly spoke to some of the troops, however, and snippets of testimony found their way into his chronicle.

The abbey of St Albans – like that of Saint-Denis in France – had a long tradition of historical writing and, well situated, only some 20 miles from London, received a host of important visitors. Walsingham himself was an enthusiastic and well-informed reporter of political issues and author of a chronicle that had spanned over 40 years. He described events with impressive factual detail, consulted official documents and sometimes transcribed their contents, and spoke with considerable conviction. His friendship with a number of captains who had fought under the Black Prince gave him an interest in military affairs and an understanding of the qualities of a successful war leader.

If Henry's chaplain brought to life the pain of the English army's march to Agincourt, Thomas Walsingham brought alive the pain of the previous 40 years of military failure and defeatism. Walsingham hoped that Henry V would provide a new beginning. On the king's accession, the chronicler recorded, Henry 'changed suddenly into another man, zealous for modesty, honesty and gravity – there being no sort of virtue that he was not anxious to display'. Walsingham's evaluation of Henry's leadership was entirely positive:

There was no one like him amongst Christian kings or princes ... He was pious in soul, taciturn and discreet in speech, far-seeing in council, prudent in judgement, modest in appearance, magnanimous in his actions, firm in business, persistent in pilgrimage and generous in alms, devoted to God and supportive and respectful of prelates and ministers of the church. War-like, distinguished and fortunate, he won victories wherever he fought. He was generous in constructing buildings and founding monasteries, munificent in his gifts and above all pursued and attacked enemies of the faith and the church.

And when Walsingham said that on the Agincourt campaign Henry fought 'not so much as a king but as a knight', he could not have bestowed a greater compliment – he envisaged him picking up the mantle of the Black Prince, England's much lamented war hero.

Walsingham seems to have gathered information from returning soldiers about a host of matters: the state of the army before battle, the French threat to mutilate English archers, the all-important condition of the ground (the chronicler was the first English source to point out the soil was newly sown and soft, and thus exceptionally muddy) and how difficult it was to move across it. All this makes his chronicle both useful and insightful.

Thomas Elmham also interviewed aristocrats returning from the campaign. Originally a monk at St Augustine's, Canterbury, he became prior of the Cluniac monastery of Lenton in Nottinghamshire in 1414. Lenton enjoyed royal patronage and Elmham's appointment showed that he had forged court connections and probably become personally acquainted with Henry V. In 1415 Henry recommended him for the post of vicar-general of the Cluniac order in England, and he in return dedicated his own work, the *Liber Metricus*, to the English king – a verse history of his reign, based on eyewitness testimony, that was brought out a year after the chaplain's history.

Elmham was particularly interested in the ritual that Henry employed before battle, and the effect it had on his soldiers, how the king 'stood in his army without fear', and 'put a [battle] crown upon his head', and then 'signing himself with the cross, bestowed upon his men a courage comparable to his own'. And it was Elmham who heard reports, from the battle's participants, that St George was seen in the sky fighting on the side of the English.

Other military testimony was gathered later, after Henry V's death, in the 1430s – by two Italian humanist scholars employed and commissioned by Agincourt veterans. Tito Livio dei Frulovisi (better known as Titus Livius) entered the service of Henry's brother, Humphrey, Duke of Gloucester, in 1436, and was encouraged by the duke to write a life of the king – which draws on many of the Agincourt recollections of Humphrey himself. And another, anonymous Italian humanist scholar compiled an additional work on Henry (known by the cumbersome title of 'the Pseudo-Elmham') under the patronage of Walter Lord Hungerford, now promoted to the baronage – the man who had famously asked for more archers before the battle.

All these accounts were in Latin – but there were also works in English, the vernacular Brut and London civic chronicles, that on occasions vividly catch the voices of ordinary soldiers. Together they allow us a unique window on the Agincourt experience.

But on the night of 24 October monastic libraries and historical writing seemed very distant. The French were lighting celebratory bonfires and throwing up blockades to prevent the English army escaping their clutches.

'Heavy rain continued to fall the whole night through,' the chaplain said.

And when our adversaries noted how still we were, and thinking that, being so few, we were overcome by fear, and perhaps intended to flee during the night, they lit large fires and guarded all the tracks and roadways across the fields. And it was said amongst our men that the enemy were so confident of victory that night that they spent their time throwing dice for who would have captor's rights to our king and nobles.

Henry knew his Vegetius (the Roman military writer whose ideas held such sway over the medieval mind). 'Cornering an opponent makes him brave,' Vegetius wrote, 'for despair can quickly change into courage. A good general always leaves his opponent a chance to escape, for thus men can be easily defeated. Whoever entertains the thought of flight loses heart and might.'

However, the English king now had to form a plan of battle. In order to do so, he needed to gather more information on the likely field of combat. Successful reconnaissance had always been the hallmark of good English generalship in the Hundred Years War. Sir Thomas Dagworth, Edward III's lieutenant in Brittany, was an expert at it – and although his campaigns took place in the fourteenth century they were widely written up in the chronicles of the time and Henry V was likely to have known of his exploits. When French forces under Charles of Blois drew up to meet him at La Roche-Derrien on 12 June 1347, Dagworth had already gained good knowledge of his opponent's use of terrain and the strength of his army.

'The lord Charles had made great entrenchments round about him,' Dagworth wrote in a dispatch to Edward III, 'and outside his stronghold had caused to be levelled and razed, for half a league of the country round about him, all manner of ditches and hedges, whereby my archers might not find their advantage over him and his people, but they needs must in the end fight in the open fields.'

Although Sir Thomas Dagworth's army was much smaller, some 300 men-at-arms and 400 archers, accurate intelligence enabled him to draw up a highly effective battle plan. Realising that the French army was encamped in four main positions he struck at dawn, attacking and defeating each force in turn before they could reinforce one another. The result was a dramatic English victory, in which Charles and many of his nobles were taken prisoner, and Dagworth estimated that 'between 600 and 700 men-at-arms of the enemy' had been killed.

The Black Prince had used thorough reconnaissance of the ground before all his campaigns. The chronicler Geoffrey le Baker was struck by his prudence during the 1356 campaign:

> *Nor did he fail in the attributes of a wise commander, for he appointed the distinguished knights John Chandos, James Audley and their companions, all skilled in warfare, to act as scouts in the enemy countryside lest they laid ambushes in the woods for our men.*

Throughout his own campaign Henry would have been mindful of such earlier examples – and he used reconnaissance himself to keep one step ahead of the enemy. The anonymous Italian humanist (the source known as the 'Pseudo-Elmham') related:

> *The king, in his royal wisdom, sent out certain troops – strong in the fight by reason of their great bravery – to inspect the neighbouring territory, to consider its state and to bring victuals into the army.*

On the eve of Agincourt, the Italian continued:

> *Around the middle of the night, the king, believing a sense of the site ahead would be most useful to him, sent some valiant knights by moonlight to examine the likely field of combat. And from their report he drew up his battle plan, setting out the disposition of his forces.*

These 'valiant knights' were almost certainly the king's reconnaissance team: Sir John Cornwall, Sir Gilbert Umfraville, Sir William Bourchier, Sir John Gray, Sir John Holland and William Porter.

Several days earlier, the Duke of Orléans had sent Henry a formal challenge to battle: Orléans said what he knew about the English king:

> *... that ever since he had left his own realm, his desire had been to have a battle against the French. And so, the princes born of the royal blood were ready to relieve him, and fulfil his desire, and perform that which he sought; and, if he would care to name a place and date where he would fight them, they would be happy to meet him there, and representatives of each side would choose and notify [the actual site] so that it did not offer any physical advantage to one or the other party.*

Orléans was using the wording of a tournament challenge, as if he wanted to perform a joust or feat of arms – even to the point of referring to Henry's '*désir*' to do battle and the French princes' wish to relieve him of it. The duke loved such chivalric wordplay. But the English king had no wish to perform a joust; he was fighting to save his army.

Henry chose not to embroil himself in chivalric protocol. At the beginning of the Hundred Years War, a similar chal-

lenge had been issued between Philip VI of France and
Edward III of England. But at La Capelle in 1339, Philip had
refused to attack the English position because it had been
heavily fortified; the letter of challenge had stipulated the
absence of ditches and hedges, and that the battle was to take
place on even, open ground. But Henry – considerably outnumbered by the French – did not want a battle on even,
open ground. He needed to turn every feature of the terrain
to his advantage, to find protection for his archers and possibly also to spring a surprise on his opponent.

Henry could not ignore the challenge – it would appear
cowardly, as if he was running away from the French – but he
could not risk accepting it either, for it gave too much advantage to the enemy. So he remained non-committal. Jean Le
Fèvre witnessed his response:

> *The English king sent back two of his own heralds with the fol-
> lowing reply. He wished [the Duke of Orléans] to know that
> since he had left the town of Harfleur he had sought, and was
> still seeking, to return to his kingdom of England, and he had
> not barricaded himself up in any fortified town or castle. So, if
> the princes of France wished to fight with him there was no need
> to appoint a time or place because they could find him any day
> they liked in open country and without any hindrance.*

Henry knew that the French wanted to bring him to battle.
But when they did so, he intended to meet them not as some
lover of the tournament but with the resolve of a professional
soldier.

After a while the reconnaissance party returned. Sir John
Cornwall and his comrades had done the English king ster-
ling service throughout the campaign, but this was their most
difficult and dangerous assignment yet, carried out in poor

light, torrential rain, thick, cloying mud and with a large French army alarmingly close. They told the king that the Calais road climbed slightly and then passed through a natural funnel, bordered by woodland on either side, and with the land dropping away towards the villages of Agincourt and Tramecourt. Beyond the funnel, in the direction of Ruisseauville, the French forces were camped. If Henry occupied the narrow end of the funnel, which lay closest to the English army, he could secure greatest protection for his archers and fight in the most advantageous position.

At Dupplin Moor, in 1332, the small English army had drawn up in a defile, with their men-at-arms holding a narrow front some 200 yards wide, and the archers on slightly higher ground on either side of them. The key to their position was its funnelling effect. The Bridlington chronicle noted that they could only be approached through a 'straite [constricting] passage', beyond which the men-at-arms were formed up, 'with the archers disposed so that they could attack the enemy from the flank'. When the English line held firm, the Scottish forces collided with each other, losing momentum and coherence, and presenting an easy target for the bowmen.

The impact of dense clouds of arrows on the cohesion of an advancing army was overwhelming. The sheer weight of fire would cause the enemy formations to bunch and compress, as the outer ranks moved away from the hail of arrows and pushed and collided with their fellows, who became increasingly unable to fight effectively. If the terrain further accentuated this – its cumulative impact would be even more powerful.

At Crécy on 26 August 1346 Edward III had chosen the site carefully. A ridge or terrace funnelled the charging French men-at-arms into a restricted killing zone in front of the Black Prince's division – where the fighting was fiercest.

At Agincourt Sir John Cornwall and his group warned the king about the state of the ground. The fields had been newly sown with wheat, and were exceptionally muddy. The rough, churned-up soil was soft underfoot – so much so that one sank deeply into it. It would be very difficult for either side to advance across the battlefield. Ideally, Henry needed to keep his forces at the narrow end of the funnel and let the French attack. Here the ground was unploughed – and firmer underfoot. In such a position, the English longbow could be used to maximum effect.

At Halidon Hill on 19 July 1333, another English victory against the Scots, that perfected the archer formation Edward III would employ with so much success during the Hundred Years War, King Edward had deployed his men on high ground two miles north of Berwick. 'The Scotsmen arrayed themselves soundly', noted the chronicler Andrew Wyntoun, 'but they had not considered the terrain. There was a large, marshy creek-bed between them and the enemy.' This creek-bed was not visible from the Scottish camp – or from where they assembled in the valley in front of the English position. Its existence was masked by an abrupt decline, with rising ground on either side of it. 'They could not see it before-hand,' Wyntoun wrote bluntly, and as they had done no battlefield reconnaissance they would stumble into it entirely by chance.

But Edward III, with his exceptional eye for terrain, had not only seen it but decided to incorporate it into his battle position. He had realised, as Wyntoun was quick to point out, that the Scots would be forced 'to clamber down the steep slope, and then climb up towards his soldiers, on a nar-rowing slope where a single man might defeat three'.

The first Scottish division rushed forward confidently. But as it approached the hidden defile, the English 'shot arrows as thickly as the rays in sunlight'. The muddy creek fatally slowed their advance. The Lanercost chronicle stressed the effect of the withering fire. 'Now the Scots marching in the first division were so grievously wounded in the face and blinded by the host of English archery, just as they had been before at Dupplin, that they were helpless, and quickly began to turn their faces from the arrow flight and fall back.' Edward had ensured that his men were well stocked with ammunition – we know that the sheriffs of London had dispatched to his army some 195 sheaves, each containing 24 arrows, and that was only a small proportion of what was required. The effect was devastating.

Henry V had to anticipate a scenario where the French did not move either, but remained drawn up across the Calais road, simply waiting. They knew, after all, that the English army was starving and growing weaker and weaker while on their side fresh reinforcements were arriving all the time.

Edward III's system of deployment for his armies – which Henry was seeking to emulate – worked best from a prepared defensive position. At Crécy Edward had placed his men on a natural ridge with woodland behind it and ditches in front of it, where agricultural terraces protected the centre of his army. He then waited for the French to attack.

It was far harder to move on to the offensive using a formation with men-at-arms interspersed with archers. The archers would be much more lightly equipped, and thus able to move more quickly, but the whole body of troops would need to be kept in alignment as it moved forward. And, as it did so, the archers on the flanks would lose the protection they had enjoyed and become increasingly vulnerable.

If the French simply held their position, Henry V would be faced with a predicament. The English would be forced to leave their advantageous position, move forward and try and provoke their opponents to fight. It would be a hard manoeuvre to pull off. Moving his entire army forward to within bow range – keeping formation and across the exceptionally muddy ground – would be very difficult to achieve safely. The alternative was to use some of his archers as a rapid attacking force, to provoke the French, while the rest of his army made a more limited advance. (The English had succeeded in doing this once before, at the battle of Neville's Cross in 1346. Wishing to hold their own position, but facing a Scottish army unwilling to leave theirs, a select force of bowmen ran ahead of the main English army and by shooting at the Scots provoked them to attack.)

Finally, Cornwall told Henry of a small, hidden meadow within the woods on the Tramecourt side of the battlefield, close to the French lines. It would, in his opinion, be ideal for setting up an archer ambush.

There was much here for the king to consider. His mind may have turned to the story of Najera in 1367 – his grandfather, John of Gaunt, had commanded the vanguard in that earlier battle. The English army had once again been in dire straits, exhausted and hungry after its march across the Pyrenees and down on to the plains of northern Spain. But its commander, the Black Prince, had found the right tactical plan and strongly motivated his men, riding in front of his troops and addressing them all – aristocrats and commoners alike – as 'seigneurs': making clear that to fight for him with distinction was an ennobling act in itself.

Medieval commanders thought about earlier battles to draw inspiration and comfort in the present. At Maisoncelles, Henry V may well have reflected on another, which showed both the power of the French and an abiding weakness. A small force of English troops under Henry's half-uncle, John Beaufort, Earl of Somerset, had joined a crusading army against the Ottoman Turks and witnessed the debacle that followed.

The battle of Nicopolis was fought on 25 September 1396 by an allied force largely consisting of Hungarians, Wallachians and French, against the invading masses of the Ottoman Turks. This was one of the last great crusading encounters of the Middle Ages and a terrible defeat for Christendom. The French contingent showed great courage in rallying to this call for help and undertaking a difficult and dangerous march. But for all their bravery, they demonstrated complete unwillingness to adhere to any chain of command, and this was to be their downfall – and the downfall of the entire Christian army.

As the campaign got underway, the French contingent was under the nominal command of John de Nevers, the eldest son of the Duke of Burgundy (who in 1415 had succeeded to the dukedom as John the Fearless). Both Marshal Boucicaut and the experienced warrior Enguerrand de Coucy were appointed as 'counsellors' of Nevers; indeed, Nevers was given a long list of 'counsellors', and an additional list of other French lords, whom he could consult 'when it seemed good to him'. This was campaigning by committee, and an extremely large one at that.

French pursuit of honour and renown would override any sensible military dispositions. This was revealed early in the proceedings, when a meeting of the French noblemen drew up a list of ordinances governing their conduct that included the fateful provision: 'Item, that in any battle the count [Nevers] and his company claim the *avant garde*' – revealing that the French chivalric code required knights to prove their valour by always leading the attack.

This impatience for honour began to take precedence over all other considerations. At the first full allied council of war at Buda a waiting strategy was proposed by Sigismund of Hungary, who assured the French crusaders that the Ottoman sultan Bayazid would come this far, and it would be better to let the Turks do all the hard work, rather than undertaking a long march to find them first.

Enguerrand de Coucy roundly declared: 'The Sultan's boasts [of attacking Hungary] should not prevent us from doing deeds of arms and taking the initiative against our enemies, for that is the purpose for which we came.'

As that campaign progressed, the French showed themselves unwilling or unable to work under anyone else's authority. Approaching the fortress of Rachowa, and frustrated by a lack of opportunity to show their bravery, the French undertook a forced night march to reach the town before their Hungarian allies, and launched a premature attack on Rachowa's walls before Sigismund had even arrived. They then ignored Sigismund's attempts to negotiate a treaty of surrender with the defenders, claiming that the Hungarians were trying to rob them of glory.

When the French reached the town of Nicopolis, their intoxication with the cult of valour overrode even the importance of military technology. Remarkably, they began the siege without any proper equipment, Boucicaut – younger and more impulsive than the seasoned veteran the English would face in 1415 – making the astonishing declaration that 'scaling ladders were easily made, and worked far more effectively than any catapult when used by courageous men'.

As the relieving Ottoman army of Sultan Bayazid approached Nicopolis, Sigismund drew up a battle plan, in which Wallachian foot soldiers – experienced in battle against the Turks – would form the vanguard of the crusading army. The French would be held back to lead the main attack. But the French Count of Eu was having none of this, denouncing the proposal as demeaning to his fellow knights, who would be forced to follow peasant footmen into battle: 'to take up such a position – behind these men – is a dishonour to us,' Eu declared, 'and will expose us to the contempt of all'. Instead, Eu claimed the right for the French of leading the allied army.

As the rival armies came into view, the Christian forces first waited – to allow reconnaissance riders to report on the numbers and disposition of their enemies. But then the French lost patience and launched a charge. They crashed through the ranks of Bayazid's untrained conscripts, but came under sustained archer fire from Ottoman bowmen protected by rows of sharpened stakes – a deployment that had been hidden from view by a screen of Turkish cavalry. Their horses were brought down by the stakes and the arrow fire – and for all their bravery, the French were then overwhelmed by their foe.

Sigismund would later state bluntly to the Master of the Hospitallers: 'We lost that day through the pride and vanity of the French.'

However difficult Henry's position was, the terrible example of Nicopolis offered him a ray of hope, if the French once again threw away their cohesion and discipline. But to exploit such a possibility, Henry had to devise the right plan and inspire his men to follow it. To do this, he needed to invoke the glory days of Edward III and the Black Prince, when English soldiers truly believed they held mastery over the French.

Sir Thomas Gray – the grandfather of the Sir John who had returned from the reconnaissance party – wrote in his *Scalacronica* how a mood of exhilaration had swept the country in the 1360s – as men signed up to the war effort:

They came in astonishing numbers, all of them on their own account, without any leader. And yet they were nothing but a gathering of commoners, young men who until this time had been held of little account, who became rich and gained experience from this war, many beginning as archers, and then becoming knights and captains – and it has not been possible to detail all of their battles and successes because of the sheer number of them.

The Anonimalle chronicle noted happily that after victory at Poitiers, 'A hundred Frenchmen neither dared to meet twenty Englishmen in the field, nor to give them battle.'

It was no easy matter to rekindle such a martial flame and in the hours before battle at Agincourt the king needed advice and support. Henry now reached out to his close friend, one of the senior commanders in the army – the 42-year-old Edward, Duke of York. The author of *Knyghthode and Bataille,* a fifteenth-century translation of Vegetius, advised all commanders before battle to listen to the words of veterans 'of trusted wisdom'. At Crécy, Edward III took the advice of Sir Reginald Cobham, a veteran of the battles of Halidon Hill and Morlaix, before choosing the most suitable site. And Jean Froissart noted that before Poitiers the Black Prince had sought the counsel of Sir James Audley, who advised him on the drawing up of the English positions, 'for he was a most wise and valiant knight'.

York had originally been Henry's hunting tutor. His political career was chequered – as a favourite of Richard II he had jumped ship at the very last moment, and his allegiance during the reign of Henry IV was sometimes under suspicion. He was implicated in the anti-Lancastrian plotting of his sister, and was even imprisoned for 17 weeks in Pevensey Castle. But in his earlier service in the war in Wales he had won the trust of Prince Henry, who now stood as guarantor for his release. In the parliament of December 1407 the prince made a spirited defence of his fellow fighter.

Henry spoke of York's reliability and trustworthiness in the clashes against Glendower. 'If it had not been for the duke's good advice and counsel,' the prince began, 'he and others in his company would have been in great peril and desolation.' At times of great hardship, he continued, York put aside his own personal suffering, and did his very best to give courage and comfort to others:

He laboured in such a way as to support and embolden all the other members of the company, as if he had been the poorest gentleman in the realm, wishing to serve amongst them in order to gain honour and renown.

The duke was in all things, Henry concluded, 'a loyal and valiant knight'. It was a powerful, and highly personal, intervention – and it saved York's fortunes.

An example of York's ability 'to give courage and comfort to others' had occurred in the war in Wales, some four years earlier, when the duke was faced by a company of soldiers in a state of near-mutiny for lack of wages. He entreated them to continue a few weeks longer, taking the remarkable step of mortgaging all his Yorkshire estates in order to raise a loan, and pledging to his men that 'on his oath, as a true gentleman' he would not receive any of his revenues until his soldiers got paid. The duke kept his word, his troops received their money and a disaffected and disillusioned force was transformed into one that was motivated and loyal.

That was the mettle of the man and the forge of his friendship with Henry Prince of Wales. In the autumn of 1409, with Glendower's revolt in its dying stages, the two travelled together from Cardiff to Hanley Castle (Worcs), close to the

Welsh border. Here Prince Henry and his small riding household stayed with York, dining with him at his table, in an atmosphere of easy informality – the duke on one occasion paying for the repair of a silver wine jug that Henry had broken. They clearly enjoyed each other's company. In December Henry and York rode to Tewkesbury for seven days of hunting, York paying the costs of the prince's pages and horses on the trip.

The duke's household account contained frequent references to the care of horses, dogs and falcons used to 'sport and hunt' – and Henry evidently felt at ease in the company of York's huntsmen. Robert Morton of Bawtry (Yorks) was the duke's master forester of Hatfield. The prince stood as godfather to Morton's son Henry, and once he became king appointed Robert his master falconer.

Henry's recommendation of York in Parliament was thus entirely genuine and, as a mark of gratitude, the duke dedicated a treatise on hunting to the prince, who as he well knew keenly enjoyed the sport. It was called *The Master of Game*. In his preface he described it as a 'simple book', but it was an exceptional work in many ways. The duke, like many aristocrats, was passionate about hunting – and, unusually, the book was not written in French, the language of chivalry, but English. Much of it was a translation of a famous hunting manual by Gaston Phoebus, Count of Foix – but York edited the count's text and added five additional chapters, based on his own experience as master of the royal hart hounds.

A man of literary tastes, familiar with and able to quote from the works of Geoffrey Chaucer, the duke loved hunting. For him it was not simply a pastime, but a battle of wits and skill against a respected quarry, and an instinctive sense for the lie of the land.

For when the hunter riseth in the morning, and he sees a sweet and fair morn, and clear weather and bright, and he heareth the song of small birds, which sing so sweetly with great melody and full of love ... and when the sun is arisen, he shall see fresh dew upon the small twigs and grasses, and the sun by his great virtue shall make them shine ... wherefore I say that hunters go into paradise when they die, and live in the world more joyfully than other men.

York knew his sport inside out and it showed. He adapted the French text to suit English skills and customs, customs that were found both in the organised hunt of the nobleman and in the hunting way of life in the forests which supported it.

One of the beautiful illustrations to Gaston de Phoebus's *Livre de Chasse* (written between 1387 and 1389) showed archers – clad partly in green – shoot at oncoming deer. The type of hunting depicted here was 'bow and stable', where the archers would each take a station close to a tree, and await the game driven towards them by beaters and dogs.

Yet Gaston de Phoebus did not feel entirely comfortable with hunting with the bow, and his chapter on the subject ended on a rather dismissive note:

I know little of hunting with the bow: if you want to learn more, you had better go to England, for there it is a way of life ... In hunting with the bow you take the beasts without really working the hounds – you set your traps, you put in your men to beat and make a noise through the wood, and the deer run out towards the bowmen.

In contrast, the most significant addition Edward, Duke of York made to his original source was the space he devoted to the bow – and the respect he showed for it. In a new chapter on the breaking and killing of deer, he remarked that while the huntsman looked after the hounds it was the woodman (a hunter of forest game) who stalked the deer with his bow:

I say woodmanly, for it is a point that belongs to a woodman's craft, and though it may be well fitting to a hunter ... nevertheless it belongs more to a woodman than to a hunter ... and there is no good woodman or good hunter in England who cannot already do it well, and far better than I could teach them.

York chose to praise the home-grown knowledge and practicality of the English forest bowmen. He deliberately wrote in English, employing the same language as them, and, despite the social divide, was not condescending and respected their skill. And when faced with the elaborate French procedure for stripping down the carcass, York simply edited down Gaston de Phoebus's text – the implication being, there and elsewhere, that it was too showy for English taste.

The majority of men authorised to carry bows were the numerous foresters and verderers (keepers of those parts of the forest set aside for hunting) who administered these areas, on behalf of the king or of lords who possessed their own woods and deer parks. Foresters played an important role in patrolling these areas and in working with those of the lord's household responsible for hunting. As *The Master of Game* explained:

The master forester ought to show [the master of the game] the king's standing, if the king would stand with his bow, and where all the remnant of the bows would stand. And the yeoman for the king's bows ought to be there for the king's standing, and remain there without noise until the king comes.

The forester's equipment included not only a bow but also a hunting horn – used in the chase as well as for summoning assistance when arresting poachers in the forest. Such was the equipment of Chaucer's Yeoman in the Prologue to *The Canterbury Tales*, who with his bows, arrows, horn and green clothing was the archetypal forester.

In response, the majority of the poachers hunted in groups, usually with bows, and were not just from the peasantry but the yeoman and gentry classes as well – as the popularity of the Robin Hood ballads in the late Middle Ages made clear. While the crown wanted to protect the king's game and limit poaching, there was also an opportunity to recruit skilled archers from such forest areas. An English king was able to kill two birds with one stone by pressing those caught poaching into military service. Some 300 outlaws were among those whom Edward I recruited, in return for a pardon, for his wars in Aquitaine in 1294 (the first known instance of resorting to this practice). A generation later, the archers who fought with such success for Edward III at Halidon Hill included poachers from Sherwood Forest, pardoned on condition of entering the king's army.

From the records of the forest assizes it was evident that foresters and poachers alike used longbows, and that Chaucer's Yeoman was as much a soldier as a forester. To Chaucer's contemporaries a vivid portrait of a skilled woodsman with his bow would have carried a strong resonance – not only with the tales of Robin Hood but also the great victories of the recent past, achieved with the longbow in the armies of the Black Prince in France and Spain. Indeed, familiarity with the tales was such that a Robert of Shirwood appeared as an archer in the English garrison of Edinburgh Castle in 1335, and a 'Robyn Hood' was enrolled as one of the archers defending the Isle of Wight in 1403.

Given their skill with the bow, foresters were naturally among those selected for military service. In 1373, John of Gaunt drew heavily on those administering his parks and forests to furnish men for his expedition. His Yorkshire receiver was given the name of three park keepers presumably because of their renown with the bow, while the keeper of the forest of Leicester was ordered to offer recruits two oaks each as an incentive to join up. And many forest outlaws continued to enlist with the king's armies, to gain wages and pardons for their offences.

There was thus an intimate connection between war and the hunt, and it extended down from the ranks of the aristocracy to those gentry and yeomen administering the forests and those yeomen and peasantry poaching their game. A wall painting behind the tomb of Sir Oliver Ingham at Holy Trinity church in Ingham (Norfolk) showed two hunters, equipped with horn, longbow and arrows. Sir Oliver had enjoyed a distinguished military career under Edward III as seneschal of Aquitaine – the juxtaposition of hunting scenes with his military effigy showed how closely the two were connected in the minds of contemporaries. It was a shared language and experience – and one that spanned the social divide.

In *The Master of Game* we see not only an aristocrat who was passionate about hunting, but a man who could reach out to the ordinary bowman, whether on the hunt or in an army, speak his language without condescending to him and respect his skill. We see an aristocrat who valued French culture and prowess without being overawed by it, who admired their gifts but felt that many of their ways were showy, elaborate and unnecessary. And we find a man who felt more at home with the English way of doing things – whether in the beauty of the English language or an

147

Englishman's skill with the bow. And above all, a man who instinctively trusted English practicality – the gift of doing things well without ostentation or fuss, the ability of all classes to pull together for a common cause and gain a quiet pride in their common achievement.

These were the values shared by duke and king. And these were the reasons that king had said of York on campaign: 'He laboured in such a way as to embolden all the other members of the company, as if he had been the poorest gentleman in the realm.'

Henry and York now looked to devising a plan that would blend military tactics with the psychology of the hunt, one that would make every soldier in the army feel a part of their enterprise and – while recognising the bravery and strength of their opponents – would play on their pride and social elitism.

While the two men were contemplating the battle ahead, the French were conducting an elaborate procession through their war camp, and planting a succession of banners in the ground, as if they had already gained the victory and were now commemorating it.

Before the battle of Poitiers in 1356 the French had thoroughly investigated the English position and reported back in detail:

> They have chosen a road strongly fortified with hedges and undergrowth, and have posted their archers along this hedge on both sides of the road, so that one cannot approach to attack the army save between these rows of archers. This road has no other entry or issue, and is only wide enough for perhaps four men-at-arms to ride abreast. At the end of the hedge, among the vines and thorn bushes, where one cannot go on foot or ride, are their men-at-arms, all on foot; and they have placed their men-at-arms behind their archers. All this, it seems to us, is most skilfully

148

planned, for if we could fight our way to that point we could not
penetrate further without coming up against the archers, whom
it would be no light task to dislodge.

On 24 October, Marshal Boucicaut had sent a reconnaissance party under the Count of Nevers to seek out and find
the English army. When Nevers returned with news of its
whereabouts – that it was approaching Blangy-sur-Ternoise
– Boucicaut knighted him, but that night they undertook no
further investigation of the battlefield. They seemed to regard
the result as a foregone conclusion.

CHAPTER 5

Breakfast at Agincourt →

Motivation and Morale

06.00–08.00 (25 October 1415)

On the morning of battle a medieval commander and his chief captains would first celebrate Mass, and then eat lightly – taking breakfast – before going into combat. Contemporaries, mindful that a battle's result could be the verdict of God on one side's particular failings or fault – believed this a time of good or ill omen, with every moment scrutinised carefully.

Sometimes the proximity of religious observance to the mayhem of war allowed a little dark humour. Thomas Walsingham produced a tongue-in-cheek paean of praise to the warrior Sir Hugh Calveley for delaying his sack of Boulogne (1377) so that 'he could have Mass celebrated by his chaplain there, and in his bold way he heard it through to the very end'. Once it was completed, 'he burnt the town, and made off with prisoners and plunder'.

It was genuinely felt important that Mass be taken correctly and in unhurried fashion. A reminder of what might happen if it was neglected was the battle of Courtrai in the early fourteenth century, something of a medieval *cause célèbre*. On 11 July 1302 a Flemish army of common labourers, fighting on foot, routed the strongest force in Europe, the French cavalry – the very epitome of chivalry. The Flemish leaders prepared a good defensive position. Small rivers protected their flanks, and ditches had been dug across their centre to break the force of the cavalry charge. The French were running a considerable risk in attacking such a strong site. However, its natural strength allowed a different weakness, that flight from the battlefield was impossible, and they had the chance to destroy totally their opponents.

The contest was fiercely fought. Many of the cavalry were able to jump the ditches, regroup and charge the enemy. Units of horsemen penetrated the ranks of the infantry and came close to breaking their formation. They were forced back by sheer weight of numbers and driven into the rivers with appalling slaughter. In terms of the rank, kudos and training of medieval warfare, it was an inexplicable result: mounted knights had never before been beaten by peasant infantry. Their failure to do so was a devastating shock.

Commentators were struck by the expensive armour and equipment of the French, their heraldic banners, the golden spurs won at tournaments, and noted incredulously that their opponents had virtually no armour at all. Yet they had somehow managed to triumph. News of this resounding French defeat spread all over Europe. Something quite incredible had happened. Contemporaries showed their astonishment and disbelief by likening Courtrai to biblical or mythic triumphs of the underdog: the Greeks defeating the Trojans, or the victories of the Israelites under King David. Indeed, the battle achieved such notoriety that chroniclers soon felt it unnecessary to repeat the details of the story, since they were so well known already. They were familiar to Henry V and his soldiers – found in English prose translation and even popular poetry.

Inevitably, writers attempted to make sense of the battle's outcome. Although the French commander, Robert, Count of Artois, seemed to have fought with courage and determination, disturbing images were quickly circulated by the writers of the day. Portents on the morning of battle included

153

Artois's valuable warhorse falling as the count tried to mount, his dog attempting to pull off his armour and a toad (a creature of ill omen) crawling out of the Flemish ranks to spit venom at the French.

And in one account, Artois was unable to celebrate Mass before going into combat. The count had wished to take it privately and his priest had promptly begun to read the Mass. However, when Artois was about to receive the host, it had disappeared and could not be found anywhere. The count impetuously railed against this incident of misfortune, exclaiming to his followers: 'What I have decided to do today, I will bring to an end, come what may.'

Whether this story was true or not, it made a broader point. Artois was being punished for his pride – and the pride of his army. They were puffed up with their own glory and had failed to humble themselves before God. And as a result, they were not fighting with God on their side – and faced His judgement on the battlefield. This powerful rendition of a David (the Flemish) bringing down a mighty Goliath (the French) was not lost on Henry V.

These themes were familiar to Henry's contemporaries. Thomas Walsingham described the failure of a Franco-Breton attack on Dartmouth in 1404 with barely concealed delight. The French noblemen had been roundly defeated by an English rural levy. Their leader, Guillaume de Castel, had – as Walsingham said frankly – 'been killed by opponents for whom he had the utmost contempt, the peasantry, and the men who landed afterwards were immediately overwhelmed by those same peasants and at once taken captive or killed'. Three lords and 24 knights were taken prisoner, and Walsingham concluded emphatically: 'God on that day brought low the pride of the haughty, and gave victory to the ordinary people.'

For Henry to take Mass in an unhurried fashion he needed to rise at around 6 am, allowing himself a little over an hour before sunrise. Once daylight arrived, he would have little time to spare. The 'hour' of 'prime' (in autumn from 7 to 8 am) would be needed for his army.

At Agincourt both sides celebrated Mass properly. And the mass of French aristocrats was a frightening prospect. Fear is contagious and among soldiers it can spread particularly quickly. In its worst form – absolute terror – it can paralyse the will and sap the resolve of an army. Early on the morning of 25 October Henry V's chaplain, who often allowed us to glimpse the feelings of the ordinary soldier, related that many of the troops were terrified. The sheer number of the enemy, he emphasised, was 'really frightening'.

Jean Le Fèvre said simply: 'During that night, all who could find one, made confessions to a priest. Thomas Elmham confirmed how: 'That rainy night, the [English] people there, without bread or any food, overflowed with the offering of prayers and vigils to the Lord.' Thomas Walsingham also recalled: 'The English, much fatigued and weakened ... spent the night in prayers and confessions.'

Many had already taken confession the previous afternoon, when the two armies had faced each other at Blangy. Determined that God would hear them, they were now making their confessions again – and again. Thus was the power of numbers and repetition to the medieval mind – and a way of staving off the terror of battle.

Most of the English archers came, as we have established, from the ranks of the peasantry. They were skilled in using the bow, through regular practice, but only a few could afford any expensive equipment to accompany it. The majority would count themselves lucky with a makeshift helmet and light chain mail shoulder coverings, and just a leather jerkin or jacket underneath. As the rival armies roused themselves at dawn, the class system was all too clearly represented in their weaponry and armour – or the lack of it. The French chronicler Pierre Cochon had described the arrival of Henry V's archers at Harfleur with barely concealed disdain:

All with bare feet and no shoes, dressed in scruffy doublets made out of old bedding, a poor skull cap of iron on their heads, a bow and quiver of arrows in their hand and a sword hanging by their side. That was all the armour they had.

And the Burgundian Monstrelet emphasised how at Agincourt most of the English archers:

... were without armour, dressed in their doublets, with their hose [trousers] loose around their knees, hanging axes or swords from their belts. Many had bare heads and were without headgear.

The French seemed genuinely shocked that such poorly dressed men had the presumption to go into battle at all. In contrast, Jean de Waurin, present with the opposing army at Agincourt, described its participants turning up in all their finery, as if they were going to a tournament. The French were now adhering to a strict dress code, arranging their ranks 'by invitation only' and pushing their squires and servants to the rear. The English archers, in contrast, were only too visible: described by their opponents as 'scum', 'unworthy' and 'vile'.

Pride in armour, seen in the late Middle Ages in tombs and memorial brasses, was thus a socially divisive marker, reminding us of the horrible dangers in battle for those lower down the social scale, with the least protection. In the terrible shock of impact, as one army clashed with another in the mêlée, the hand-to-hand combat between dismounted soldiers, the most lightly armoured were by far the most vulnerable. At this critical stage of the fighting, aristocrats often showed scant interest in the fate of ordinary peasant soldiers and the instinctive reaction of these unfortunates was often just to get out of the way and run from the field. But Henry V had a very different vision for the forthcoming battle, one which would bridge the divide of class and equipment within his army and forge a greater whole.

As Henry's army awoke in the cold early morning light, the king needed to reach out to all his soldiers. This could not be done by a long-winded speech – which would not be heard by the majority of his troops anyway. Nor was it a moment for learned arguments, offering a justification of the war with France. The message needed to be simple and to the point. Henry and York had a special plan for the English archers; they now enabled their men to overcome fear by turning the emotion to anger instead.

The Roman writer Vegetius, author of the soldier's bible in the Middle Ages, warned the commander to look out for fear in his men – in their facial expressions, language and gestures. Once discovered, it was vital to get them angry: 'Say anything by which the soldiers' minds may be provoked to hatred of their adversaries, by rousing their anger and indignation.'

Henry instinctively understood Vegetius's advice. He used the arrogance of their opponents to stir a fury among his men that overcame their anxieties. The English were keeping relatively quiet so the sounds of the enemy camp would be easily overheard, and men would inevitably listen, and wonder what their opponents might be doing or saying. Some chroniclers related French boasts that they would mutilate captured archers, cutting off their hands and fingers, or auctioning them for a derisory sum of money. Such alleged boasts were almost certainly passing around the English war camp, and Henry exploited them directly.

Jean Le Fèvre remembered that Henry deliberately circulated stories that 'the French had boasted that if any English archers were captured they would cut off three fingers from their right hand so that no man would be able to draw a bow again.'

Thomas Walsingham corroborated this: 'The French proclaimed that they wished no one [among the English army] spared, except a few named lords and the king himself, announcing that the rest would be killed or have their limbs horribly mutilated.'

Walsingham told how the threat of death or mutilation at French hands spread quickly through the ranks and men put their fear behind them. The English troops, he said, 'hot with indignation ... forgot all their misfortunes, exhaustion and weakness'. Anger now fired up the army: 'Our men were much excited to rage and took heart, encouraging one another.'

The threat of mutilation seems genuine, a reflection of the antipathy of the aristocrat towards the humble archer, born out of class consciousness but also a fear of his weapon. The Leicestershire chronicler Henry Knighton recorded in an obituary of Sir James Douglas – the long-serving lieutenant of Robert the Bruce, killed fighting the Moors in 1330 – that he was in the habit of cutting off the right hand of any archer he caught, or putting out their right eye, taking terrible revenge without mercy 'on account of their bows and arrows'. And at the battle of Valmont in March 1416, when a small force under the Earl of Dorset was confronted by a much larger French one led by the Count of Armagnac, John

Strecche noted that Armagnac gave Dorset the chance to surrender: his men-at-arms would be ransomed, his archers would lose their right hands. Dorset chose to stand and fight – and turned the tables on his adversary.

This was instinctive generalship on Henry's part. And once the king had got his archers angry, he needed to keep that anger directed towards the enemy. There was a risk that his bowmen, once roused, might turn their fury towards aristocrats in their own army. For noblemen, as the archers well knew, would be ransomed if taken prisoner, while they themselves were more likely to be put to the sword. Stories circulating were therefore at pains to show the French treating everyone with equal contempt. The popular English chronicle, the Brut, related one version:

> *All the night before the battle the French made many great fires,*
> *and with much revelry and shouting, played for our king and*
> *his lords with dice, and bid for an archer with a blanc of their*
> *money [the smallest possible coin], for they intended to have*
> *them as their own.*

The enemy was apparently painting a waggon to haul the captive English king back to Paris and gambling for who would win the most aristocratic prisoners. As the king's chaplain said disapprovingly: 'It is said that the French thought themselves so sure of us that night, that they cast dice for our king and his nobles.' Henry wanted his men to know that they were all in this together – and unite his army in its anger at the arrogance of the French.

In terms of a broader message, Henry needed to build on this emotion and put his case across simply and clearly, riding along the line himself, repeating it to clusters of men, backed up by some sort of visual display – rather like a modern-day promotional company video – so that the ideas could be quickly digested and understood. With an army largely drawn from peasant stock and thus mostly illiterate, the effectiveness of such symbols would be all-important.

To bring this into effect, the king needed the support of his captains. Before the battle of Poitiers, Robert Ufford, Earl of Suffolk 'passed through each rank, encouraging his men, restraining the young knights from advancing against orders and bidding the archers not to waste their arrows'. Sir Thomas Erpingham performed a similar role before Agincourt – and could transmit tactical ideas and also encourage the troops.

This was a very different language – where powerful sentiments were elaborated by ritual and gesture, and their meaning passed on to rank-and-file soldiers by the commander, his captains and priests. It began when the English king chose to hold a dawn religious service, as Titus Livius recalled: 'At dawn, prayers, supplications, matins and masses were completed and sung by the royal priests according to religious observance, with all proper devotion.'

Henry now made an inspired decision, dedicating the battle that morning to the two saints – Crispin and Crispinian – whose day it was, and commemorating the clash of arms in their name.

Thomas Elmham recalled how the English were 'passionately reminded how Crispin and Crispinian willingly took up their [spiritual] weapons in the name of Christ'. The invocation of St Crispin's Day, as a way of remembering the battle and the deeds of the English soldiers who fought there, was captured memorably by Shakespeare:

> *This day is called the Feast of Crispian.*
> *He that outlives this day and comes safe home*
> *Will stand a-tiptoe when this day is named*

And rouse himself in the name of Crispian.
He that shall see this day and live old age
Will yearly on the vigil feast his neighbours
And say, 'Tomorrow is Saint Crispian'.
Then he will strip his sleeve and show his scars
And say, 'These wounds I had on Crispin's day'.
Old men forget; yet all shall be forgot,
But he'll remember with advantages,
What feats he did that day. Then shall our names,
Familiar in his mouth as household words
...
Be in their flowing cups freshly remembered.

And then the theme is powerfully reiterated:

This story shall the good man teach his son,
And Crispin Crispian shall ne'er go by
From this day to the ending of the world
But we in it shall be remembered.

This powerful oration was based on solid historical fact. Such was Henry's veneration for these saints (the two, Crispin and Crispinian, were commemorated together) that he ordained that they should be celebrated in his daily Masses in his own chapel for as long as he lived. He also ensured that their day, 25 October, would be properly observed in England on each returning anniversary of the battle. As one contemporary emphasised:

Because that day was the commemoration by the church of the blessed Crispin and Crispinian, and it seemed to him it was through their intercession to God that he had obtained so great a victory over the enemy...'.

161

The explanation for this seems simple enough. The medieval calendar was based around its many saint's days, and these were carefully set out in the beautifully illuminated books of hours that record the days and months, and whose scenes present to us an enduring image of medieval life. Since Agincourt fell on the saint's day of Crispin and Crispinian it was an obvious way of remembering it, particularly because Henry wanted the outcome of the battle to be surrendered to God's will.

But it was a surprising choice nonetheless, for Crispin and Crispinian were *French* saints, cobblers from Soissons who in the third century were martyred for their Christian beliefs. The story was well known in France, and was depicted in a fine early fifteenth-century painting on the altarpiece of St Sepulchre's church in Saint-Omer, not far from the Agincourt battle site. In short, it was a French way of remembering the battle, subsequently brought out on the tomb memorial to one of the French slain, Jean, Count of Roucy, giving his date of death as 'the day of Sts Crispin and Crispinian'. Henry, who had always resolutely preferred English saints, and used English symbols to foster a sense of unity within his army, had made a most unusual dedication on the morning of battle.

Another saint's day fell upon 25 October, and it seemed a far more appropriate choice for a battle commemoration: the feast of the translation of St John of Beverley. St John of Beverley was an English saint, whose piety was extolled by Bede and who had been canonised in the eleventh century. In a clear martial precedent, his banner was used by Edward I, alongside that of St George, to encourage his soldiers on campaign to Scotland – and it was proudly borne on the king's expeditions of 1296 and 1300.

St John of Beverley was closely connected to England's ruling Lancastrian dynasty. When Henry's father, Henry IV, had landed at Ravenspur in Yorkshire in 1399, in his bid to take the throne, it was believed that the saint had shown approval of his actions: witnesses at his shrine claimed that his body had distilled drops of oil at the time of Henry's return from exile. As a result, St John of Beverley was venerated by Henry V's family circle, and prayers to him are found in a number of their books of hours.

This was an impressive pedigree. St John of Beverley was one of the king's three favourite saints, alongside St George and St John of Bridlington, and Henry had gone on pilgrimage to St John of Beverley's shrine in the aftermath of his siege of Aberystwyth. Remarkably, according to Adam of Usk, the saint was also said to have given a premonition of the fight at Agincourt, again sweating out clear drops of oil at the very time battle was raging in Picardy.

Yet while St John of Beverley was acknowledged in the aftermath of Agincourt, it was Sts Crispin and Crispinian to whom 'the English people owed so much' – as the Archbishop of Canterbury put it – who were singled out for special veneration. To favour French saints against such a notable English one was a quite extraordinary choice. And once we realise Henry was making a choice, we can look for an underlying meaning to make sense of his actions. The key was that Crispin and Crispinian were *martyrs* of Soissons.

As we have already learned, before Henry V had invaded France the country had been in the throes of a vicious civil war as the aristocratic house of Orléans and the Duke of Burgundy jostled for power – and the English had, from time to time, provided military assistance to one or other of the warring parties. In 1414 the Orléanist faction regained Burgundian-held Soissons, and subsequently put many of the garrison and ordinary townspeople to the sword. The incident became notorious, and was well known within

Henry's army. According to Jean Juvenal des Ursins, when English soldiers entered the town of Harfleur they reassured its inhabitants: 'Fear not that we shall do you any harm! We shall not behave towards you as did your countrymen towards the people of Soissons, for we are good Christians.'

Crucially, within the garrison of Soissons had been a contingent of English archers. They had gone into the service of the Duke of Burgundy and, as foreign auxiliaries, should have been protected under the law of arms, the medieval equivalent of the Geneva Convention. But according to the Burgundian chronicler Monstrelet they were massacred in cold blood. This terrible deed could only have reinforced the prejudices of the ordinary bowmen: that they were not treated as proper combatants and were seen by the aristocracy as easily expendable.

The story of the cobblers Crispin and Crispinian carried real resonance for the English archers. They had helped the poor, and repaired their shoes for no financial charge. Before being killed for their faith, both had been tortured – and their hands, upon which they relied for their craft, were deliberately mutilated. The Saint-Omer altarpiece graphically depicted a scene showing their arms clamped to chairs, and spikes then being inserted under their nails. As Henry well knew, his bowmen feared similar mutilation if the French won the battle.

'May these saints, Crispin and Crispinian, be always in bliss, for they bore their wounds for us,' wrote the soldier John Hardyng in his account of Agincourt. By invoking Crispin and Crispinian on the morning of battle Henry was venerating the slain archers of Soissons and honouring them as martyrs to the English cause. It was an astonishing mark of respect for England's bowmen. The king was reminding his men that, if the massacre at Soissons was anything to go by, they could expect no mercy from their opponents and therefore should not consider surrender or flight. Rather, they were fighting to avenge their fallen comrades. Here is evidence of the king's instinctive gift as a commander, one that he shared with the Duke of York; he knew how to bring his whole army together and give it a strong sense of common cause.

The Norman chronicler Thomas Basin spoke with English and French soldiers after the battle. He related how Henry's invocation of Crispin and Crispinian had an incredible effect on his troops, stoking the fires of their courage and giving them real belief in victory. Basin was struck by the English king's 'annexation' of two French saints, fearing that their resting place had been desecrated during the sack of Soissons in 1414 and that God would now punish the French army for it. His words were written with hindsight, but show the real power of Henry's action. The morale of the English army was being transformed.

York wrote in *The Master of Game* that hunting provided an essential training for war. It taught courage, mental quickness and an ability to formulate strategy – sentiments echoed by the soldier John Hardyng: 'From hunting and trapping deer one learns hardiness [physical endurance], and from that springs courage, quick-wittedness and instinctive cunning, qualities of great use on the battlefield.' Henry and York now fashioned a tactic to express their army's anger, one borrowed from the hunting bow rather than any military textbook. A German knight, Guicennas, wrote a treatise on deer hunting – and listed the abilities the huntsman needed:

> *He must need to shoot well with the bow; to train his scenting-hound to follow a trail of blood; to stand properly by his tree; to remember the placement of the archers – which is the most important thing of all in this form of hunting; to observe the*

165

wind, by which he may know the direction the beasts will take and where to place his archers; to cut arrow shafts; to make a bow string if necessary; to skin and cut up his hart; to direct his scenting-hound well, which needs much experience; to sound a horn in all the ways a hunter needs.

In the fifteenth century, Edward, Duke of York made a long addition to Gaston de Phoebus's earlier work, with a new chapter entitled 'on the manner of hunting when the king will hunt in forest or in park for the hart with bows, grey-hound and stable'. The operation revolved around the arrival of the king and queen. Much had to be done in advance of their arrival.

And if the hunting shall be in a park, all men should wait at the park gate … And early that morning the master of the game should be at the wood-side to see that all be ready … And then the master forester or parker will show him the king's stand, and if the king will stand with his bow and where all the remaining bowmen shall be positioned.

When the king and queen were installed, and the other archers were at their places, the master of the game blew three long notes on his horn for the uncoupling of the hounds. What followed was known as the 'drive' – the goading of the beasts into a flight towards the huntsmen. The *Ritual Book* of Holyrood Abbey captured the scene:

The king and his huntsmen rode between two hills, to the place where he thought the beasts would be most likely to flee from the hounds. The huntsmen went into the forest with their hounds, so as to drive out the beasts from the depths of the woods by their craft, and the cry of their hounds, and soon the baying of the

hounds and the shouting of the huntsmen filled the whole air
with melody. The king waited silently, withal his nobles dis-
persed around with their dogs, after the manner of hunters.

The terrible but strangely powerful lyricism of ritual killing
is described well in the 'hunting of the deer by Sir Bertilak',
in the fourteenth-century poem *Sir Gawain and the Green
Knight*:

Huntsmen uncoupled their hounds.
The forest was woken and stirred
By the echoing notes of the horn.
The wild beasts quivered at the cry of the questing hounds:
Deer ran through the dale, distracted by fear,
Hastened up the high slopes, but hotly were met
By the stout cries of the stable, staying their flight
...

Then the shimmering arrows slipped from the bowstrings,
*   and slanted,*
Winging their way from every tree in the wood.
Their broad heads pierced the bonny flanks of brown;
The deer brayed and bled, as on the banks they died.
The hurrying hounds still chased them, and harried them still;
Hunters came after with high hue of the horn,
Cleaving the cliffs with the clear note of their cry.
The beasts which ran on and broke through the ranks of
*   bowmen*
Died at the resayt, seized and dragged down by the dogs;
They were harried from the slopes and teased down to the
*   streams,*
So skilled were those who stood at the sets,
And the greyhounds so great and so swift to grip them
And to fling them down ...

The terrain governed the position of the archers: the drive was down a wooded valley, so that the flight of the deer was confined and channelled towards the bowmen; the deer tried to escape up the sides of the valley, but were turned back into it by the shouting of the stable, stationed in a line along the upper slopes on each side; the hounds, hunters and beaters drove the deer between two parallel lines of stable, and the archers did their work; deer which ran on behind the archers again tried to take refuge by climbing the slopes; they were chivvied out again; they came down to the water – a desperate last refuge – and were caught by the larger greyhounds, the receivers, waiting at the receiving station (the 'resayt').

The role of the 'stable' – a hunting term referring to a line of archers or auxiliaries – was to guide the deer along a predetermined route, whether in the wild or enclosed hunting areas or deer parks. 'Hayes', or long nets, set on poles, were used either as a means of capture or to prevent the beasts from escaping, so that they could only run towards the hunters waiting in ambush. The progress of the hunt was signalled by horn blasts. As the arrows flew, and the frantic deer were dragged down by the greyhounds, the carcasses were carried through the trees on carts and lined up for the final ceremonies.

As with the hunt, so with the battle: the power of the plan lay in its visual imagery – a clear sequence that drew on men's everyday experience and instinctive skill, created a sense of group identity and tapped into their shared anger. That anger would drive the sequence forward.

The king and queen arrive: the army assembles for battle. The master of the game inspects the woods and sees all is in order: the troops are organised in military formation, around an enclosed space. A blast is made on the horn: a signal is given for battle to commence. The hounds are uncoupled;

specialist squadrons of archers run towards the enemy. The 'drive' begins: the French are provoked by the archer squadrons – including some placed in ambush – and the derisory calls of the English, into a fateful advance across the battlefield. The 'drive' is down an enclosed valley: the French are confined and channelled towards mass archer fire from the remainder of the bowmen. The archers do their work: the enemy suffer terrible attrition. The 'last refuge': the French collide with the line of English men-at-arms at the 'receiving station'. They are caught by the larger greyhounds: the whole English army encloses the French and destroys them.

All was to be played out to the terrible melody of the hunt – one that drew on the everyday experience of nobles, knights and peasantry, whether authorised or illicit, and bound the army together in an act of ritual killing – one that sated the fury of men derided by their foe as 'unworthy' and 'vile', men threatened with mutilation – who remembered the fate of their comrades, killed in cold blood at Soissons and would now fight for their memory. This battle would be for them.

All knew the sounds of the trumpet, bugle and horn – men recognised the different notes and could imitate them. These sounds would hold the army together and signal the progress of the battle. In *The Master of Game* Edward, Duke of York also provided additional material on horn calls – the 'motes' by which the hunt's progress was signalled and directed, the hunting party held together and the ritual moment of kill declared. John I of Portugal wrote lyrically on this subject:

> *When one's hearing is blunted by listening to unpleasant things, it is refreshed by the pleasant things to be heard in the hunt, for it is a thing of beauty to hear the huntsman blow to the scent, and then to hear the cry of the hounds as they find it, and are all*

running together – a beauty beyond all reckoning … Then there is the blowing of the horns, and the hue and cry of the huntsmen after the hounds … All these are as effective in refreshing one's ears as rhubarb in restoring the liver!

'There are diverse kinds of horns,' York began, and gave information on a practical horn for the huntsman – again, indifferent to showy or luxurious items, such as the one ordered by Louis, Duke of Orléans in the early fifteenth century, a large, unwieldy horn mounted in gold and silver, beautiful to look at but impossible to use. He described a particular fanfare, known as the '*menée*' – the note sounded on the horn when the hunted stag is to be driven towards the archers, and the deer provoked into full flight. The 'strake' or 'stroke' was the horn call; 'huer' was to imitate the horn – hunters using oral calls that mimicked the horn blast. In an audacious ploy, these hunting techniques would be transferred to the battlefield.

The co-ordination of the English bowmen was vital to the plan's success. The Brut chronicle recalled how York 'went forth and ordered and commanded for every man to provide himself with a stake, sharpened at both ends, and put in the ground in front of him at an angle, so that the French horsemen could not overrun his position'. But, ironically, most detail on the deployment of the archers is found in a French source, not an English one.

We have three eyewitness accounts of the battle on the French side. Arthur, Count of Richemont was in the thick of the fighting – and later became constable of France, fought with Joan of Arc, organised French military reforms and was one of the commanders who defeated the last English army in Normandy in 1450. A chronicle of his life was later compiled by one of his servants, Guillaume Gruel, probably after

170

Richemont's death in 1458. It is derived primarily from Richemont's oral testimony, from which we learn that he returned to the battlefield in the summer of 1436 and that 'he explained to those who were with him how it had been fought'. He placed particular emphasis on the terrain, the narrow, constricting effect of the battlefield as the French advanced. Sadly, the information contained in the chronicle is tantalisingly brief.

Ghillebert Lannoy made a passing reference to Agincourt in one of his works, although he only described an episode within it (involving his own capture) rather than the battle as a whole. Once again, in the midst of horror and killing, Lannoy seemed to be leading a charmed life. But the moment he depicted opens a window on a highly controversial moment within the fight.

Jean de Waurin was a 15-year-old page at the time of the battle. He would later – during the days of the Anglo-Burgundian alliance – fight on the English side at the battles of Verneuil (1424) and Patay (1429), and his accounts of these clashes are fascinating. But for Agincourt he largely relied on another's completed history (Enguerrand de Monstrelet) and his own recollections – sometimes interesting – are fragmentary.

There is also the moving testimony of Edmond de Dynter, the Duke of Brabant's secretary who arrived at the battle site two days later, with the remainder of the duke's retinue, only to search for and find his master's dead body. Deeply shocked by the carnage still around him, over time Dynter was able to reconstruct, from conversations with surviving eyewitnesses, the last tragic moments of the duke's life.

Two sources acknowledged they had interviewed soldiers in the aftermath of the battle. Jean Juvenal des Ursins, a lawyer in Paris at the time of the battle, who later became bishop of Beauvais (1432), Laon (1444) and finally Archbishop of Rheims (1449), was a prolific researcher and political writer, with a great interest in documentary sources – and committed to the Valois cause. As with the Monk of Saint-Denis, he was very interested in the decision-making process, on the French side, that led up to the battle. He also addressed – obliquely – the issue of John the Fearless, Duke of Burgundy not attending the battle.

And there was also Thomas Basin, a child at the time of Agincourt, whose family were from Caudebec in the Pays de Caux. Basin studied canon law at the University of Paris. In the last days of English-held Normandy he became Bishop of Lisieux (1447) and president of the Norman treasury (*chambre des comptes*) a year later, but quickly switched allegiance when Charles invaded the duchy in 1449. Basin was able to talk to French and English veterans about Agincourt, although his account was brief and saw the outcome of the clash as the judgement of God. And the chronicle of Ruisseauville contains valuable local information about the battle.

Then there were chronicles from strong supporters of Charles VI (the Berry Herald) and the Duke of Alençon (Perceval de Cagny). But pride of place goes to the chronicles of the Burgundian, Enguerrand de Monstrelet. Monstrelet was from a minor noble family in Picardy, who went on to become *bailli* (town governor) of Compiègne and *prévôt* (royal administrator) of Cambrai. He saw himself as a successor to Froissart – writing a monumental history of the second phase of the Hundred Years War.

Monstrelet completed his work in 1444 and presented it to the Duke of Burgundy three years later. It was widely read by his contemporaries. While lacking Froissart's imagination and infectious enthusiasm, he was a thorough and conscientious researcher, determined as far as possible to be impartial and to get his facts right. Monstrelet believed that English archers were vital to the victory at Agincourt, and he did all he could to gather information about their role. And, crucially, his account is dynamic rather than static – he provided an all-important sequence of events. Through these, we see how Henry V and the Duke of York intended to put their plan into effect.

In *The Master of Game*, the first complete treatise on hunting in the English language, York made a request:

> *I ask of every person who reads this little treatise, or comes to hear of it, whatever their estate or condition, that in plain and simple language they will add to it anything they find useful and remove all that seems superfluous ... so that this work may always grow through the advice and counsel of all hunters, and with this in mind, I tried to set out, as simply and clearly as I knew, what I understood of this craft, for the use and remembrance of all.*

Here it is – a gift to all those who love hunting, one that is modest, defers to the life experience of others and asks for their guidance, whatever their rank and status, is inclusive and never condescends, and is always practical, favouring instinctive skill over unnecessary show. It offers a shared vision that will bring all together and give every man his place and sense of value. It evokes a band of brothers, bound together in a common cause.

That sense of brotherhood would now be transferred to the battlefield.

CHAPTER 6

A Touch of Harry in the Morning

Battle Ritual

08.00–09.00 (25 October 1415)

IT WAS NOW just after sunrise – the first hour of light, known from the monastic daily regimen as 'prime'. Henry could expect the French army to start assembling before 'terce', that is at 9 am, so he had about an hour to gather his troops and prepare them for combat, and then march the short distance to the southern end of the funnel and take up his battle position. The king joked that the end of prime would be a good time to move his army, telling his men 'the whole of England will be praying for us'.

We have already seen how Henry V motivated his men, but what the king did in the next hour or so would be crucial. Shakespeare allowed Henry to express it aptly: 'All things are ready if our minds be so.'

The rituals of preparation performed by commanders are often instinctive and thus do not fall into set patterns. But we are not on the battlefield with Henry and his soldiers, and for us to imagine what that might have been like, some sort of structure will be important. It was generally recognised that the king did something very special. Shakespeare made this idea famous, showing the king doing the rounds the night before the battle, talking to his men:

> ... who will behold
> The royal captain of this ruin'd band
> Walking from watch to watch, from tent to tent
> ...

176

For forth he goes, and visits all his host.

...

And calls them brothers, friends and countrymen.

This was certainly a characteristic action of the king. During the siege of Harfleur men noted how Henry often chose to walk around his war camp at night, chatting to his soldiers. At Agincourt, the chronicler Thomas Elmham said something significant had happened before the battle – the king had given courage to his men. Titus Livius spoke of a rousing exhortation: 'Be brave in heart and fight with all your might!' But the most impressive tributes came from the French. As they were reluctant to praise Henry – for obvious reasons – it is striking that here they chose to do so nonetheless.

The Monk of Saint-Denis described how the king urged his men 'to be mindful of the valour of their ancestors' at Crécy and Poitiers:

> ... and rather than being scared of doing business with so many [French] princes and barons, be of firm hope that their large numbers will turn, as in the past, to their shame and perpetual confusion.

Juvenal des Ursins gave a quite remarkable tribute. Henry had urged his followers to be 'good men in battle and do their duty'. He also 'inspired them', and 'boosted their courage enormously'. The king's message had reached the whole of the army:

> His words were received with enthusiasm, and not only by the leading men; for the common soldiers also promised to fight to the death.

When Shakespeare showed us Henry mingling with his men – 'a little touch of Harry in the night' – and then, in his St Crispin's Day address, transforming his army's fears and doubts, he captured a fundamental truth about the battle. To explore it, I want to weld the fragments and snippets preserved by contemporary witnesses and chroniclers – our voices from the battlefield – into a coherent whole.

The Roman military writer Vegetius expressed a timeless truth: 'An army gains its courage and fighting spirit from the advice and encouragement of its general.' If the precise detail of what Henry said to his men and how he put it across remains unknowable, it is possible, nevertheless, to catch something of its content and sense its power. It reveals a psychological strategy common to all effective battle ritual: a sequence of actions whose effect is cumulative.

Henry and the Duke of York had already begun to transform his soldiers' fear into anger, and, by reminding them of the martyrdom of Sts Crispin and Crispinian, and thus the murdered English bowmen in the sack of the town in 1414, given them a powerful rallying call to fight for. Benefiting from York's counsel, he now built upon this.

Firstly, the king reminded his soldiers, in clear and simple terms, that his cause was just. The dignity of his claim was emphasised through parading the royal regalia in front of his soldiers. On the march from Harfleur to Agincourt, Henry was travelling light, but he nevertheless chose to carry precious items of his regalia with him, including a crown and a sword of state. Some of these items were displayed outside Harfleur, when the king sat in majesty to receive the surrender of the town. They then seem to have been carried with his army, strongly suggesting that Henry intended a pre-battle ritual in front of his soldiers before he took on the French.

Henry had assembled a stunning treasure trove for the journey: a precious crown, a sword of state so valuable it was rarely seen, a gold cross set with precious stones, a piece of the True Cross set among rich jewels and an orb used for the coronation service itself.

The man responsible for supervising the transport of this priceless cargo was probably John Feriby. He had a useful pedigree of royal service, having organised the supplies for Henry IV's expedition to Scotland in 1400, and three years later, after the battle of Shrewsbury, he was given the important task of moving the royal pavilions, armour and artillery. Henry V recognised his gifts and brought him on the Agincourt expedition.

The visual impact of this would have been enormous – with men craning their necks as the king processed along the battle line to catch a glimpse of the priceless sword or the coronation orb. The excitement felt among his soldiers would be akin to the crown jewels being shown to the public for the first time – and there is a point to this comparison, for the last relic of this pre-battle ritual can be seen in the Imperial State Crown displayed at the Tower of London. (Although the crown itself was made in 1937 for the coronation of George VI, it contains a red pear-shaped jewel, known as the 'Black Prince's Ruby'. This was believed to have been given to the prince by Dom Pedro of Castile as a token of gratitude for his victory at Najera and subsequently worn by Henry V in the circlet crown, welded to his helmet, at Agincourt.)

Henry then told his men he would rather be killed than taken prisoner – he would never burden his countrymen with the payment of his ransom. He made a pledge in front of his men: 'As I am true king and knight, this day England shall never pay a ransom for me.' To show this was more than bravado, he then donned a helmet with a jewelled circlet crown welded to it, making him a conspicuous target. This was leadership from the front and his troops got the message. They called out in loyalty and real affection: 'Sir, we pray God give you a good life and the victory over your enemies.'

Leadership through personal example is incredibly powerful. During the battle of Poitiers in 1356 the exhausted army of the Black Prince discovered a fresh division of Frenchmen advancing on them. One of the Black Prince's followers counselled retreat, fearing they would be overwhelmed by the enemy. 'You lie, you fool!' the prince retorted, 'and speak the worst slander, if you say that I would be defeated whilst I am still alive.' The force of this declaration – 'If I don't win I will at least die in the attempt' – united his men behind him. The line held, and the English went on to secure a remarkable victory.

Henry then offered his men a vision – that they were destined to be brought together for the battle, to achieve something truly memorable. This was the stroke of genius in his reply to Sir Walter Hungerford the previous afternoon, that the chaplain recorded for posterity: 'I would not, even if I could, increase my number by one. For those I have are the people of God.'

This of course was the genesis of Shakespeare's memorable St Crispin's Day speech. But at Agincourt itself, Henry genuinely created a band of brothers. The gift of a great leader is the ability to turn a disadvantage into a source of inspiration. In one account it was recalled how the king told his men:

They should remember that they were born in the realm of England, where their fathers, mothers, wives and children now dwelt – therefore they ought to strive to return there with great glory and fame.

According to Thomas Elmham, Henry now invoked the memory of Edward III and the Black Prince, and their triumphs against the odds. By drawing on the 'military memory' of Crécy and Poitiers, the king showed that success was achievable: English armies had done it before. His soldiers were reminded of the love and support of the nation as they prepared to fight:

Now is a good time, for all England is praying for us. Therefore be of good cheer and go into battle.

The French were seen as puffed up with pride. The Dominican friar John Bromyard, whose writings were an important influence on Henry, warned of such worldly arrogance before battle. He singled out in contrast an historical example: Charlemagne's careful spiritual preparation before going into combat. Charlemagne would always hear Mass before going into battle – and if he achieved victory, he 'took no credit for it, but rendered thanks to God'.

Henry followed Bromyard's teaching. He now exhorted his men to throw themselves and the battle's outcome on the mercy of God. Henry heard Mass again, this time in front of his troops, and then made the sign of the cross, 'thus giving courage to his men', as Thomas Elmham related. Then priests were commanded to come up before the army and pray continually: 'Remember us, O Lord! Our enemies are gathered together and boast in their might. Scatter their strength and disperse them, that there is none other that fighteth for us, but only thou, O God.'

Already on campaign, the soldiers had been encouraged to pray to St George for help against their enemies, Henry's chaplain remembering that as the army marched along the River Somme, with morale faltering, troops sought the protection of 'the blessed Saint George, to mediate for us between God and our poor people'. The king now solemnly called upon the help of the saint on the morning of battle: 'In the name of Almighty God and Saint George advance your banners. Saint George, give us this day your help.'

The battleground itself was consecrated and the poet John Lydgate caught the moment: 'The king kneeled down, Englishmen on every side, and thrice kissed the ground, saying "Christ, as I am thy knight, this day save me for England's sake".' Then all the soldiers fell to their knees and made the sign of the cross on the ground with their hands, placed their lips on the earth and kissed it, and then took a piece of soil in their mouths. The preparation for combat was complete.

Men now readied themselves for the short march to the battlefield. The Brut chronicle related: 'Edward, Duke of York came to the king and asked that he might have command of the vanguard that day.'

This would mean that York held the right flank of the line of men-at-arms forming the army. This was an 'honour' position – and a dangerous one. Both York and Henry intended to lead by example and, in doing so, make themselves targets for the enemy. The king assented.

It was sometimes hard to get men raised on ideas of chivalric prowess and personal pride to take secondary positions within the army. Thomas Elmham recorded the story that Henry originally intended that the duke should guard the baggage train, and hence the army's rear. This was not a demotion – rather, the king was worried that the French might try and attack their forces from behind, and wanted someone he could really trust to guard against that danger.

There is an echo here of an earlier incident, at the battle of Auray in 1364, where Sir John Chandos requested that Sir Hugh Calveley command the rearguard, which had the essential task of reinforcing the line wherever it was hardest pressed, but Calveley indignantly refused, wishing instead to win honour in the front rank; he finally and only reluctantly consented after much pleading by Chandos. What is significant here is not that Calveley complained but that he eventually agreed – the army's discipline and cohesion was seen as more important than an individual's reputation. At Agincourt, the king revised his instructions, realising that his army would gain more by seeing York visibly occupying a prominent position in the line.

The royal banner, and those of the principal aristocrats, Lord Camoys and Michael de la Pole, Earl of Suffolk, on the left, the Duke of York on the right, would be focal points in the fight ahead. The banners were markers in the terrible surging clash of the mêlée, the fight between dismounted men-at-arms when, as Jean de Waurin recalled, armoured soldiers collided with each other with all the force of waves hitting a breakwater. This was a heavyweight slugging match, and, within it, banners served as vital rallying points. Men would look up and see how the lord and his chief retainers, grouped under their banner or standard, were fighting. It was a source of encouragement when the standard was resolutely defended; despondency, when it was seized by the enemy.

Immediately before the battle of Najera, in 1367, the Black Prince promoted Sir John Chandos to the rank of knight banneret by giving him the banner with the words, 'God grant that you may do nobly with it'. Chandos's herald, who witnessed this event, continued:

> So Chandos took his banner, and set it up among his comrades saying, 'Sirs, here is my banner, guard it as if it were your own, for it is yours as much as mine.' His companions were delighted by this. Then they continued on their way, not wanting to wait any longer for battle.

At Crécy in 1346 the Black Prince, only 16, had asked his father, Edward III, to place him where the combat would be the most dangerous. His banner – raised above the heads of his fighting comrades – became a target for the charging French cavalry, who on one occasion breached the English line and surrounded the young Edward. As the riders surged towards the dismounted English knights, the prince was knocked to the ground, badly concussed, and his banner toppled. The exultant French, believing Edward dead, seized the banner and taunted their foes. But Edward hauled himself back to his feet and his soldiers regrouped around him. He fought with true distinction that day and displayed such remarkable courage that it left a deep impression on contemporaries. One chronicler wrote:

> In the heart of this ferocious battle, the noble-spirited Edward of Woodstock, King Edward III's eldest son, who was at this time sixteen years old, was showing the French his admirable bravery at the head of his division. He stabbed horses, killed knights, struck helmets, snapped lances, craftily parried blows, aided his men, helped up fallen comrades and encouraged all to do good deeds by his own example. Nor did he cease from his noble efforts until the enemy retired behind the mound of his dead.

'The Prince truly won his spurs that day,' observed the chronicler Jean Froissart. And Edward did not forget to reward one of his retainers, Thomas Daniel, with a life annuity of £20 'for retrieving our banner from the French'.

Such encouragement, and the raising of morale, had to be ruthlessly backed up by strict discipline. There was no place for impulsive or rash gestures. At Cocherel in 1364 the English were defeated when John Jouel rashly led his men down from a strong defensive position in pursuit of the retreating forces of Bertrand du Guesclin, heedless of the Captal de Buch's orders, and his warning that this could be a ruse.

At Crécy, Edward III combined cheerful encouragement with the command that 'on pain of the noose, none should break ranks, nor seek gain, nor despoil either living or dead without his leave; for if the affair went in their favour, each would have time enough to pillage, and if fortune turned against them, then nothing they could do would gain them anything'.

Keeping tight and well-ordered ranks was vital, particularly if the English were outnumbered; if soldiers broke ranks or ceased fighting to pillage the dead, or take prisoners for ransom, there was a real danger that the enemy might quickly exploit such gaps in the line, with catastrophic results.

Only the army's commander could permit the cry 'Havoc', allowing soldiers to break ranks to plunder and to take prisoners at will, and the ordinances of war of Henry V punished the unauthorised use of this cry by beheading.

Even after nightfall, following the battle of Crécy, Edward III had kept his men to arms and in their ranks, as there were still substantial French units at large, and Henry V had shown a similar discipline in his march from Blangy to Maisoncelles, and the setting up of his war camp. Similarly, in mid-September 1356, when he was readying his soldiers for imminent battle at Poitiers, the Black Prince gave orders 'that none, upon pain of death, shall proceed without permission in front of the troop of marshals' but instead retain their position within the army.

In his treatise, Vegetius stressed the importance of keeping good order, ranking it above all other things. Vegetius had been first translated into English in 1408, on the request of the Gloucestershire nobleman Thomas Lord Berkeley, although copies of his work in French were widely available from the late thirteenth century. The English king understood its precepts, and so did a number of his soldiers. Sir John Fastolf, first off the boats at Harfleur, would become a lifelong devotee of the work, which he carefully read and studied. And Vegetius emphasised that an army's approach to combat should always be methodical, carefully planned and disciplined.

The insights of Sir John Fastolf, his secretary William Worcester and other members of his circle evolved over time, through Fastolf's own ongoing war experience and reflection on its broader implications. We cannot be fully sure, from the documentary evidence, whether Fastolf was actually on the battlefield at Agincourt or had been left behind, as a member of the important and substantial garrison at Harfleur. Not all English soldiers reflected so deeply, and with such thorough recourse to classical literature, about the war they were embarking on, and yet, for all that, the ideas formed by Fastolf and Worcester give us a glimpse of the mentality of the army gathering itself for battle on 25 October 1415.

Fastolf believed in the importance of military training and a professional approach to war, and he found such principles echoed in the work of Vegetius, a copy of which he owned. Organisation was the bedrock of military success – and could counter the superior numbers of the enemy. Looking at the wars of ancient times between Rome and Carthage, he took heart from the fact that large armies could suffer defeat at the hands of smaller ones, if they were better trained, disciplined and led. As his secretary William Worcester wrote: 'Men well learned and exercised in the profession of arms are a greater treasure than any precious stones.'

Fastolf understood that to win an army must act together, as one. For him, true nobility, or 'noblesse', was not about rank or status but an attitude of mind, the willingness of a soldier to put the common good before his own individual interests. He made an all-important distinction between a 'manly man', a fighter who saw himself as a servant, through training and discipline, of a common cause and a 'hardy [foolhardy] man', a warrior who put his own pursuit of wealth or glory before everything else.

The French were well aware of such principles. Within their army, copies of Vegetius were owned by the Dukes of Orléans and Bourbon, and Arthur, Count of Richemont. The biographer of Louis, Duke of Bourbon, the father of Duke Jean at Agincourt, claimed that he always ate his meals in silence, 'listening to readings from the histories of great men' – although it is unclear whether such a worthy routine had rubbed off on his son. And within the realm there had been a blossoming of literature on the Roman way of war. In 1389 the Provençal lawyer Honorat Bovet brought out his *L'Arbre des batailles* (Tree of Battles), a complex treatise on just wars, which argued for a reinstatement of Roman values in public and military life. And between 1399 and 1410 Christine de Pizan had completed a wide range of works on knighthood and warfare, again strongly influenced by the classical texts and traditions.

Vegetius's overarching belief in military discipline was successfully applied in the practical arena, in the 1370s, by Bertrand du Guesclin, who had been made constable of France by Charles V. Shortly after being appointed to the office, du Guesclin used good military intelligence to surprise and then destroy an English army at Pontvallain, shattering the myth of the nation's invincibility. The following year a Franco-Castilian fleet defeated the English at sea, at La Rochelle, enabling the constable to start raiding England's southern coast. After another land victory, at Chizé on 23 March 1373, du Guesclin was able to reconquer much of Poitou and Brittany for the French crown. He also began, in concert with Charles V, to introduce much-needed military reforms and encourage the use of the bow.

However, du Guesclin, for all his skill, was low-born, and many aristocrats refused to serve under him. After his death in 1380 his more professional approach to war was all but discarded. The French turned away from the 'advice literature' that encouraged them to study the Roman way of war, and the practical experience of the 1370s, and instead embraced an increasingly hedonistic courtly and chivalric lifestyle, where the pursuit of honour at all costs became the overarching goal.

The lessons of the *Bal des Ardents* (Ball of the Burning Men) and the defeat at Nicopolis (1396) – which, as the Monk of Saint-Denis bluntly observed, 'was caused by arrogance and lack of discipline' – were largely ignored. In an act of supreme self-indulgence, on 6 January 1400 the French aristocracy created a 'cour amoureuse' – a 'court of love', with 600 members, presided over by its own 'Prince', holding regular festivities and poetry competitions praising the beauty of women (an act that echoed Marshal Boucicaut's founding of the equally indulgent Order of the White Lady on a Green Shield for the protection of virtuous women). Books owned by the wives of Charles, Duke of Orléans and his brother Jean, Count of Angoulême were full of courtly poems, signed by a wide circle of friends.

The French were losing all touch with reality. In the summer of 1413 the Burgundian duke John the Fearless left the French capital and retreated to his Burgundian heartlands. The return of Charles, Duke of Orléans and Jean, Duke of Bourbon to Paris on 31 August 1413 after a number of small-scale military successes was greeted with rhapsodic praise. Even Christine de Pizan – that author of sober reflections on good military practice – quite forgot herself. The Duke of Bourbon had returned from a 'hault voyage' (a 'great campaign') where he had covered himself in glory. Jean de Bourbon's success owed nothing to military discipline, but, rather, his 'valiant deeds' were inspired by his great love for his lady (Marie de Berry), and by her continuing love for him. Although the duke had been far away, his lady's love had been unfailing, strengthened by the news of his 'great victories' (a fine example of poetic licence) and her awareness of the heavy responsibilities he had had to bear.

In November 1413 the Duke of Bourbon captured the Gascon town of Soubise from the English. The small garrison was in no condition to resist and, as the Monk of Saint-Denis noted, terms were agreed after just two days. But this episode was recast as 'an epic struggle' showing 'great knightly prowess', and the duke lost no time in sending an inflated report of his endeavours to Paris, where a celebratory Mass was held to honour his achievement. The French indeed seemed lost in a world of their own.

The Monk of Saint-Denis believed that the French army at Agincourt had succumbed to a state of euphoria, where the cult of honour had subsumed all other considerations. He noted that the Duke of Bourbon had accused the constable, Charles d'Albret, of failing to respond quickly enough to the English siege of Harfleur. This charge was unfounded – the French were simply not strong enough to challenge Henry V at this stage of the campaign – but it pushed d'Albret on to the back foot, and he was now joining the plethora of aristocrats in the vanguard to vindicate his reputation, rather than exercise any meaningful command and control of the French forces.

The canonical 'hour' of 'terce' – 9 am – was approaching. The sun was now out, and with so much rain the previous night the pools of water everywhere were glistening. There was great bustle of activity, as men cared for their horses, donned their armour, checked their weaponry, brought up provisions and called words of encouragement to each other. Sheets of water ran down the tent awnings as men shook them, hung out the material to dry and unfurled their banners. Soon both armies would be on the move, drawing themselves up on opposite ends of the funnelling escarpment, bordered by trees, that would form the battlefield.

The English king had taken great care, on the campaign and before the battle, to encourage his men, and he had grounded that encouragement in a sequenced ritual that left his army focused and determined.

In the French war camp men were also strongly motivated, but as a result of a high-octane adrenalin rush rather than thorough emotional and spiritual preparation. The gathering together of so many former enemies – Burgundian and Orléanist – had created an overwhelming sense of euphoria, both heady and exciting. It was not, however, a reliable basis for cool-headed decision-making in a life or death situation. One chronicler caught the intoxicating atmosphere well:

> Some of them kissed and put their arms around each other's necks in making peace, and it was moving to see this. All troubles and discords which had been between them, and which they had in the past, were changed into great feelings of love.

The French had united against a common invader and these feelings were strong enough to dictate the shape of the battle. The atmosphere was exceptionally volatile as a mood of reconciliation swept the army. The English army had kissed the soil and taken a piece of it in their mouths, in imitation of the rite of communion – and now stood together – sober and resolute; the French were ascending higher and higher, with all the exhilaration of a helium balloon. Agincourt would be a battle between two armies – and also two hugely contrasting emotional states.

The Field of Battle —

Terrain

09.00–11.00 (25 October 1415)

A s THE TWO armies came into view a little past the 'hour' of 'terce' – shortly after 9 am – the panoply of French nobility was now on display. Their army contained four royal dukes: Orléans, Alençon, Bourbon and Bar (and the Duke of Brabant was on his way); twelve counts (Vendôme, Eu, Richemont, Nevers, Vaudémont, Blanmont, Salm, Grandpré, Roussy, Dammartin, Marle and Fauquembergues); and innumerable lords. All the great military officials of France were in attendance: Constable d'Albret, Marshal Boucicaut, the two admirals (Clignet de Brabant and Jacques de Châtillon), the master of the crossbowmen, David de Rambures, and the grand master of the royal household, Guichard Dauphin. Local officials from many of the towns of northern France had also arrived, together with their militias.

Unlike the French force, where there were so many banners that some had to be taken down and put away because they were blocking the way forward, the English ones were few and far between. Four nobles had been invalided home at Harfleur: the Duke of Clarence, the earl marshal, and the Earls of March and Arundel. That left two dukes – the king's brother, the Duke of Gloucester, and Edward, Duke of York – and two earls, Oxford and Suffolk. Sir John Holland, who was sometimes referred to as the Earl of Huntingdon in later accounts of the battle, in fact was only restored to the earldom in 1416.

The last moments before battle held a powerful sway over the medieval imagination. One encounter in particular had an enduring fascination, the battle on the plains of Troy between the Greeks and the Trojans. This distant martial episode became something of a late medieval bestseller, translated into numerous languages, with its manuscript histories beautifully produced and illustrated. The word 'history' was very much a contemporary euphemism, for these deeds of arms had long passed into the mists of mythic imagination. What was important was not whether they had actually happened but the effect they invoked in their audience.

The clash of arms outside Troy was a roll call of honour. Enormous care was taken in listing those present on both sides, the captains of renown and their great achievements, a form of description also used by heralds in their relation of medieval battles. The skill lay in creating and building atmosphere in the narration.

Time and movement were quietened, instilling a sense that all eyes were watching the assembled armies. The massing onlookers gathered on the Trojan ramparts. All were to be witness to an extraordinary dramatic spectacle. Perception was then intensified through the capture of significant detail: the vivid colouring of a shield hanging from the wall, a flash of sunlight on burnished armour. And in the last minutes before the armies engaged, language was stilled. The power of the battle would be drawn from the silence that preceded it.

What followed was an exhilarating cacophony of sound: the guttural roar of the combatants as the lines suddenly surged forward; the crashing din of impact as bodies collided and blows were exchanged. The best medieval accounts of battle understood this truth, forgoing analysis and explanation and employing rhyme and alliteration to imitate the terrible noise of war.

This was a compelling yet terrifying arena. Humanity was brought to it through individual deeds of valour that were recalled and commemorated, how men conducted themselves in a struggle for life or death. The best and the worst were related, the moments of incredible courage, the moments of cowardice and dishonour. Here would be the inspirational act that could push an army forward and give it fresh reserves of strength. But here also would be the betrayal that would undermine its resolve and corrode its unity. Lessons would be learned for the future. The Trojan Hector fought with great tenacity and none could withstand his onslaught. But in a moment of greed, he turned to plunder the rich helmet of a fallen opponent. It was this lapse of concentration that allowed the Greek champion Achilles to slay him.

The continuing popularity of the Trojan War in medieval times showed that people cared about how battles were fought, along with their eventual outcome. Thomas Walsingham referred to the Black Prince as 'a Hector for his people – invincible in warfare'. John Lydgate was inspired enough by Henry V to create his own *Troy Book*. But the field of Agincourt was no plain of Troy. Conditions resembled a mud bath.

At around 9 am Henry V led his army out of the village of Maisoncelles, and, moving northwards, lined up his men at the top of a slight ridge. On either side was woodland, which surrounded the villages of Agincourt to their left and Tramecourt to their right. The ground formed an escarpment, dropping away quite steeply towards both villages, and funnelling towards the English position. Henry took up position at the narrow end of this funnel.

The king drew up his forces as effectively as he could. Here, some of the battle accounts are not easy to interpret. The chaplain, who by his own admission was sitting in the baggage train as Henry deployed his troops, and thus unable to see things at first hand, described the king placing 'wedges' of archers in between the line of men-at-arms; Jean Le Fèvre and Jean de Waurin, both present on the actual battlefield, told how Henry instructed Sir Thomas Erpingham 'to draw up his archers, and place them in front, in two wings'. Probably the king placed the majority of his archers on his flanks, where the woodland gave them some protection, interspersing other clusters of bowmen among his line of dismounted men-at-arms. All his men were on foot.

The archers hammered their protective stakes into the ground. Very much a novelty in Anglo-French warfare, these must have given a morale boost to the bowmen, a 'secret weapon' against the feared enemy cavalry. Armies normally marched and fought in three divisions, but Henry had to put his men-at-arms, who probably numbered about 1,500, in a single line, 'in view of his want of numbers', as the chaplain bluntly put it. There was no reserve.

Henry had great respect for his bowmen. The longbow – the yew bow used by his archers – had a draw weight of well over a hundred pounds and thus called for real strength and skill to be used properly. This weapon was very accurate in the hands of a person properly trained, and also very powerful. A bow with a draw weight of 150 pounds could drive a heavy 60-gram arrow 230 yards, a lighter arrow 300 yards. A broadhead arrow – of the sort commonly used against horses – would penetrate mail with ease, while a narrow pointed 'bodkin' shaft could be lethal even through plate armour.

These were the great strengths of the longbow, and, rather than representing an 'underclass', as some of the French seemed to imagine, they were – in military terms – an elite corps. Their weakness was their vulnerability once hand-to-hand combat commenced.

197

While the wealthiest bowmen might own a cheap armour breast plate – known as a 'brigandine' or 'jack' – or mail shirt, contemporary illustrations of warfare, which showed most of the archers in armour, presented an idealised picture. As we have learned, the reality was very different, for there was great diversity in archers' equipment and the vast majority had very little, as Monstrelet had recalled before the battle, 'being without armour, dressed in their doublets, and without any headgear'.

So within the English army the archers needed to be properly protected to be fully effective – and it was important for Henry to take advantage of any features of the terrain to achieve this. At Crécy in 1346 Edward III had chosen a superb site for his bowmen – a ridge shielded by the woodland behind it and man-made ditches in front of the archers' position. At Agincourt, Titus Livius noted, alongside the woods, the main bodies of archers had an additional safeguard: 'On the two flanks hedges and thorn bushes also protected the army from assault by the enemy.'

The dangers of leaving the archers exposed were shown in another fourteenth-century battle – at Mauron in Brittany in 1352. The English commander, Sir Walter Bentley, was outnumbered by the French and the battle site was unpromising, 'upon the open fields, without woods, ditches or other defences'. The French cavalry were able to break into the archers' position, killing many of them and creating panic. Bentley managed to counter-attack and win the victory, but in the battle's aftermath he 'ordered thirty of the archers to be beheaded, because at the height of the battle, frightened by the numbers of the French, they had fled'. This grim piece of military discipline demonstrated that, to fight against the odds, the cohesion of the army was vital: everyone had to hold together.

On the morning of Agincourt, the English war camp at Maisoncelles had contained a mass of waggons. Commanding a relatively small force, Henry needed to fight with maximum economy, using everything at hand – including his baggage train. The previous night, at dusk, a group of French cavalry had attacked a surprised unit of English archers, and the vigour of their action warned the king that on the day of the battle enemy horsemen might ride around his position – skirting the far side of the woods – and attack his army from the rear. So he brought up his baggage train, close behind his battle line, to act as a defensive shield.

The chaplain recalled that on the morning of battle the king ordered all his waggons to move up behind his soldiers. Henry was too short of men to spare a proper reserve, so the baggage train could only be held by a scratch force of pages and a few archers. The danger was primarily from the French mounted combatants in their third line. These men could easily ride around the battlefield – such an enveloping manoeuvre had been seen at a recent battle, at Othée in 1408, when the Burgundian commander John the Fearless sent several hundred horsemen around his opponent's position. It had been envisaged by Marshal Boucicaut, in his original battle plan against the English, that a force of 200 picked cavalry would perform the task and if they met a defence line of carts they would attempt to break through it.

Men were still being lost to dysentery – and according to Thomas Walsingham many had been surviving on drinking water for days before the battle – so we can only guess at the exact total of the English army. The calculation of Thomas Elmham, who estimated it had been reduced to about 7,000 men, was probably right.

Ahead of them were the French. Their army was drawn up about a thousand yards further north, at the wide end of the funnel between Agincourt and Tramecourt. Here the ground broadened, giving them greater room to deploy. There were open fields, and beyond these the abbey of Ruisseauville. They were blocking the Calais road – leaving the English no option but to fight.

Their exact number was probably not even known to them. A number of the chroniclers (the Monk of Saint-Denis, Thomas Basin and the anonymous chronicler of Charles VI) believed their force was around four times the English army, and the strong consensus that Henry was heavily outnumbered was well sourced and founded.

The French heavily outnumbered the English in men-at-arms – the chronicler of Ruisseauville said that here they held a 10:1 advantage. We can give their whole army a notional strength of around 28,000 men. Allowing for around 1,000 mounted men-at-arms, posted on either flank, there would be around 14,000 of them dismounted in the first two divisions. Behind them, in the third line, were the lighter armed combatants (known as the *gros valets*), many of whom had horses and reasonable military equipment, and the crossbowmen.

Henry rode along the line to maintain morale and his lords and captains did likewise among their own retinues. The king would hold the centre, with the experienced soldiers Thomas lord Camoys and Edward, Duke of York to the left and right. Now he watched the French in front of him. Earlier in the campaign he had expected to meet a smaller army, close to the crossing point of the Somme at Blanchetaque, commanded by the renowned crusader Marshal Boucicaut. The encounter had never happened – and now, looking at the army opposing him, it seemed that Boucicaut was no longer in sole command.

Only remnants of the marshal's original battle plan now survived. The French had pushed their crossbowmen to the rear. There was still some cavalry on the flanks but their huge vanguard occupied most of the space ahead. It was crammed with aristocrats. Their squires and servants were also relegated to the back of the army, along with the crossbowmen. The vanguard and the division following it, both dismounted, would consist entirely of noblemen. As the chronicler Pierre Cochon said frankly:

> *The French thought that they would carry the day because of their great numbers, and in their arrogance had proclaimed that only those who were noble should go into battle.*

As he surveyed the fevered press of Frenchmen ahead, Henry grasped the possibilities opening up for him. Without opposing crossbowmen, or a really strong cavalry presence, he could use his archers to their best effect. The French now had no overall commander – neither the king nor the dauphin was present, and judging from the array of banners most of their chief aristocrats were in the vanguard, leaving other parts of the army virtually leaderless. The Monk of Saint-Denis, as we have heard, described the situation with wry humour:

> *Each of the leaders claimed for himself the honour of leading the vanguard. This led to a considerable debate and so that there could be some agreement, they came to the rather unfortunate conclusion that they should all place themselves in the front line.*

Their appearance, however, was still daunting. The modified French plan was simple and was to be carried through on sheer instinct. The cavalry would distract the archers and the main body of men-at-arms would assail the English line with

201

the force of a battering ram. According to Titus Livius, the line of English men-at-arms was no more than four men deep. Against them the opposing French were more than 30 men deep. The enemy seemed supremely confident of victory.

These were worrying odds.

The disparity between the men-at-arms of either side was far greater than at Crécy or Poitiers. The French noblemen were fired up by the aristocratic code of honour and were resolved to smash through the English position, which looked alarmingly fragile. Their numerical superiority meant they could afford to sustain considerable casualties and the English arrow storm, however effective, could only operate for a limited period of time.

Each bowman would have two sheaves carrying 48 arrows. Allowing for some supplies in reserve, kept in waggons behind the archers' positions and brought up by the pages as the fighting commenced, the arrow storm could only maintain its full intensity for around 12 minutes or so. A skilled archer could let loose at least seven or eight arrows a minute to good effect. It was likely that these volleys would be carefully controlled – the psychological impact of massed, co-ordinated shooting would be far more terrifying than 'firing at will'. But when the French men-at-arms reached the English position the archers would have to fight hand-to-hand with the far more heavily armoured and better equipped men-at-arms in the desperate combat which would follow.

Henry knew, too, that he had to make the battlefield terrain work for him. The ground was waterlogged and the mud heavy and clinging. This was crucial – for as Thomas Walsingham related, because of the softness of the ground, 'it was extremely difficult to stand or advance'. The chronicler Pierre Cochon told how men-at-arms 'sank into it by at least a foot'; the Monk of Saint-Denis recorded that it was 'up to their knees'. Juvenal des Ursins made it clear that men 'could scarcely move their legs and pull them out of the ground'. In such terrible conditions it was vital that the French be made to do the work and attack the English position. But the enemy showed no sign of doing this.

The French still seemed content to adopt a defensive position, knowing full well that the English were tired, hungry and desperately short of provisions and could not wait there indefinitely.

In the intervening wait, Henry requested a last parley with the French. He sent out his heralds, and appointed trusted envoys to meet the French representatives. The enemy's choice was distinctly provocative. Colart d'Estouteville, Lord of Torcy was the brother of the defender of Harfleur, Jean – now on parole as Henry's prisoner. Jean Malet, Lord of Graville also had a grudge against the English king – he had lost lands around the town because of the English invasion and occupation.

These discussions were held in the muddy field, at an equal distance between the two armies. Jean Le Fèvre, who had witnessed the whole bizarre interlude, wondered what terms, if any, had been on offer. Some French chroniclers would later claim that the English king, realising how desperate his position was, offered to give back Harfleur and also pay the French compensation. This seems unlikely. Le Fèvre's own version is rather more plausible, even though he freely admitted it was based on hearsay:

> The French offered, as I have heard said, that if he would renounce his pretended title to the crown of France, and never take it up again, and return the town of Harfleur which he had recently captured, the king [Charles VI] would be content to allow him to keep Aquitaine and Calais. The king of England,

or his people, replied that if the king of France would give up to him the duchy of Aquitaine, and five named cities which belonged to us, together with the county of Ponthieu and the king's daughter Catherine in marriage, and 800,000 écus for her jewels and clothing, he would be content to renounce his title to the crown of France and return Harfleur.

Whatever offers were really made, the negotiations were brief and were rejected by both sides. For two hours the armies then surveyed each other across the muddy battlefield. Henry had prepared his men well but he knew a long delay would start to sap their spirits. The king needed to commence the action.

Some French chronicle accounts consistently played up the desperation of Henry's position. They claimed that he had reneged on an agreement to meet in battle, at Aubigny, two or three days earlier, and that he had offered the most desperate terms to the French to try and extricate his army from their grip. Neither assertion seems likely. But one claim does deserve serious consideration – that before the battle Henry set up an archer ambush.

The chronicler Enguerrand de Monstrelet gave the most detail on this ploy. Unlike more partisan sources such as the Berry Herald, anxious to portray things in the best light for the government of Charles VI and to diminish the English achievement, Monstrelet was genuinely concerned about presenting an accurate battle narrative. He focused on the ambush because it seemed in itself significant, and also because, in his eyes, it formed part of a broader archer deployment that was both novel and effective. Always concerned with historical accuracy, he was careful to verify his material before using it – and, having checked his sources, he drew attention to the ambush not as a way of belittling Henry V but as an explanation of the battle's outcome:

The king of England sent about 200 archers around his army, so that they would not be spotted by the French. They secretly entered a meadow near Tramecourt, quite close to the enemy's rearguard, and held themselves secretly there until it was time to shoot.

Jean Juvenal des Ursins added:

The English had chosen a good battle position, between two areas of woodland. In front of them, but a little way off, there was another wood – where they put a large ambush of archers.

Jean Le Fèvre, with the English army, felt compelled to investigate this tactic. Le Fèvre said that he had heard about the ambush, but when he questioned one of Henry's soldiers, the story was denied: 'It was certified as true by a man of honour, who was there that day in the company of the king that nothing like this had happened.'

The reference to a 'man of honour' is significant because setting up an ambush before battle might have been regarded as an underhand tactic. The soldier Jean de Bueil addressed such a dilemma in his book *Le Jouvencel* (the Youth). De Bueil acknowledged that an honourable knight would not want to win a battle through a ruse – but went on to emphasise that knowledge of such matters was essential if one was to be successful in war.

In chivalric convention the importance of adhering to codes of conduct outweighed thinking 'outside the box', by acting unexpectedly and cleverly. A 'man of honour' may have found the ambush unpalatable – and thus difficult to admit to – but Henry probably knew of similar surprises in famous battles of the fourteenth century: the sudden attack made by the Black Prince behind the French third line at

205

Poitiers (1356), which brought the English victory, and its imitation in the victory of Sir John Hawkwood at the battle of Castagnaro in 1387.

At Poitiers, the Black Prince sent the Captal de Buch, Jean de Greilly, to swing round the French forces with a force of 60 men-at-arms and several hundred mounted archers, using the terrain to obscure his movements. He then launched a surprise attack on the rear of the French army, where 'the archers he had taken with him wrought great havoc'. The Captal's sudden onslaught was the turning point of the battle, for the Prince took it as a signal to launch an all-out charge – and the French battle line was completely broken up.

On 11 March 1387 the English captain Sir John Hawkwood, faced by a determined Veronese army near the small town of Castagnaro, executed a similar manoeuvre, sending a mounted detachment – hidden from view by steep canal banks – round the back of their forces, and supporting their surprise attack by a barrage of archer fire and a general order to advance.

These stratagems were well described in contemporary chronicles, and in all likelihood Henry V was prepared to emulate them, for there were no hard and fast rules here. Thomas Walsingham could at one moment strongly complain that the Brecon gentleman Davy Gam – a tough campaigner against Glendower's rebellion, victor at Pwll Melyn (1405) and now in the king's own retinue at Agincourt – had been captured by the rebels 'by a trick, rather than a fair fight' (this incident took place in 1412 and Henry quickly secured Gam's release), and then in the next breath applaud a similar 'trick', when the English discomfited the French, after the shipman John Prendergast arrived incognito in Creil on market day and made off with thousands of cattle belonging to the Count of Saint-Pol.

Indeed, if a ploy or ruse embarrassed the French it was usually warmly welcomed. When Harry Pay and 15 small merchant ships appeared outside La Rochelle harbour and captured the entire French trading fleet by running up the royal ensign and pretending to be the advance contingent of Henry IV's naval expedition, Walsingham praised Pay's enterprise rather than censuring his use of deception.

On balance, the claim appears plausible. On the morning of 25 October, Henry needed to use any trick or stratagem he could find. For if the French did not move, he had to find a way of provoking them into battle.

In the meantime, both armies continued to watch each other. Medieval warriors liked to read about the battles of ancient Rome, and in one, on the plain of Cannae in 216 BC, the Carthaginian commander Hannibal had drawn up his troops, made his battle plans and was now staring at the mass of Roman legions ahead of him. Realising that this view of the enemy was demoralising, Hannibal resorted to joking with his captains. They laughed, the tension was broken, and his men, seeing their officers in such good spirits, laughed as well – a huge belly laugh that swelled through the ranks.

Jokes may well have done the rounds among the English captains as well – taking their minds off the sheer number of the French. Charles, Duke of Orléans now appeared to have nominal command of the army – where every aristocrat of note seemed to be taking his place in the vanguard. Edward, Duke of York and Sir John Cornwall had both met the young duke two years earlier, and both were struck by his inflated self-confidence: he was 'exultant' and 'believed himself unbeatable', as Thomas Walsingham recorded.

In this regard, he appeared rather like his father Louis, the man whose assassination in Paris in 1407 by an agent of the

Duke of Burgundy had sparked – in the absence of any real governing authority from either the king, Charles VI, or the dauphin – the intermittent French civil war. Walsingham once described Louis, Duke of Orléans as 'insufferably proud and arrogant' with an 'exalted sense of his place in the world'. Amusing stories of his conduct during the siege of Bourg in English-held Gascony, earlier in 1407, may have circulated as Henry V's army waited for battle.

Topically, one anecdote described how, during a heavy downpour, Orléans was seen processing through the siege works with four knights carrying a cloth of gold awning above his head, so that he did not get wet. Another involved his attempt to disrupt the English wine fleet, about to set sail from Bordeaux, downriver from Bourg. Orléans dispatched a fleet of 30 ships along the River Garonne but the English, forewarned of his intentions, safely unloaded the wine and replaced it with soldiers, armed to the teeth. Orléans's ships were captured – and the most expensive vessel then sent back to the duke in flames.

Humour, as it has always been, was an important way of taking men's minds off combat. And by making Charles, Duke of Orléans and his father Louis the butt of their jokes, they were also reminding themselves of the absence from battle of the one man the English really feared, the Duke of Burgundy. As preparations for recruiting the French army had begun, in late September, both Orléans and Burgundy had been told to stay away and send military retinues instead. Both men were seen as politically divisive figures and the quarrel between them had not been properly resolved. Henry, who was worried that Burgundy might join the French war effort nonetheless, had maintained diplomatic contacts with him even as his campaign was underway – but remained uncertain of the duke's ultimate intentions.

Within fifteenth-century France, the Dukes of Brittany and Burgundy, while remaining vassals of the French crown, administered their own lands, had their own treasuries and imposed their own taxes, raised their own armies – and often pursued a semi-independent foreign policy. The Duke of Burgundy was a particularly important player because of the wealth of his territories (formed into two blocks: in the north, centred around Picardy, Flanders and Holland, administered from Lille and Brussels; and in the south, the region of Burgundy proper, administered from Dijon) and the income they generated from the wool and wine trade.

The Duke of Burgundy was thus able to enjoy a large income, preside over a lavish court and raise a substantial number of troops – and to reach Calais Henry had to march through his northern lands. One of the duke's brothers, Philip, Count of Nevers, had joined the French with his retinue; another, Anthony, Duke of Brabant, was on his way. It would be a different matter entirely if Duke John appeared with the complete Burgundian army.

Duke John the Fearless was the one French commander who had fully learned the lessons of Nicopolis. He respected the part archers could play in a battle's outcome and recruited thousands for his own army. The duke imposed good discipline on his troops, was up to date with the latest military technology (even employing hand-gunners) and followed a clear battle plan. At Othée, in 1408, he had defeated forces from Liège in a consummate victory. He was thoroughly professional, never underestimated his opponents, and in a letter to his brother, Anthony, Duke of Brabant, said of the enemy:

Experienced people say they have never seen men fight so well as they [the Liègois] did; for the battle lasted one and a half hours and, for a least half an hour, no one knew which way it would go.

In truth, Duke John's battle plan worked admirably. Archers shot from the flanks into the Liègois army, an attack from the rear was made by 400 mounted men-at-arms and then an infantry advance decided the day. Once Charles, Duke of Orléans took overall command of the army it was clear that John the Fearless would not be attending, and the English can only have breathed a collective sigh of relief. John the Fearless was one of the most accomplished fighters of his age; Charles of Orléans's main claim to fame would be the invention of the Valentine's Day card.

It was now midway between the 'hours' of 'terce' (9 am) and 'sext' (midday). Soon the English would need to begin proceedings. The Duke of Brabant was fast approaching, and the Duke of Brittany might also make an appearance. At 3 am (a time carefully recorded by the town notary of Amiens in the municipal accounts), one of the duke's knights, Sir Bertrand du Blois, had clattered into the town, claiming that more Breton troops were on their way and demanding to be led out to the battlefield. Sir Bertrand had now taken his place among the throng of French in the vanguard – the English could not afford the risk that thousands more Bretons might join him.

All had been thoroughly prepared. Henry and his captains agreed they would wait a little longer, so that the autumn sun would shine directly in the faces of the French opposite them. Then they would advance, and put their plan of provoking their opponent to the test. In the meantime, they would hold their ground.

And now the French knight Jacques de Créquy, lord of Heilly, entered the fray. De Heilly was not lacking in self-confidence. Two years earlier, he had gone to Gascony 'to fall upon the English and drive them out of the country'. Events turned out rather differently, as Thomas Walsingham related:

De Heilly, with many nobles, men-at-arms and other troops, numbering more than four thousand soldiers, laid siege to a town in Aquitaine, which the Englishman Sir John Blount was holding. Sir John – with only 300 auxiliary troops – routed and put to flight the whole French army, capturing de Heilly, twelve other noblemen and 120 more of good birth. De Heilly was sent to Wisbech Castle with some of the other prisoners.

Once Henry set sail for France, de Heilly managed to escape from this remote stronghold in the Cambridgeshire Fens, because of 'slackness amongst the guards', as Walsingham believed, or patriotic fervour, as de Heilly claimed. Whatever the explanation for his escape, he was a prisoner who had breached the terms of his parole, a solemn chivalric oath, but rather than keep his head down he joined up with Charles, Duke of Orléans and marched on Agincourt. Ostensibly one of the negotiators in the parley, he suddenly appeared before the English king, demanding an audience.

About to begin battle, Henry was scarcely obliged to meet this insistent Frenchman, but, sensing the ridiculousness of the situation, Henry saw an opportunity to amuse his captains and allowed de Heilly come before him and speak his mind.

What followed is recorded by Titus Livius from the personal reminiscences of Humphrey, Duke of Gloucester, who would have been standing next to the king. About to face a momentous battle, Gloucester found the encounter with de Heilly so memorable that, many years later, he relayed it in some detail. Just as Hannibal was able to lift the spirits of his commanders before Cannae, the English king now engaged in a wonderful piece of knock-about comedy that brought heart to his men.

Henry began by expressing surprise that a man who had escaped from prison should now show up before his whole army. De Heilly looked most irate, and exclaimed that although he had broken his chivalric oath, he had done so for patriotic reasons:

> It has often been reported within your kingdom that I fled away in a most common manner, shamefully, and in a fashion unbecoming to a soldier and a knight. I deny this most strongly.

Men around Henry were beginning to smile. It was all so pompous – and so very French. The king, seeing how de Heilly was puffing up with indignation, waited – and then let him continue.

De Heilly rounded on Henry and his captains, his voice rising in a crescendo:

> I deny this to you and all your men, and if anyone dares to say such a thing he should prepare himself for a duel – right now – so that I can prove to your Majesty and all those about you that such an accusation of dishonourable conduct should never be brought against me.

Everyone burst out laughing. This ridiculous man seemed to have entirely overlooked that their two armies were about to go into combat. And looking around at each other, in this moment of shared humour, it was all made so very clear: this is who we are a fighting against. An army so blinded by its grandiose, inflated sense of honour, that one of its knights, in pursuit of that honour, can actually forget about the very battle he is supposed to be participating in.

And then Henry became serious and brought things to a close. The king said that there would be no duel.

'And we trust in God,' he added, 'that as you have escaped from us, having no regard for the honour of a knight, as this day ends you will either be brought to us as captive once more, or else by the sword you shall finish your life.'

It was 11 am. Battle was about to commence.

CHAPTER 8

Banners Advance! —

The Armies Close In

11.00–11.30 (25 October 1415)

ALL ALONG THE English line men were looking at each other. The sense of expectancy was tangible. After 17 days on the march, after nine days without proper food, bread and meat, after three days of dread at encountering the French, after two hours of waiting on the battlefield – at last this tired bedraggled army was going into action.

In these last few moments the soldiers remembered fellow fighters who had not made it, those sent home during the siege of Harfleur, those who had died of dysentery – at Harfleur and on the march. Theirs was a small army – and yet, one united in its desire to goad and provoke the French. As the soldier John Hardyng wrote in his notes on the Agincourt campaign, in a strikingly apt metaphor: 'Who may cast off his running hounds and many hunting dogs without losing some of them?'

This was do or die – and everybody knew it. All could see the size of the French army opposing them and yet fear had been put aside. The troops had been galvanised by the battle plan they were about to enact, encouraged to see the whole army lining up, ready for the fight. Men looked at the banners – those of the king, York, Suffolk, Camoys – mumbled a last few words of prayer, spoke a few words to the soldiers around them, ran their hands along armour, sword hilt or bow.

It was 11 am. Henry and his army could wait no longer. The king prepared to move forward towards the enemy.

The formal order was passed along the line: 'Advance banners!' There was a sudden surge of energy. As this command was relayed, Henry turned to the men around him and said simply: 'Fellows, let's go!'

Now the signal was given to the archers. Sir Thomas Erpingham – who had become marshal of the army after John Mowbray returned home with dysentery – had ridden along the English line with two followers, inspecting the archers' positions, giving a few words of praise to some, joking with others. Men were reassured to see Erpingham. They were fond of this grizzled old veteran and respected his toughness and composure. They all knew that he had extricated himself from difficult situations before. And they could see that this old warrior – who had all but retired from public life before the Agincourt campaign – was up for the fight.

Suddenly Erpingham threw his marshal's baton in the air. After this dramatic gesture he then shouted a word that puzzled foreign chroniclers.

Jean de Waurin recalled:

> The king of England ordered a veteran knight, called Sir Thomas Erpingham, to draw up the archers, and put them in the front, in two wings. Sir Thomas exhorted everyone – on behalf of King Henry – to fight with vigour against the French. Then, after he had carried out the deployment, he rode with an escort in front of the formation of archers and threw in the air a baton that he had been carrying in his hand. Then he called out 'Nestroque', which was the signal for the attack.

Enguerrand de Monstrelet added an important detail. A body of archers had been drawn out from the main English line – and had been placed in front of the massed ranks of men-at-arms and archers.

'Nestroque' has sometimes been thought to mean 'Now strike!' or 'Knee stretch!' – but this makes little sense with the English army so far out of bow range from the enemy. It was far more likely to be '*menée* stroke' the signal to sound the hunting horn. 'Strake' or 'stroke' was the word used for a horn blast; '*menée*' the notes or signal when the deer were to be herded into the 'drive', the narrow ground that led to the 'resayt', the 'receiving place', where they would be bunched together and killed. All had a part to play in this outcome.

Everyone in the English army now had a simple sequence of images in front of them, drawing on their own life experience and feeding off a corrosive anger against the French. The archer squadron in front of the main English line would play the part of the hounds – and together with the ambush placed in the Tramecourt woods and the derisory sounds and cries from all the army, 'chivvy' (goad or provoke) the enemy into making their attack. The main body of bowmen, on the flanks of the army, would play the part of the archers and beaters in the hunt, driving – through sustained, enfilading arrow fire – the foe forward, into the funnel of the battlefield and compressing his formations. The line of men-at-arms drawn up at the narrow end of the funnel, the 'receiving ground', would play the part of the great hounds, who would make the final kill. At this point, the main units of bowmen, having unleashed all their arrows, would pick up hand weapons, swords and daggers, and strike at the flanks of their opponent, compressing his ranks still further, and creating a 'press' or crush, eroding his capacity to resist.

In the hunt, and on the battlefield, terrain was vitally important. For these tactics to work, the main English army would need to make a limited advance of some 50 yards or so, keeping the advantage of the dry ground, the unploughed land that formed a ridge at the narrow end of the Agincourt funnel, and staying close to the archers' wall of stakes, which for the most part had not been dismantled but remained in its original position. The purpose of making this limited advance was through noise and action to start goading the French. But in the battle's opening stage, the advance archer squadron was exposing itself to the most danger and taking the greatest risk. This is where all Henry's work, on campaign and before the battle, to motivate his men would pay off.

Straight away, as the main line of English troops was slowly and purposefully starting to move towards their foe, the squadron of bowmen in the forward position ran quickly towards the French – and then put them under arrow fire. The chronicler of Ruisseauville gave most detail on this sudden advance: 'The archers in front came very quickly, without armour and their breeches loosened, always firing on the French.'

The 'running hounds' were unleashed. Such a manoeuvre had been used by the English before, against the Scots, at the battle of Neville's Cross in 1346. One chronicler described how, prior to the main engagement, '500 English archers ran on in advance, and by piercing them through many times with their missiles, forced the Scots to abandon the place they had occupied, and provoked them to seek battle.' Another noted that while the Scots were deploying, 'some of the English archers ran up so near, so they could shoot amongst them'. Whatever their exact formation, what is clear is that the English – desiring to remain on the defensive – succeeded in goading the Scots to attack. And as this was a notable battle, in which the king of Scotland had been captured, this tactic would have been well known to Henry V and his captains.

At Agincourt, at the same time that the squadron of archers ran up to the French, the archer ambush hidden in the woods – on the Tramecourt side of the battlefield – after hearing the hunting horn and the shouts of the army, also opened up on the French. And the main English battle line, with its men-at-arms and the remainder of the archers, 'let out a great cry, which was a source of much amazement to their opponents'.

The 'many hunting dogs' were making their presence felt. This was no ordinary war cry, which the French would have expected – it was the din of a braying pack. The chroniclers used words like 'huer', 'brayer' and 'crier', a cacophony of odd and alarming noises, braying, honking and chanting. These were the sounds used in the hunt to goad the prey forward.

Hunting had long been regarded as a good training for war. After the battle of Poitiers the Black Prince escorted the captive French king, John II, from the south coast of England to London. As they passed through a forest, 500 men suddenly appeared, bearing bows and arrows, swords and shields. The French king was amazed. The Black Prince told him: 'they were men of England, foresters ... and it was their custom each day to be thus arrayed'. This shamelessly stage-managed event was a piece of 'chivalric sport': the image being conveyed to the French was that England was a country full of hardy bowmen, living rough, but ready to follow the Black Prince back to France should he so command.

The experience of hunting was important, for the word used by a number of the French chroniclers, 'huer', had a specific meaning, 'to shout while hunting', a vocal imitation of the hunting horn. Jean de Waurin and Jean Le Fèvre – both present at the battle – described the English making a 'grand hué'. In 1327, during the Wearsdale campaign, the chronicler Jean Le Bel told how English archers taunted Hainaulter men-at-arms with the hunting cry of 'hahay, hahay!' – the cry used to drive deer towards the nets.

The incident – in which Jean Le Bel was actually caught up, and thus a witness to at close quarters – occurred on

7 June 1327, starting out as a brawl between some English archers and the men of John of Hainault's company, and quickly escalating into a serious skirmish. Le Bel recalled:

All the other archers of the town and the remainder, who were encamped around the Hainaulters, gathered up their bows, [making the animal noise] hahay, hahay, and wounded many of their opponents and forced them to retire to their hostels. And these archers ... had the devil in their bodies, for they shot with amazing skill – to kill everyone, whether lords or esquires.

Rather like the affray at Salisbury at the beginning of August 1415, involving the bowmen of Sir James Harrington's company and some of the townspeople, the archers knew how to look after themselves and were quick and instinctive in their response, using hunting calls as signals and working together as a group. Edward, Duke of York was right when he said it was not necessary to instruct forest bowmen on hunting techniques, they had all the necessary skills in place anyway – and to harness these skills on the battlefield was a stroke of genius.

At Agincourt, the violent din was described by Thomas Elmham as a 'noise which penetrated the heavens'. And Monstrelet added that, as the English moved forward with this great cry, 'the hidden archers also raised a great shout and began shooting hard and fast at the French'. This was the point of the archer ambush, set up with such care in the hidden meadow within the Tramecourt woods: it could now begin shooting at the flank of the French army. The screen of archers sent by Erpingham to within bow range – some 300 yards from the French line – were also firing as fast as they could, and the French had no missile-bearing troops to counter this, as they had all been sent to the rear of the army.

And the main English line, which had noisily advanced some 50 yards or so from its original position, taunted their opponents as well.

These were the goading tactics of the hunt – devised by Henry and Edward, Duke of York – upon which the whole success of their battle plan depended. The cries were deliberately provocative – as were the banners displaying the French royal coat of arms alongside the English, which were impudently waved in the enemy's direction. The archers – so disparaged by the aristocrats opposing them – now brayed and shouted as if they were pursuing a pack of animals. For a moment the French were dumbfounded by such blatant cheek. As Monstrelet emphasised: 'The English cry was a cause of great amazement.'

And the provocation worked. Many of the chroniclers related how the French now reacted quickly. The chaplain said that when Henry began to advance, 'the enemy, too, advanced towards him'. Thomas Walsingham believed that when the English first moved forward, the French 'considered the moment was favourable to attack'. One version of the Brut chronicle noted that when the command 'Advance banners!' was given to the English army, 'then the French came rushing down, as if to ride over our men'; another that when the English started to advance, 'immediately trumpets sounded, and the French came galloping down'. Similarly, the Monk of Saint-Denis observed that when the English began to move forward, 'at almost the same moment the French advanced against their opponents'. French patience had snapped. They launched their cavalry charge against the English archers. The main body of dismounted men-at-arms would then follow up behind them.

The English had achieved a first success. It was a powerful moment – as the army, for so long harried by the French, now took the battle initiative. The weeks of frustration, hardship and suffering were put behind them and the last remnants of fear swept away in a surging, cathartic release of sound.

However, for the tactics devised by Henry and the Duke of York to be effective, the French cavalry would have to be neutralised. Sir Thomas Erpingham had inspected the main archer positions before battle commenced, encouraging the men and making sure the stake wall was properly in place. Erpingham had fought for the Black Prince in France, and took care to see that the bowmen's experience in that phase of the Hundred Years War would now be replicated on the field of Agincourt.

In fourteenth-century France, well-armoured cavalry had always been more than a match for peasant levies. During the Jacquerie, a series of popular revolts in the mid-fourteenth century, a peasant army under Jean Valliant was completely routed at Meaux by a small force of only 24 knights, who launched a surprise sally from the town. The following day Guillaume Cale drew up his peasant rebels in a defensive position at Silly, northeast of Paris. He protected his flanks by carts and trenches and placed his archers in front of the two divisions of his small army. But when the French mounted men-at-arms charged the position the archers fled in panic and were easily cut down. This demonstrated that poorly trained artisans and labourers, even if equipped with bows, were no match for seasoned troops in open combat.

But Henry's men were well trained and disciplined and they were shooting from a protected position. At Crécy, the archers – protected by a series of ditches and the infantry formations around them – had struck at the French horses using barbed arrows (with hooks on the arrowhead to rip open the flesh). Jean le Bel related the terrible result:

223

The archers used barbed arrows so effectively that when the horses were hit by these some would halt in their tracks, others leapt into the air as if maddened, others balked and bucked horribly, others turned their rumps towards the enemy — regardless of the urgings of their masters — or fell writhing to the ground.

At Poitiers (1356), Jean Froissart recalled Eustace de Ribemont urging King Jean II of France to select a picked body of cavalry (about 500-strong), to force their way through the English archers' position stationed by the gaps in a thick hedge. Ribemont said the horses should be 'well-barded' to protect them from the arrows, and 'the boldest, toughest and most enterprising riders should be chosen'.

But Ribemont, unlike the French at Agincourt, proposed supporting his cavalry attack with crossbowmen and infantry armed with javelins providing covering missile fire, and additional German cavalry moving up behind. That was the intention behind Marshal Boucicaut's original battle plan, to use his missile-bearing troops to support the assault of his horsemen. And Boucicaut envisaged a mass attack of around a thousand men, creating the weight and momentum to smash the English archers' position. The experienced leader he had recommended for this job, David, Lord of Rambures, who had fought with him in Gascony, was now in the front line of the vanguard with all the other aristocrats of note.

In 1415, the numbers of the French cavalry should never have been allowed to drop so low. The small numbers involved reveal the suddenness of the English provocation, for if Henry V's line of men-at-arms and archers had slowly traversed the muddy battlefield, pausing at frequent intervals to keep in alignment, until they were within extreme bow range of the enemy, hammered their stakes back in and only then opened fire – an operation that would have taken well over half an hour – there would have been ample time to recall all the cavalry.

The absence of so many French horsemen from their posts exposed a lack of leadership within the French army. With all its senior aristocrats in the first ranks of the vanguard there was no one left to oversee the situation and give clear orders. There was also an issue of morale. Having a place in the vanguard had become such a matter of prestige that those assigned to other units probably felt relegated to being bit players in a drama now largely taking place elsewhere.

In 1356 and in 1415 the French cavalry was only barded (armoured) at the front. And on both occasions the English archers would find the right tactics to deal with this. At Poitiers, Geoffrey le Baker noted:

> *The archers of our vanguard were safely positioned on the edge of a marsh, where the enemy's cavalry could not reach them. But [it became evident that] they were of little use there. For the [French] cavalry, designed to ride down the bowmen and protect their compatriots from them, only offered the archers a target on their fore-quarters, which were well-protected by steel plates and leather shields, so that the arrows aimed at them either shattered or glanced off heaven wards, falling on friend and foe alike … So the bowmen moved to one side, and shot at the horses' hind-quarters. When this was done, the wounded chargers reared, throwing their riders or turning back on their own men, throwing not a few of their masters to the ground … Once the cavalry was out of the way, the archers took up their previous position and shot directly at the French flank.*

At Agincourt, the English archers possessed a number of advantages as the French cavalry attacked: the accuracy of their fire, its rapidity, and the fact that they were on dry ground and could manoeuvre easily.

Accurate fire had become the hallmark of English bowmen in the Hundred Years War, forged by regular practice at the butts. In 1342 a force of men-at-arms and archers sallied out from the walled Breton town of Hennebont under Sir Walter de Mauny (a remarkable soldier of fortune, present at the great victory of the longbow at Dupplin Moor, who would later go on to found the London Charterhouse) and destroyed an enemy siege engine, 'for the archers shot so well that those who guarded the machine fled'.

The shooting of well-aimed and co-ordinated volleys at the enemy made the longbow a particularly potent weapon. Jean Froissart described how, during the siege of Castelnaudary in Languedoc, during the Black Prince's campaign of 1355, groups of English archers shot volleys of arrows so dense that the defenders could no longer hold their positions on the walls.

Crucially, at Agincourt the bulk of English archers remained on dry ground, the unploughed land at the base of the funnel, whereas the enemy cavalry were approaching them through the churned-up mud of recently ploughed and newly sown fields. In an engagement fought at Calais on 2 January 1350 Edward III had employed a similar feature of the terrain, positioning his archers to one side of his men-at-arms on dry islands within an area of marshland, so that the heavily armed French horsemen would not be able to reach them without sinking into the mire.

The lightly clad archers could manoeuvre easily, and with units posted in the woodland and also interspersed among the men-at-arms, could fire at the flanks and rear ends of the horses, which were not protected by armour.

The French, seeing the English pull back to their prepared position, may have thought that they were retreating

– and they could simply charge them down. At the battle of Homildon Hill, in 1402, the Earl of Douglas had succumbed to a similar impulse, believing the English bowmen to be out of position, and he led a cavalry attack to try and overrun the archers. He was moving downhill, so that his charge could gather momentum – and he saw an opportunity to overwhelm the bowmen. But as Thomas Walsingham observed bluntly, 'he trusted too much in the strength of his armour – and that of his men's'. Walsingham described what followed:

> *The [English] archers pulled back, firing so vigorously and effectively that they pierced the armour, perforated the helmets, pitted the swords, split the lances and penetrated all the [Scottish] equipment with ease. The Earl of Douglas was wounded in five different places, notwithstanding his elaborate equipment.*

The leading horsemen were killed or captured and the remainder fled. Walsingham concluded: 'In this battle the flower of Scottish chivalry was reduced to captivity.'

In 1415, the French also hoped to ride down the English archers, but the order to charge them was given with their cavalry units seriously undermanned. It was said that many of the horsemen had wandered off during the long wait, to find water and provision for their mounts, and could not quickly be found again. They envisaged two flank attacks, traversing the sides of the battlefield closest to the woodland, and aiming at the main archer positions placed on the sides of the English army. In normal conditions, with reasonably dry ground, they would have had the distance to build up proper momentum. But these were not normal conditions. The French were riding across cloying mud which, with the weight of the riders, would make it very difficult for the horses to gather speed. One wing did not even reach the English position. Two hours earlier, Clignet de Brabant had assembled 800 men for the charge. Now fewer than 140 could be found.

As Clignet de Brabant's group moved forward, the screen of archers sent ahead by Erpingham pulled back into the woods to the right and left of the battlefield, and fired on the French cavalry. But the Frenchmen's target was the main body of archers on the right (Tramecourt) flank of the English army, which had advanced some 50 yards or so with the rest of Henry's main battle line.

The French may have assumed that once the English archers began to advance, the stakes, which had been knocked into the ground to defend them, would have been pulled out again and were being dragged forward to the new position. That being the case, the cavalry attack would catch them unprotected.

Once again, the chronicle accounts are unclear at this point. Titus Livius put the fixing of the stakes after the order to advance. However, the chaplain said the stakes were set in place, and the advance happened later. He made no reference to a repositioning of the stake wall. It would not have been easy to do this quickly when knee-deep in heavy mud. The Monk of Saint-Denis commented on the novelty of archers carrying lead-covered mallets – in other words, it was necessary to hammer them into the ground. And the anonymous Italian humanist commissioned by Sir Walter Hungerford (the source known as the Pseudo-Elmham) said that they were left behind when the archers moved forward, emphasising, perhaps on Hungerford's own recollection: 'The archers, leaving behind them in the field their sharp stakes, which they had before prepared in case they met the French horsemen.'

As the stakes clearly served an important military purpose, it would be surprising if they were simply abandoned. It is far more likely that the English bowmen employed a trick. The squadron of archers that ran forward to within range of the French line may have carried their stakes with them, and replanted them further forward, before they began firing (as Titus Livius recalled). But the main body of bowmen had only moved a little way in front of their still intact stake wall. And this protective wall was now in the ground behind them, hidden from view. As the cavalry rode forward, the archers were able to retreat behind this wall and start firing once the enemy came within range.

This ploy had been used in an earlier battle, at Nicopolis in 1396, when the Turks put a screen of troops ahead of a row of thickly planted stakes, obscuring them from the French horsemen. On this occasion, the renowned French crusader Marshal Boucicaut was fighting on the opposing side – and ironically the English may have learned about this trick, one that had not been used before in medieval warfare, from reading the book about the marshal's deeds.

Boucicaut had been the architect of the original French plan, which intended to use cavalry to bring down the English archers, and Henry had ordered his men to carry sharpened stakes as a response to this threat. The stake wall hidden by archers set up a trap for the French horsemen, rather like the concealed nets used by huntsmen to bring down deer in a forest. Once again Edward, Duke of York's expertise in hunting – well brought out in *The Master of Game* – was important, for, as one version of the Brut chronicle had believed, it was he who suggested to the king that every archer should use stakes against the enemy.

Clignet de Brabant's squadron of horsemen, under strength as it was, had not picked up much momentum as it closed within range of the English bowmen. The horsemen now rode into a devastating arrow storm. As Thomas Walsingham noted: 'The French sent mounted men ahead, who were to overwhelm our archers by the barded breasts of their horses, and to trample them under their hooves.'

The attacks came to grief almost immediately, despite the horse armour and the bravery of the commanders.

> *The archers simultaneously shot arrows against the advancing knights so that the leading horses were scattered in that great storm of hail ... the horses were pierced by iron; the riders, turning round by means of their bridles, rushing away, fell to the ground amongst their own army.*

The Norman chronicler Thomas Basin emphasised the power of the arrow storm:

> *Raising horrible cries, the English began to bend their bows with all their might, and to let fly arrows into the enemy in such quantities that their density obscured the sun, just like a cloud.*

'The French came rushing down, hoping to ride over our men – but God and our archers made them stumble,' the Brut chronicle recorded happily. 'Our archers shot no arrows off target; all caused death and brought to the ground both men and horses. For they were shooting that day [as if] for a wager.'

The other wing of horsemen fared little better. There were rather more of them, perhaps around 300 in all, and few managed to penetrate the archers' position – but they were quickly surrounded and pulled off their horses or shot down. 'All that the French cavalry attempted was in vain,' Monstrelet said bleakly. 'Horses were becoming unmanageable, and threw their riders on the ground.' Some turned back; others forced their way on, only to collide with the stake wall. The chaplain put it simply:

> *The French cavalry were forced to retreat under showers of arrows and fled to their rearguard, save for a very few who — although not without losses in dead and wounded — rode through between the archers and the woodlands, and save too, of course, for the many who were stopped by the stakes driven into the ground and prevented from fleeing very far by the stinging hail of missiles, which brought down horses and riders in their flight.*

According to Jean Le Fèvre, the leader of the second mounted contingent, Guillaume de Saveuse, had his horse brought down by one of the stakes and was killed as he lay on the ground:

> *Then Sir Guillaume de Saveuse, a very valiant knight, took the Agincourt side [charged the archers on the left flank of the English position] with about 300 mounted men; and with only an escort of two he advanced ahead of all the others, and attacked the English archers, who had their sharpened stakes placed in front of them. But the ground was very difficult to move through and the stakes brought their horses down. The rest of their company was forced back [because of the arrow fire] and Saveuse and his two companions lay helpless in the mud, where they were killed by the archers.*

The Monk of Saint-Denis was unimpressed by the fleeing French cavalry who had abandoned their commander:

> *At the first volley of arrows which the archers caused to rain down upon them, they turned and fled, to their eternal shame, leaving their leaders stranded in the middle of the enemy.*

In truth, some of the French may have lacked resolution but it was the effectiveness of the English bowmen's tactics, striking at the unprotected parts of the horses, which drove them back. The sights and sounds must have been terrible, as agonised horses, maddened by pain, careered across the battlefield. Some of the riderless mounts, crazed by their wounds, even charged straight into the oncoming French dismounted knights, 'causing great disarray, and breaking the line in many places'.

Both wings of horsemen had been beaten off. There was no French commander in a position to take stock of events, regroup his forces, give instructions to his third line of squires and servants, many mounted, who were still in a position to ride round the far side of the woods and strike the English from behind, or make effective use of his missile-bearing troops, his crossbowmen and archers.

The absence of a proven war leader of the calibre of Duke John the Fearless was sorely felt. The French cavalry attack – so important in Marshal Boucicaut's original plan of battle – had failed. Now all would depend on the massed ranks of infantry following up behind.

CHAPTER 9

Impact!

The Mêlée

11.30–12.00 (25 October 1415)

THE TIME WAS now approaching noon, or 'sext' in the canonical hours of devotion. As the French cavalry retreated, a densely packed formation of dismounted men-at-arms was now advancing on the English position. The two armies were a little under 1,000 yards apart. Jean de Waurin, as a page in the French army, had helped equip many of these men, and he remembered:

> *The knights were armed with long coats of mail, reaching below their knees and being very heavy. Below these they had leg harness and above white harness [plate armour]. In addition they had bascinets [helmets with visors] with aventails [chain mail collars].*

The strength of this armour offered real protection against the English bowmen over most parts of the body, and was vital in the heavyweight slugging match between two lines of dismounted men-at-arms, the mêlée. The mêlée was the most physically intense and exhausting form of combat, where all a man's years of training came into play. It was about physical valour and prowess, watching the backs of the fighting comrades closest to you and the collective discipline of holding the line and keeping in formation. For if the line broke or was punctured, individual groups of men would be surrounded and overwhelmed with all the speed and force of a tidal wave sweeping over islands in the sea.

Sometimes this man-to-man combat was all over quickly. At Neville's Cross in 1346 it went on for hours, and men became so exhausted that short breaks in the fighting were organised, signalled by trumpet blast. There were three such intervals in the fighting. But here the French were all focused on a quick and decisive outcome. Most of their leading aristocrats were now crammed into the vanguard, determined to win renown by smashing through Henry's army. The Monk of Saint-Denis recollected:

The illustrious dukes and counts of France invoked the help of heaven and made the sign of the cross, embraced each other and then advanced towards the English, each at the head of his men-at-arms, boldly calling out the traditional war cry 'Mountjoye! Mountjoye!' It was a moment of delirious joy.

Jean de Bueil, whose father and two uncles were at the battle, would later become a professional soldier himself. He wrote a semi-autobiographical book about warfare, *Le Jouvencel* (the Youth), and he said of moments like these:

You love your comrade so much in war. When you see your quarrel is just and your fellow soldiers are fighting well, tears rise to your eyes. A great sweet feeling of love and compassion fills your heart … And then you prepare to enter the fray, to live or die by their side – and for love, not to abandon them. And out of that arises such a feeling of exhilaration that he who has not tasted it is not fit to say what a delight it is. Do you think that a man who has experienced this fears death? Not at all – he feels strengthened; in fact he is so elated he does not know where he is. Truly he is afraid of nothing.

French chivalry was an intoxicating draught. English knights would have understood and admired the sense of comradeship that Jean de Bueil evoked here. But when Sir John Fastolf spoke about the virtues of the 'manly' man, in *The Book of Noblesse* (written by his secretary William Worcester), concern for one's fellows was tempered with the Roman virtue of prudence, a mindfulness of the state of the army as a whole and how best to defeat the enemy. For Fastolf, and many like him in the English force, a man 'so elated he does not know where he is' would not be regarded as an asset on the battlefield.

Arthur, Count of Richemont looked at the men around him. There were good Breton knights gathered under his standard – Bertrand de Montauban, Geoffrey de Malestroit, Oliver de la Feuillée, men with whom he had fought and whom he entirely trusted. Further along the line was David de Rambures, the king's master of crossbowmen, but neither with the crossbowmen nor the cavalry. Rambures, who traced his ancestry back to a knight who had fought in the First Crusade, at the end of the eleventh century, had seen his father killed in battle with the English at Merck on the Calais marches eleven years earlier. This would be the moment of revenge – and he had brought three of his four sons with him to witness the triumph. They would all fight together under the Rambures banner.

Robert, Seigneur de Boissay, one of the great figures of French chivalry, and the oldest knight in their army, even had his two grandsons, Charles and Colart, jointly bearing his standard. De Boissay had been a companion of Bertrand du Guesclin, the Breton squire who rose to become constable and a national hero for leading the French recovery after the battle of Poitiers. He had been by du Guesclin's side when that great warrior died at the siege of Châteauneuf-de-Randon in 1380; now, 35 years later, de Boissay had taken up arms again, to resist the English invasion.

They were two French formations of infantry moving forward, the vanguard and, a short distance behind it, the second division. The latter force was now leaderless, as the Duke of Alençon, who had been entrusted with its command, had on impulse decided to join the vanguard instead, 'carried away by foolish passion and an overwhelming desire to be in the forefront of the fight'.

At the beginning, all went well. The chronicler of Ruisseauville described the French vanguard advancing 'in very fine fashion, without rushing'. In a contest between dismounted men-at-arms, it was vital that the attackers kept in alignment, so at the moment of impact they brought maximum force to bear without presenting any weakness to their opponent. There must have been an initial surge of optimism as the French moved forward in good order.

But soon they began to struggle through the heavy, cloying mud, under the weight of all their armour. 'They foundered on the grain fields,' the chronicler of Ruisseauville noted grimly. An English chronicler further observed: 'The French were becoming worn out by the sheer quantity of equipment they were wearing.' The Monk of Saint-Denis commented:

The fields – newly sown with grain – were inundated ... Marching through a huge mud-pit, where with each step they sank up to their knees, they began to be overcome by fatigue even before they got within striking distance of the enemy.

Pierre Cochon added: 'The ground was so soft that men-at-arms sank into it by at least a foot.' Other chroniclers were also at pains to emphasise this. Jean Juvenal des Ursins remarked: 'The mud rose high up their legs, to the mid-calf, so that they could scarcely pull their feet out of the ground.' And the chronicler of Ruisseauville observed: 'Their feet sank very deeply into the earth.' It was clear that the French were already in trouble. Jean de Waurin, watching proceedings anxiously from behind the advancing troops, said: 'So soft was the ground, and so heavy was their armour, that soon some could scarcely carry their weapons.'

Scientific tests carried out on the soil of Agincourt have shown that it sucked in and absorbed water, rather than letting it run off or soak through. Following heavy rain this type of soil would have been particularly muddy and sticky, creating a strong suction effect as men equipped with plate armour tried to move across it.

Full plate armour weighed about 60 pounds. But, in addition, the French men-at-arms at Agincourt wore heavy coats of mail, down to their knees, which would have added another 20–30 pounds. Medieval infantry forces always tried to move forward slowly, 'by the small step', so that their formation would remain in good order. Ordinary parade-ground pace for French infantry in the eighteenth century was 40 yards a minute. Here, the French were more encumbered, and it would probably have taken almost half an hour to close in on the English position.

In such atrocious conditions it was the job of the pages and squires to help the men-at-arms. The Burgundian nobleman Olivier de la Marche later recounted that at the battle of Dendermonde in Flanders (1452) the men-at-arms were so exhausted that they leaned on the pages for support, lest they fall and be unable to get up again. But at Agincourt, Waurin continued:

Most had no one to help them, because they had not wanted to take with them any of the lower ranks, for the gentlemen wanted to have all the honour deriving from the battle.

Any knight who slipped and fell was in grave danger of being trampled by the massed ranks pushing up behind him.

As the vanguard pushed on, horsemen from the failed cavalry charge, and riderless horses, no longer carrying their masters, careered straight into their path and broke up their formation.

Jean de Bueil would go on to fight in numerous battles in the Hundred Years War, and gain a keen appreciation of military tactics. Drawing on testimony of those who had survived the battle, and his own military experience, he made a more sober assessment of Agincourt. Of the French advance he said:

> Our men-at-arms marched across a large stretch of fallow land, with mud up to their knees, before meeting with the enemy. Their line was broken up and many were exhausted and out of breath when there was still a considerable distance between them and the English … It is no good, in these circumstances, trying to fight on foot.

It was as if de Bueil had awoken from his own reverie about the exhilaration and elation of combat and, in the cold light of day, plainly realised that it was a good idea to know where you were and what you were doing. Richemont, advancing with his Breton knights, had a soldier's instinct that something was wrong. The battle line was losing its order and cohesion, and the ground was narrowing ominously. 'Soon,' Richemont thought, 'it will become too restricted to fight.'

The French, who were 'becoming increasingly worn-out and exhausted', as Thomas Elmham put it, were about to stumble into a living nightmare. For they now had come within range of the English bowmen. Volley upon volley of arrows rained down upon them.

Thomas Walsingham reported:

The air was filled with a terrifying sound. A cloud burst in all directions, and iron sounded on iron, as the volleys struck helmets, breastplates and cuirasses.

At the beginning, the sheer weight of plate armour the men-at-arms were wearing protected them. Jean Juvenal des Ursins recalled: 'Initially, the French were scarcely harmed by the arrow fire of the English, because they were so well-armoured.' Duke John the Fearless had survived a number of arrow strikes at the battle of Othée (1408) simply because of the quality of his equipment. But then the English bowmen switched from high- to low-trajectory firing and deliberately aimed for the faces of their opponents.

This was always a very effective tactic. At Dupplin Moor in 1332: 'The English archers, by continuous volleys of arrows, so bloodied and wounded the first division of Scots in the face that they were left helpless.' And at Poitiers (1356), against French soldiers better armoured and protected, the bowmen deliberately aimed at the helmets of their foe, knowing the vulnerable spots – particularly the 'aventail', the chain mail collar, which could be pierced by a bodkin arrow (an arrowhead in the form of a square metal spike).

At Agincourt, the French were particularly vulnerable because they were suffering from shortage of breath. As the arrows rained down, they would be forced to lower the visors of their bascinet helmets. Even this did not offer complete protection, for eye slits and ventilation holes were also vulnerable to the narrow points of bodkin arrowheads, so – almost as a reflex action – they would lower their heads as well.

With the visor down, the effect of the bascinet was rather like putting on a diver's helmet – but without the oxygen supply. The wearer was plunged into disorientating darkness, with vision restricted to a single, horizontal slit, about half an inch wide. Although the visor projected outwards, like a pig's snout, and was punctured with ventilation holes, the circulation of air was very restricted. But if a struggling man-at-arms lifted his visor briefly to get more oxygen, he risked getting an arrow full in the face, just as Henry V had done at the battle of Shrewsbury.

And yet, soldiers were struggling so much in the difficult conditions that they were forced to do this. Richemont remembered: 'The arrow fire was so thick it broke up our line, just when we needed to close in on the English.' And Thomas Walsingham added: 'Men fell to the ground and soon heaps of them were piling up, all pierced by arrows.'

The main English line of men-at-arms, interspersed with small groups of archers, now braced itself for the shock of their opponent's assault. It was clear that the battle plan was working. And yet, as the French approached, their strength in men-at-arms, as Titus Livius related, was 32 men deep; the English line only four men deep. For victory to be won, they must not let the enemy through. In a remarkable spontaneous gesture, Henry and his captains tore up their aristocratic surcoats and passed pieces of the fabric all along the line. In the fight that followed all men would be noble, all would be brothers-in-arms.

The sun was now shining directly in the eyes of the advancing French, and according to Jean Juvenal des Ursins it shone so brightly, even through their visor slits, that their soldiers lowered their heads still further. Jean de Waurin added: 'The English fired so vigorously that none of our soldiers dared look up.'

Men bowed their heads under the sheer weight of the arrow storm. The French were sustaining heavy casualties but they kept pushing forward. As they closed in they switched formation, from line abreast to three columns, as the chaplain grimly described:

> *The French nobility, who had previously advanced in line abreast and had all but come to grips with us, either from fear of the missiles whose very force pierced the sides and visors of their helmets, or in order to sooner break through our strongest points and reach the standards, divided into three columns, attacking our line of battle at the three places the standards were.*

This may have been partly a response to the arrow storm, but seems to have been an intentional manoeuvre nonetheless – and, if so, it was an extraordinary feat, given the hail of missiles and the heaviness of the ground. The shock of the impact pushed back the English line, as the chaplain emphasised:

> *In the mêlée of weapon-fighting which then followed, they hurled themselves against our men in such a fierce charge as to force them back almost a spear's length.*

The English fought back strongly. As an anonymous chronicler at the court of Charles VI related:

> *The French had struggled over newly worked land, which was very difficult to cross. They were heavily armed and the ground was soft, and they were exhausted and much troubled in their advance. When they engaged with the main English battle line some were so exhausted that they could scarcely move.*

The chronicler continued, 'The English were fresh and unwearied, *for they had not moved from their advantageous position* [my italics]. They began to strike in a most violent fashion – and knocked to the ground many who could not get up again.'

As the remaining French men-at-arms crashed into the English line there was less and less space for them to use their weapons, as the troops coming up behind were funnelled into narrower and narrower ground, and pushed into the men ahead of them. This funnelling, along with the effect of the cloying mud, was making the terrain a great ally of the English – a vital reason why Henry and the Duke of York had wanted to provoke the French into advancing in the first place.

For this stage of the battle contained all the elements of a major crowd disaster. On either side of the English position the land fell away sharply, restricting the room for fighting. One recent study has suggested that the available space may have dropped from about 900 yards at the wide end of the funnel to a little over 500 yards at the narrow end, a reduction of nearly 50 per cent. As the French soldiers moved down the funnel, the mass of people and the effect of the constriction would push people towards the centre. Men would start jostling at the back, unable to easily move, with still more coming up behind them. A deadly calibration was occurring: too many people, not enough space, a quick reduction in space, a massive increase in density, a sudden restriction of forward movement.

When people fell over it would create a domino effect, with others – unable to get out of the way – falling, too. The science of crowd control reveals that when the density of the French vanguard reached four men per square yard, the soldiers would not even be able to take full steps forward, lessening the speed of their advance by 70 per cent. At that point, others would crash into them from behind, and the sheer pressure of men trying to move forward without room to do so would become life-threatening.

The Monk of Saint-Denis said: 'The vanguard, comprising about 5,000 men, now found itself so tightly packed, that those in its third rank could scarcely use their swords.'

This was the creation of a 'resayt', the receiving station or killing ground. At Crécy the English had exploited agricultural ridges and terraces to funnel French troops into a killing zone opposite the Black Prince's division, where, in the words of Geoffrey le Baker, 'many were crushed to death, without a mark on them, in the middle of their own army, because the press was so great'.

And still the English bowmen were inflicting terrible damage. 'The Count of Vendôme,' the Monk continued, 'a man of bravery and renown, was seen struggling in the face of the arrow storm, with several of his best men slain and others wounded.'

The French wanted to bring down the English banners, kill the commanders fighting under them and then punch their way through the line. In the ferocious onslaught which followed, the Duke of York ordered his men not to retreat even a foot from his standard. His men clustered around him, trading sword thrusts with their opponents. Axe blows were raining down upon York's helmet. On the other wing, the young Earl of Suffolk's banner was down – he had been slain by the enemy. French knights now converged on the king's own standard.

Arthur, Count of Richemont and his followers were approaching Henry's banner: 'Here there was particularly fierce and hard fighting,' Richemont recalled. 'Men were dying all around the king.' Henry showed astonishing courage, wielding a battle axe and trading blows with the enemy. Thomas Walsingham said:

> Henry fought not so much as a king as a knight that day, as he flung himself against the enemy, giving and receiving blows, and giving an example to his men through his bravery.

When his brother, Humphrey, Duke of Gloucester, was wounded and dragged towards the French, the king stood over his body and fought them off. Titus Livius writes:

The king did not spare himself from the danger of the fight. And like a lion he battled amongst the enemy, receiving blow after blow to his helmet. When his brother was thrown to the ground half-dead, Henry put his feet astride his body, and fought off the French, so that he might not be carried off by the enemy, but retrieved by his own followers.

'The Duke of Gloucester, brother of the king, was brought down with a sword blow to the head,' Richemont remembered. 'Henry stood over him, fearing that he might be killed, and received such a blow to the [circlet] crown on his helmet that he too fell to his knees.'

Jean de Waurin elaborated:

Eighteen knights, serving together under the Lord of Croy, had sworn an oath that when the two sides met in battle they would try with all their might to get as close as possible to the king of England, and knock the crown right off his helmet, or die in the attempt. They did indeed do this. When they got right up to the king one of them, with an axe in his hand, struck such a heavy blow on the king's bascinet that it knocked off one of the rubies of his crown. But all eighteen of these knights were cut to pieces – not a single one survived.

Ordinary soldiers pitched in to protect their king. Later tradition had it that one of them, the Welshman Daffyd Llewelyn, known by his soldier's nickname of Davy Gam, died saving the king's life – and Llewelyn's story lay behind the creation of Shakespeare's memorable Welshman Fluellen. The legend may have some truth in it, for contemporary sources told of Henry's knighting two men during the battle – the other was Roger Vaughan, Llewelyn's son-in-law, who also died in the fighting – and such a gesture was reserved for acts of outstanding valour.

The French second division was now approaching the English line. Jean de Longueval, who was in this force, remembered seeing the vanguard ahead of him start to break up and disintegrate before his eyes because of the constricted space. But still there was hope of victory if the French could break through the hard-pressed English men-at-arms. On sheer adrenalin, Longueval and his comrades pushed on.

It was shortly after midday – and the crisis point of the battle had been reached.

CHAPTER 10

Bowmen of England →

The Rout

12.00–13.30 (25 October 1415)

FRENCH MEN-AT-ARMS were now frenziedly attacking the key points in the English line. The Earl of Suffolk lay dead. Henry V and the Duke of York were fighting for their very lives. If their banners went down the English might still lose the day – because their opponents would then punch through their battle line and – even with their reduced strength – envelop Henry's forces. In such a scenario, the narrow end of the funnel would become a trap rather than a battle-winning advantage, especially if some of the cavalry from the French third line also rode around the field of combat, broke through the baggage train and attacked the English army from the rear.

For a medieval general, commanding a battle was about the conscious acceptance of risk. And, at the moment, the terrain was working strongly in Henry's favour. The English army had gathered itself and was acting – with the battle plan in mind – not as disparate entities but as a unified whole. And it was fighting with extraordinary power.

The chaplain, situated well to the rear of Henry's army, was trying to gauge the progress of the battle through the sounds that he heard – the cries of the soldiers, the blast of trumpets or hunting horns. He recalled this anxious period of waiting:

I, who am now writing this, and was then sitting on a horse among the baggage at the rear of the battle, and the other priests present, did humble our souls before God … and said in our hearts: 'Remember us, O Lord, our enemies are gathered together and boast to themselves of their excellence. Destroy their strength and scatter them, that they may understand, because there is none other that fighteth for us but only Thou, our God.' And also, in fear and trembling, with our eyes raised to heaven, we cried out that God would have compassion upon us, and upon the crown of England.

The men-at-arms of both sides, with visibility limited by their helmets, were also hearing the fearful din of combat, as weapons struck armour and men shouted out, in exhilaration or agony. And sounds of panic and alarm were now echoing around the battlefield.

The narrowing funnel of the battlefield was now working against the French, to deadly effect. At Dupplin Moor in 1332 – the first battle where the English longbow was fully integrated into the army's formation – the mass of the Scots, pushing into a narrow field of combat, hemmed in by their opponents, bunched together by the force of the arrow fire, succumbed to mass suffocation. The Bridlington chronicler observed:

The forward troops of the Scots, badly wounded by the arrows, and driven up close to their second division, jammed together in a small space, one being crushed by another. Suffocated by each other – and beaten by that, rather than by blows of the sword – they fell in a remarkable way, in a great heap. Pressed against each other in this way, and squeezed against each other as if by ropes, they perished miserably.

As the bodies piled up, the English men-at-arms stabbed into the heaving mass.

The narrowing ground – shaped by agricultural terracing – in front of the Black Prince's division at Crécy had a similar effect, as the chronicler Geoffrey le Baker grimly noted: 'Many of the French were crushed to death – without a mark on them – in the middle of their own army.' These were terrifying precedents. At Roosebeke, in 1382, the French had inflicted such a punishment on their Flemish opponents, using their cavalry to create a 'press', the Flemings squeezed together so that they could no longer fight, and many of them, including their leader Philip von Artevelde, succumbing to suffocation. At Agincourt, realising that they might suffer a similar fate, the French made a last, desperate effort to break through.

In Thomas lord Camoys's division the Earl of Oxford was performing wonders – fighting with a furious intensity, he would later be elevated to the Order of the Garter for his courage. Around the Duke of York, Sir John Holland and Sir William Bourchier were also performing well. The French closed in around York himself. The duke, realising the entire battle plan depended on the English line holding, did not budge an inch. He stood resolute, under his standard. Blows rained down upon him. His troops fought with fierce resolve. The muster rolls of the duke's force show more than 90 men lost their lives defending his banner – astonishingly, the majority of the English casualties suffered during the entire battle. And then York himself fell, his helmet smashed into his skull. A London chronicler caught the awful moment:

> The Duke of York was slain,
> For his king he would not retreat, even by a foot,
> Til his bascinet into his brain was brent [impaled].

His followers clustered around his body and carried on fighting. Sir John Popham, York's friend and fellow soldier, was later rewarded with a large annuity of 100 marks for the good service he did that day. The French were unable to break through.

Henry V personally beat back a number of the French. The body of the Duke of Alençon was found nearby – separated from his retinue, he had pushed towards the royal standard in a desperate attempt to kill the king. Seeing the fierce fighting around their leader, the English archers now resolved to join the fight, 'when their arrows were all used up, seizing axes, stakes, swords and spear heads that were lying about.'

This was the crucial moment. It took enormous courage for the archers to leave the protection of their stakes and enter the mêlée. If the French men-at-arms reorganised themselves and turned on them they would be annihilated. But their sudden intervention caught their opponents by surprise. They hacked and stabbed at the advancing Frenchmen and kept attacking, pushing further and further into the mass of the enemy, 'acting together and with great energy', as Monstrelet recalled. Jean de Waurin paid tribute to their determination: 'They struck whenever they saw breaks in the line.'

Henry's pre-battle motivation of his men now paid off handsomely. The Monk of Saint-Denis believed that the English 'were fighting with so much passion as they knew that for them it was a matter of life and death'. Titus Livius told of a mood of ferocious determination sweeping the army: 'The English were unusually eager to kill – for it seemed there was no hope of safety except in victory.'

The English troops now actually believed that they could see St George in the sky above them, at this vital stage of the battle, encouraging them to victory. This astonishing report was related by Thomas Elmham, who declared that during the fight 'Saint George was seen fighting on the side of the English.' Another chronicler echoed this belief: St George had helped the English and 'had been seen above, in the air, on the day that they fought'. Whether we believe this actually happened is not the point. These stories were credible enough to contemporaries – and showed the depth of ordinary soldiers' identification with the saint. Their effect on the morale of the army must have been incalculable.

The English archers' lightness and mobility gave them an advantage over the heavily armoured French men-at-arms and the mallets used for hammering in the stakes became a handy impromptu weapon. In increasingly cramped conditions, pushed into a narrow funnel of ground, the French began to recoil in disarray. This was the moment that Henry had been waiting for and he now urged his men-at-arms forward. The whole English army was fighting with remarkable discipline and cohesion and the battle now turned quickly and decisively in their favour.

The French men-at-arms felt the force of their advance suddenly slacken. Instead of pushing into the English, they were colliding with each other, floundering and falling in the mud. The squires and servants who might have helped them recover their footing had all been sent to the rear. Now men were asphyxiated under the sheer weight of numbers. A terrible pile of bodies built up around the English banners, with Henry's men clambering over the top of them to strike fresh blows against a now demoralised enemy. The chaplain grimly related:

The living fell upon the dead, and our men climbed upon these heaps, which rose more than six feet high, and slew those below with swords, axes and any other weapons they could find.

Thomas Elmham painted a vivid picture:

Men trod on their own entrails, others vomited forth their teeth
... some still standing had their arms hacked off, and all around
them, in the chaos of battle, the dying rolled in the blood of
complete strangers.

French overconfidence gave way to ghastly panic. The chaplain
remembered how 'fear and trembling seized them ... there
were some that day who surrendered more than ten times'.

The Norman chronicler Thomas Basin recounted:

It was a pitiful sight to see how, once their ranks had been
broken, confusion spread amongst the French army, and how
many of them tried to save their skins by fleeing. Ten Englishmen
pursued a hundred Frenchmen, and one Englishman ten
Frenchmen. And when they were caught by the English they put
up no resistance – they let themselves be killed or led off captive
like a flock of sheep.

'More people were killed in the press than in the fighting,'
the soldier John Hardyng said simply. The body of Arthur,
Count of Richemont was later found under a heap of the
slain. Knocked to the ground, with others then falling on
top of him, he had lost consciousness. Miraculously he was
still alive.

The mere sight of Sir William Trussell on the prowl was
enough to subdue the panic-stricken French. The ruffian
from Leicestershire who had once so violently laid into his
neighbour John Mortimer now gathered an impressive tally
of nine prisoners worth some 614 crowns. Few could rival
Trussell's haul, though many English men-at-arms netted
two or three prisoners each.

Something truly remarkable was happening – the cold,
exhausted, hungry English army was fighting with stupen-

dous power. The chaplain paid moving tribute to soldiers who had now lost all fear and were dauntless in combat: 'Nor, it seemed to our older men, had Englishmen ever fallen upon their enemies more boldly or fearlessly, or with a better will.' Henry's troops, sensing victory was within their grasp, now found fresh reserves of strength. The fight degenerated into a rout.

At this last stage of the fight Anthony, Duke of Brabant made a sudden appearance on the battlefield. The duke's secretary Edmond de Dynter related how it occurred:

On the morning of 25 October Duke Anthony had reached Lens, in Artois, where he was hearing Mass. Just as the host was being lifted up, a man brought him news that the English were to be fought before midday. The duke, and the others in his company, put the sign of the cross on their clothing and coats of arms, mounted their horses and set out quickly for the battle.

With the two sides in close combat, Duke Anthony arrived in the vicinity and stopped near a thicket, and there he dismounted with a few of his men. It was clear that the rest of his retinue would not reach him in time, nor would his equipment – his armour had not yet arrived, nor his weapons, standard or pennons. So he put on the armour of one of his chamberlains, and for his coat of arms he took the blazon from one of his trumpeters, cut a hole in it and wore it as a tunic. For a flag he took the blazon from another trumpeter and attached it to his lance. And so he entered the battle, with just a few of his followers, crying out 'Brabant, Brabant'.

The duke had intended to bring 1,400 men-at-arms with him. He had left most of these troops behind and had arrived, according to Jean Juvenal des Ursins, 'with about a dozen or so'. And the battle was clearly lost. The duke's own banner-bearer, Jean de Grymberg, took one look at the carnage and refused to advance a step further. But the others, out of loyalty, followed their master.

The anonymous chronicler of Charles VI wrote in wonderment:

> *Right at the point of defeat, the Duke of Brabant arrived with only a few men ... He threw himself keenly into the fight, in which he was almost immediately killed.*

Anthony, Duke of Brabant was *au fait* with the latest and most expensive designs of plate armour. In 1412 he had commissioned two of his armourers in Brussels to manufacture for him 'a complete harness, of a type made in the realm of France'. At Agincourt, however, he was not wearing any armour at all. As Edmond de Dynter concluded sadly: 'After the battle, he was found a long way away, amongst other dead. He had been wounded in the face and neck – he had not even been wearing a helmet.'

Yet there was to be one last, terrible event. Henry had heard that his baggage train had been attacked and plundered and now a third line of French appeared to be lining up for a charge. His men were distracted, busily capturing French noblemen. The sudden arrival of the Duke of Brabant had made everyone nervous; aware more troops might appear on the battlefield, the king feared that his small force might, even at this late stage, still be overwhelmed. He ordered that the enemy prisoners be killed in cold blood. It was an awful decision to have to make.

This incident is understandably shocking to us and was seen as horrifying by Henry's contemporaries. Jean de Waurin said bluntly: 'All those French noblemen were decapitated and inhumanely mutilated there in cold blood.' Waurin also made clear that many of Henry's solders were reluctant to carry out his command – although this was not out of moral scruple, but because they did not want to lose the ransom money for their prisoners:

> *When the king heard this, he ordered a man and two hundred archers to go into the host to ensure that the prisoners, whoever they were, should be killed. The esquire, without refusing or delaying for a moment, went to accomplish his sovereign master's will.*

We must place Henry's decision within the realities of medieval warfare. An army composed of dismounted men-at-arms and archers could not keep formation and collect prisoners at the same time. As a result, soldiers were prohibited from taking prisoners until an order or signal was given, signifying that victory was certain. During the battle of Crécy one of Edward III's German allies came to the king and said:

> *'Sire, we wonder greatly that you permit the shedding of so much noble blood: for if you were to take them alive, you could thereby make great progress in your war, and would gain very great ransoms from them.' And the king responded that they should not marvel at it, for thus it had been ordered, and thus it had to be.*

The situation at Agincourt was much the same. As Titus Livius recalled: 'The English took no prisoners until victory was certain and apparent.' Crucially, Henry's killing order was in response to French efforts to restart a battle that had seemed finished. The Monk of Saint-Denis suggested that these men were simply trying to get out of the way, not attack the English, but others told a different story. According to Jean de Waurin, many had regrouped, 'showing signs of wanting to fight, and marching forward in battle order'. Their standards and banners were unfurled – showing that battle was to recommence. Titus Livius described what happened next:

> *The king sent heralds to the French of the new army, asking whether they would come to fight or would leave the field, informing them that if they did not withdraw, or came to battle, all of the prisoners, and any of them who might be captured, would be killed without mercy.*

This was 'a moment of very great danger', as Jean de Waurin emphasised. The French third line posed a very real threat. They had been joined by men-at-arms from the failed cavalry attacks and the chronicler of Ruisseauville declared that these remaining French soldiers were of sufficient strength to take on Henry's army: 'they might have fought well against the English and all their power.' The king had to do something. If the French made a determined attack at this late stage, with the archers away from their stakes and mostly out of arrows, the men-at-arms exhausted by the fight and many soldiers preoccupied by taking prisoners, they would have stood a real chance of success.

Henry's actions were not without precedent. At the battle of Aljubarrota in 1385 – when an Anglo-Portuguese army defeated their Castilian opponents – elements of the Spanish vanguard regrouped and prepared for another assault and, as a result of this, a command was given to put the Castilian prisoners to death. In both cases there was a real danger that if the prisoners were left unguarded, as English troops regrouped, they might pick up weapons and resume fighting. Henry's order, although appalling to us, was necessary to save his army.

Military command sometimes requires tough decisions. This was one of the hardest Henry would ever face. The king broke chivalric convention by killing prisoners but even French chroniclers understood the reason, and did not blame him for it. Significantly, they instead criticised the Frenchmen who had rallied the third line, or those that had attacked the English baggage train. This is a fine example of how the story of a battle is always told in the winners' favour. Had the French succeeded, they would have been admired for their determined resistance when all seemed lost, while Henry would have been censured for failing to anticipate their actions.

When Henry put this drastic measure into effect the French third line hesitated – then slowly began to drift away. When the threat had passed, the killing order was rescinded and the remaining prisoners – and there seem to have been nearly a thousand of them – were then spared.

Ghillebert de Lannoy recalled:

I was wounded in the knee and the head, and I was laid down with the dead. But when the bodies were searched through, and seeing that I was [still alive and] wounded, and in a helpless state, I was taken prisoner and kept under guard for a while. I was then led to a house nearby with 10 or 12 other prisoners, who were all wounded. And there, when the Duke of Brabant was making a new attack, a shout went up that everyone should kill his prisoners. So that this might be effected much the quicker, they set fire to the house where we were. By the grace of God I dragged myself a few feet away from the fire …

Lannoy had made another lucky escape – he had pulled himself out of the burning building just in time. Shortly afterwards the killing order was cancelled.

'There I was when the English returned,' Lannoy continued, 'so I was taken prisoner again.' His new captor was Sir John Cornwall.

The two men regarded each other. Amid the carnage of battle, Lannoy told Cornwall he was pleased to be equipped in his best armour, and to be captured by a man of proper rank – he had feared being taken prisoner by an archer.

Now at last it was all over. A French herald told the king that the day was his. He had won an incredible victory and for a moment Henry was at a loss for words. Then he looked over to the woods on his left and asked for the name of the castle he saw. It was Agincourt. Monstrelet recorded the king's memorable reply:

> *Then, as all battles shall bear the name of the fortress nearest to the field on which they are fought, this shall for ever be called the battle of Agincourt.*

CHAPTER 11

A Band of Brothers —•

The Victory

13.30–14.00 (25 October 1415)

THE BATTLE OF Agincourt was over. The English had won a stunning victory. Thomas Walsingham said of the clash:

> Thus perished almost all the flower of French chivalry, cut down by the hands of a small band whom, a short while before, they had held in the greatest contempt. On that field fell the Dukes of Alençon, Brabant and Bar, together with five counts, the constable of France, the king's master of artillery and about a hundred other famous lords. Three thousand and sixty-nine knights and esquires are said to have been killed. The number of ordinary soldiers who died could not be estimated.

Henry V had remarked: 'This shall for ever be called the battle of Agincourt.' It was the prerogative of the victors to name the battle site. French sources had called the clash the 'battle of Ruisseauville', 'Blangy' and even 'Hesdin'. After the decisive English defeat against the Scots at Bannockburn in 1314, English sources had referred to it as 'the battle of Stirling'. But it was the Scottish name of 'Bannok' or 'Bannockburn' which stuck.

Not all medieval battles received a name in their immediate aftermath. The other battle that Henry had fought in, at Shrewsbury on 21 July 1403, still lacked a clear attribution when the king embarked upon the Agincourt expedition in

1415. The earliest sources, two newsletters written to the Datini bank in Florence, on 28 July and 9 August 1403, gave no name at all to the battle, or any indication where it had been fought, simply asking 'have you heard the big news in this country?' and detailing how the Percies had risen 'in the field' – a non-specific way of describing a battle – and that their defeat left 'their field broken'.

The first chroniclers of Shrewsbury offered a variety of local names – Harlescote being the most common – and a chancery inquisition of 1415 referred to it as 'the battle of Bull Field in the township of Harlescote'. Shrewsbury was of course a civil war battle, and did not carry the prestige of roundly defeating the French. Edward III's naval victory at Sluys in 1340 had several names immediately after the engagement, but Sluys was quickly decided upon because, as one fifteenth-century poem on the importance of keeping the sea related, 'it is named the battle of Sluys, so that one may read about it every day'.

Henry V undoubtedly hoped that Agincourt would be read about every day. At the very beginning the location held little resonance for an English audience, most people being unsure where it actually was. In one of the earliest reports, delivered to Winchester College, after the news of 'a certain battle fought at Agincourt' the scribe had inserted 'in Picardy' to give a rough sense of where it had taken place. But the news of 'dukes, counts, barons, knights and other gentlemen of France captured by our lord king of England' would have quickly lodged the name in everyone's memory. As Walsingham related:

> *Taken prisoner in the battle were the Dukes of Orléans and Bourbon, the Counts of Eu and Vendôme, Arthur, Count of Richemont, Marshal Boucicaut and about seven hundred others.*

> *The casualties on the English side were Edward, Duke of York, Michael, Earl of Suffolk, four knights, one squire called David Gam and 28 commoners.*

By November 1416, when Henry's chaplain completed his account, the name of Agincourt had become firmly established. 'The French took position in front of us,' he noted, 'in that field called the field of Agincourt.' However, contemporaries provided different accounts of how long the battle had taken. The chronicle of Ruisseauville said it was all over in half an hour. Arthur, Count of Richemont later recalled it had lasted around an hour. The chaplain, sheltering from proceedings in the English baggage train, said that it took between two and three hours to fully put the French to flight. If the initial French advance, and the failure of the cavalry attack, lasted around half an hour, and the mêlée about the same (which is perhaps what the Ruisseauville chronicler is referring to) this would correspond to the hour Richemont remembered – after which he lost consciousness. But the battle continued, with French forces threatening to regroup, the order given to kill the prisoner, which was then rescinded, and the final ending of hostilities.

The Duke of Brabant had heard battle was imminent while taking Mass at 'prime' (in autumn at 7 am) and had then ridden the 30 miles or so from Lens to Agincourt. He probably arrived shortly before 1 pm. Proceedings came to an end about half an hour later.

With the battle over, Henry called his soldiers around him and spoke to them simply and informally. The Monk of Saint-Denis caught the moment, telling how the king:

> *... assembled his victorious troops and, after making a sign that they should all be silent, thanked them for having so bravely*

risked their lives in his service, and encouraged them to preserve the memory of that brilliant success. He also urged them not to attribute their victory to their own strengths but to accord all the merit to the special grace of God, who had delivered into their small company such a great multitude of the French, and had brought low the latter's insolence and pride.

Thomas Walsingham carried on the story:

King Henry attributed all his success to God, as was right, and gave boundless thanks to Him who had given such an unexpected victory and crushed the fiercest of foes. He stayed the night by the battlefield – and the next day, a Saturday, he continued the journey which he had begun, towards Calais.

As the chronicler Thomas Elmham put it, it was a battle where 'the smaller army overcame the many thousand'. Henry's informality was a mark of his confidence – a medieval commander who urges his men forward with 'Fellows – let's go!' has a ready authority that is quickly communicated to his soldiers.

It was indeed the victory of the few against the many – and the disparity between the two armies made the result quite devastating for the French. The chronicler Pierre Cochon saw it as: 'The ugliest and most wretched event that had happened to France over the last thousand years.'

'We had persuaded ourselves that the sight of so many Princes would strike terror into the hearts of the enemy,' said the Monk of Saint-Denis,

and to win the day we had to do nothing but charge quickly and boldly ... To our eternal shame, this did not happen. And if it is consolation for men of honour to think that they have been defeated by adversaries of noble lineage, it was an even greater disgrace that we were beaten by men [we regarded as] unworthy and vile.

It was the heralds' job to count the dead, and English and French co-operated together in this grim task. Jean Le Fèvre wrote of the task he undertook:

During the battle, all officers of arms, as much on the one side as on the other, kept together, and after the battle the French heralds went their way and the English heralds stayed with their masters, who had won the battle. As for me, I stayed with the English.

Even the victorious English were stunned by the carnage. The chaplain wrote:

When the strength of the enemy had been utterly weakened, and the rigours of battle ended, we who had gained the victory came back through the heaps of the slain ... And I truly believe there is not a man with a heart of flesh, or even of stone, who had he seen and pondered on the bitter wounds inflicted on so many Christian men would not have dissolved into tears, time and again, through grief.

Others added their observations. Enguerrand de Monstrelet:

Many of the French returned to the field of battle, where the bodies had been turned over more than once, some to seek for their lords and carry them to their own countries for burial, others to pillage what the English had left. King Henry's army had only taken gold, silver, rich dresses, helmets and what was of value, for which reason the greater part of the armour was

266

untouched and on the dead bodies, but it did not long remain thus, for it was very soon stripped off, and even the shirts and all other parts of their dress were carried away by the peasants of the adjoining villages. The bodies were left exposed, as naked as when they came into the world.

The chronicler of Ruisseauville:

It was found by the tally of the heralds between 1,600 and 1,800 coats of arms [of the slain], without counting those gentlemen who did not have a surcoat. And in the defeat were killed more than 6,000 others …

The University of Paris held a special service for the dead:

The nation is inconsolable … in battle against the English at Agincourt so many princes, nobles, knights and barons of the blood of France have been killed that there are few in the whole country who have not lost fathers, brothers or friends in the fighting.

The French struggled to find words for it all. For Jean de Waurin it was 'piteous'; for Monstrelet, 'the saddest of days'. The Monk of Saint-Denis opined: 'I don't think there has been a bigger disaster in France for the last fifty years – or in my opinion one that has had worse consequences.'

Perceval de Cagny agreed: 'The battle was most wretched – and a cause of great and irrevocable damage to the kingdom.' And Thomas Basin noted with trepidation: 'We have lost the greater part of those who could have defended the kingdom from the enemy.'

The Monk of Saint-Denis concurred: 'The French court fell into bitter sadness thinking of how the kingdom had

267

been deprived of so many of its illustrious defenders – it was a time of profound dejection.'

Pierre Fenin recalled that the Duke of Burgundy was still in a state of deep distress, weeks after the battle, over the loss of his brothers Anthony, Duke of Brabant and Philip, Count of Nevers. The town records of Nevers recall the sense of devastation and loss. A messenger, Pierre Verneil, had been sent out to neighbouring towns to try to find out news of the Count of Nevers, 'whom they say has been in the battle with the English'. It was soon confirmed that the count had died, and Masses were immediately held in all the churches. His body was recovered – and buried in the church of Saint-Cyr, with Jean Traquement, a painter, being rewarded for decorating the coats of arms of the count, which were displayed all around the church and over his tomb.

The number of casualties was so high that the government of Charles VI felt morally obliged to provide financial support to the families of those slain. The accounts of the French receiver-general record a payment to: 'Perrette, widow of Georges de Saint-Sariol, who enlisted for military service at the voyage of Blangis [Agincourt], in which he lost his life, leaving his wife with four little children, one of whom bears the [Christian] name of the king, and for the sake of God and as alms, so that she may be better able to pay her creditors.'

Edmond de Dynter was now describing a different kind of itinerary. The Duke of Brabant's servants had recovered his body from the battlefield:

> They took it to Saint-Pol, where they put it in a lead coffin with spices and aromatic herbs. Then the cortège went to Tournai, where the bishop and chapter came out and accompanied it with much lamenting ... then it was taken to Brussels and put in the church of Saint-Goule, where exequies were held ... then it was

taken to Fure [Tervuren], *in the church of St John, where after a solemn requiem mass the duke was buried alongside his first wife.*

Charles d'Albret, constable of France, was buried in the church of the Cordeliers in Hesdin with 13 of his fighting companions by his side.

Jean Juvenal des Ursins captured a nation inconsolable with grief: 'In most places in the kingdom there were ladies who had been widowed and poor orphans.' And the Monk of Saint-Denis reported: 'It was a sight to bring tears to the eyes to see so many women crying bitterly at the loss of their husbands, others inconsolable at the death of their children or closest relatives.'

Christine de Pizan wrote a letter of commiseration to Marie de Berry, Duchess of Bourbon. The duchess had lost her son-in-law and three cousins in the battle; her husband, the Duke of Bourbon, and her son the Count of Eu, were now prisoners in England. Christine tried to be positive, saying that those who were killed on the battlefield had died 'with grace and valour', but in the atrocious conditions of Agincourt, where so many were suffocated or crushed to death, this was not really true.

The French poet Alain Chartier, in his *Book of the Four Ladies*, enlarged on this dimension of collective grief. Out for a stroll one fine morning, the poet meets four finely dressed ladies. But he soon discovers that all are deeply troubled. The first lady, weeping, tells of the death of her husband in battle. The second reveals that her husband has been taken prisoner by the English, and she can get no news of him. The third says that her husband is missing, and no one knows what has happened to him. The fourth admits that her husband fled from the battle, and that she can scarcely bear the shame and dishonour.

Chartier was a patriot and he believed it was right that an honourable knight should fight and if necessary die for his country. He felt that fleeing from the battlefield was a cowardly and shameful act, whatever the circumstances. Nevertheless, he evoked an emotional landscape of pain and overwhelming shock. The loss was so great it was hard to move on. The townspeople of Amiens visited the battlefield a few days later and found the tents and rich hangings of the French war camp still intact – remarkably, they had not been plundered. An atmosphere of ill omen hung over the place – as if the ghosts of its fallen soldiers were still nearby. The community of Saint-Quentin in Picardy recorded: 'Nearly all the richest and most notable members of the town have been killed or taken prisoner. Their houses are left empty and fall into disrepair ... Everywhere is silence.'

'We must all record in our hearts the cruelty of the damnable battle of Agincourt,' Chartier wrote, 'which we have bought at so dear a price.'

The Monk of Saint-Denis told how the English king ordered a battlefield burial for most of the English dead and agreed that the Bishop of Thérouanne should bless the battlefield so that it might be used as a cemetery.

Henry also oversaw the preparation of the remains of Edward, Duke of York, the highest-ranking English nobleman killed and the king's personal friend. The duke had fought and died a hero. York had asked in his will that his body be buried in the collegiate church at Fotheringhay, 'under a flat marble slab, with an image above it, made of brass'. York had founded the church in 1411 but most of it had yet to be built. In the interim, the duke's remains would be held in the chapel of Fotheringhay castle. The king spoke to York's fighting companions and ascertained that Sir John Popham had protected the duke's dead body from the French.

The day after battle, 26 October, the English army proceeded to Calais, reaching the town three days later. Henry's march across France had come to its end. The chronicler of the abbey of Ruisseauville related:

> *Then Louis of Luxembourg, Bishop of Thérouanne, blessed the ground and the place where the battle had been, accompanied by the Abbot of Blangy and made five graves, and in each grave were buried 1,200 men or more at his costs and expenses. No one knew the exact number of the dead except the bishop and the labourers – and they took an oath saying they should not reveal it to anyone. And on each mass grave was placed a great cross of wood.*

Beyond 24 Hours

O N 23 NOVEMBER 1415 Henry V made a spectacular entry into London. The city was packed – and as Henry's chaplain related: '... so great was the throng of people in Cheapside, from one end to the other, that the horsemen were only just able, though not without difficulty, to ride through.'

Celebration of Agincourt's invigorating success started soon after the event. The battle's winner was a shrewd self-publicist and Henry put out a simple but powerful idea – that of a boy David defeating a giant Goliath – in his stage-managed victory procession. As the king and his entourage reached the capital, a series of pageants were prepared so that all could see the triumph of the underdog. This motif was quickly circulated in newsletters, chronicles and even in song. The Agincourt Carol set the victory to rousing music and guaranteed that as many people as possible got to hear of it.

The ballad was almost certainly composed around the time of the king's return to the capital. A choir had gathered to perform 'a song of congratulation'. And the refrain would have been sung out lustily, to musical accompaniment:

Our king went forth to Normandy,
With grace and might of chivalry,
There God for him wrought marvellously;
Wherefore England might call and cry
To God give thanks for victory.

Nowadays we are used to such spin operations and regard them with cynicism, but here a significant point was being made. As Henry rode into London a bevy of maidens greeted him with a musical fanfare, beating drums and strumming gilt viols. This was a deliberate imitation of a biblical scene of David returning from the slaughter of Goliath and this was quickly understood by the onlookers. As Adam of Usk remarked, the whole city was *en fête* and the simple motif that followed struck everybody. As Henry approached Cheapside: 'Chanting virgins came dancing to meet him, accompanied by choirs and rums and golden viols, just as in king David's time, after the slaying of Goliath. What more can I say? The city wore its brightest aspect, and happiness filled the people – and rightly so.'

Adam of Usk was not some naïve observer, swept along by a superficial tide of emotion. Later in Henry V's reign he actually became a critic of the war, commenting bluntly: 'The lord king is now fleecing anyone with money, rich or poor, throughout the realm, in readiness for his return to France.' This outburst makes his spontaneous patriotism in 1415 all the more telling. Adam was so moved by the triumph at Agincourt that he put a poem in his text, and translated from the Latin it reads:

People of England, cease your work and pray,
For the glorious victory of Crispin's day:
Despite their scorn for Englishmen's renown,
The odious might of France came crashing down.

Here it is – the 'odious might' of the French laid low by the humble few. Another piece of London street theatre, showing a tiny figure winning victory against a huge opponent, carried much the same resonance. Thomas Walsingham underlined the point, calling it 'a triumph of a dwarf against a giant'. That was how everyone saw the battle.

And the mood of celebration in the capital was heightened because of earlier fears that the outnumbered English army might have suffered a terrible defeat. Indeed, on the very morning of the battle itself, a rumour was circulating in London that Henry and his men had been wiped out. Although no one knew what was happening, the city's *Letter Book* first recorded that the movements of the king and his army 'lay shrouded in mystery' before adding ominously that a 'lamentable report, replete with sadness and a cause for endless sorrow, had alarmed the community throughout all the city'. London's citizens feared the English army had suffered a catastrophe in France.

Now it was all so different. News of the result of the battle had reached London on 29 October. The city's *Letter Book* described what happened next:

> *And on the morrow of the Apostles Simon and Jude the Mayor and Aldermen, together with an immense number of citizens went on foot to Westminster, as if going on a pilgrimage, and with due solemnity made devout thanksgiving in the Minster there, for the joyous news that had now arrived.*

Medieval society was struck by the image of fortune's wheel, and how at its zenith, when all seemed disposed for success, it was possible to plunge to disaster. The French had been so confident on 25 October that a premature report of their success had reached the nearby town of Abbeville – one of the crossing points of the Somme – and a great feast had been prepared to celebrate the imagined victory. The reality was almost too ghastly to contemplate.

Not only had the underdog triumphed, he had done so with very light casualties. The English dead were but a handful – at most scarcely more than a hundred, while the French had lost thousands. Many of these thousands had piled up in a macabre wall of bodies, as men collided with each other, slipped in the mud and were asphyxiated by the press of fighters pressing behind them. Almost every noble family in France was afflicted with the loss of a father, brother, friend or kinsman.

And we need to remember that David pitching in against mighty Goliath was not the invention of the London victory pageant; it was consistent with the way most contemporaries, both French and English, saw the battle. Henry V's chaplain had, after all, recorded the terrified reaction of the English scout who first caught sight of the opposing French. The frightened man galloped back 'with the utmost speed his horse would carry him … and being almost breathless, said: "Quickly, be prepared for battle, as you are just about to fight against a world of innumerable people".' The chronicler Pierre Fenin put it simply: 'The French were incomparably greater in number than the English.' Clever and effective PR it may have been, but it chimed with the actual course of events.

The Agincourt Carol is rightly memorable, for setting Henry's victory celebration to music was an inspired idea. One of its contributors was likely to have been the foremost composer of the day, Lionel Power. Power served in the household of Henry's brother, Thomas, Duke of Clarence, and was accomplished in a wide variety of musical styles. He was the author of the first manuscript of titled English music – we might liken it to an early version of our modern chart toppers. Clarence encouraged him to compose a rousing *Sanctus* for the king's victorious return to London.

Clarence had his own issues with the war in France that would bring him to a tragic end. He had missed out on Agincourt, being sent home with dysentery after the siege of

Harfleur, and, whatever his enthusiasm for musical celebration, his absence from that great victory rankled. Six years later, on campaign at Baugé in Anjou, but feeling little better, he endeavoured to win some renown of his own on the fields of France with an impromptu decision to charge into battle halfway through his evening meal. In his haste he left behind most of his archers. His experienced captains remonstrated with him, but he retorted that they had been at Agincourt and he had not. The man who loved putting battles to music sadly misjudged the tempo of the occasion: his small and hastily assembled army was overwhelmed and Clarence himself was quickly slain.

Clarence's discomfort was understandable, for those who were present at Agincourt never forgot the experience. Alongside the status of these victorious soldiers, Clarence felt his own inferiority keenly. A Nottinghamshire knight, Sir Ralph Shirley, would have sympathised with his predicament. Shirley had been invalided home from Harfleur, with the king's permission, on 5 October 1415. His small retinue went on without him to Agincourt, where one of his men-at-arms, Ralph Fowne, gained the distinction of capturing the Duke of Bourbon, one of the greatest aristocrats in the realm of France. Shirley must have wished he had kept his medicine cabinet stocked up more fully.

The poet John Lydgate caught the general mood of amazement:

When, without stratagem,
But in plain shock and even play of battle,
Was ever known so great and little loss
On one part and on the other. Take it, God,
For it is none but thine!

The battle had a particularly powerful effect on one soldier. Before the campaign, John Cheney, in the retinue of Sir John Cornwall, had been worried about money. After it, we learn from his memorial brass, 'animated by ardent faith', he spent several years travelling the Holy Land, where fittingly his most celebrated deed was the slaying of 'a huge, savage giant'. Henry would have approved.

Medieval society often measured the worth of a battle by the numbers of opposing aristocrats killed or taken prisoner. After the killing order had been rescinded, the Agincourt prisoner tally remained an impressive one – and although chronicle estimates vary, the figure seems to lie between 700 and 2,000. The six most important were Charles, Duke of Orléans (Charles VI's nephew), Jean de Clermont, Duke of Bourbon, Louis de Bourbon, Count of Vendôme (both descendants of Louis XI), Charles d'Artois, Count of Eu (a descendant of Louis VIII), Arthur, Count of Richemont (brother of the Duke of Brittany) and the marshal of France, Jean le Meingre, called Boucicaut. These men were all of high public standing, bought by Henry V from their original captors, and their fate was linked not only to their ability to raise a ransom but also the English king's political objectives.

Lower down the hierarchy, the prospect of a quick profit dictated the fate of most prisoners, the majority of whom were put to ransom within a year or two of the battle and were probably never brought to England at all. The Burgundian Jean Le Fèvre, present with the English army during the entire campaign, remembered that when the troops finally reached Calais some of them, along with their prisoners, were barred from entering the town out of a fear its food stocks would run out. As a result, many soldiers sold both military equipment and prisoners to the inhabitants of

Calais at a low price simply to have enough money to eat and to return home.

Of those who were brought to England, the Duke of Bourbon and Marshal Boucicaut died in captivity there. Charles, Duke of Orléans was only released in 1440, 25 years after the battle. During his time as a prisoner Orléans wrote some of the best poetry of the late Middle Ages. For much of the month before Agincourt the duke was paying large sums of money to have his armour lined with black satin. But he should never have been in command of the French army.

Agincourt gave Henry V an international reputation. The joyous celebration in the city of London on 23 November 1415 was followed by a visit to the capital, some six months later, of the Holy Roman Emperor Sigismund, who – according to the delighted chaplain – 'gloried in the exploits of our king'. In 1417 Henry invaded Normandy with a fresh army and within two years had conquered it. 'The time of worship [honour] for young men is now,' wrote one happy soldier. The martial adventures of Sir William Bourchier, one of the heroes of Agincourt, were avidly followed by his wife Anne; writing to her friend, the prior of Llanthony, near Gloucester, she told him of her pride in his 'great prowess'.

In France, the progress of Henry's army was viewed with consternation, and sometimes outright fear. 'It is not easy to convey the sheer terror felt by the inhabitants of Normandy for even the name "Englishman",' Thomas Basin wrote. 'It was a fear so sudden and all-consuming that nobody believed there was any safety except in flight ... Indeed, people generally thought that the English were not men like everyone else, but wild beasts, gigantic and ferocious, who were going to throw themselves on them and then devour them.'

And, throughout it all, Henry remembered his fallen friend, Edward, Duke of York. York's remains had been returned to the chapel at Fotheringhay castle, until the collegiate church that the duke had received licence for in 1411 was constructed. The king ordered that building work begin immediately, under the supervision of Henry's master mason Stephen Lote, and when the work was sufficiently advanced York's remains were then moved to the choir of the new church, marked by the simple marble slab that the duke had requested, with his figure engraved in brass upon it.

The keeper of Fotheringhay castle was Sir Thomas Burton. Burton had fought with York in Wales, accompanied him in the French expedition of 1412 and fought by the duke's side at Agincourt. As a mark of respect for his deceased comrade the king granted Burton custody of the most important prisoners taken at Harfleur and Agincourt. Between June 1417 and February 1420 Sir Thomas was the keeper of Charles, Count of Eu, Arthur, Count of Richemont and Marshal Boucicaut, whom he escorted across the Channel in the summer of 1419 for a meeting with Henry. His other captives included Charles, Duke of Orléans, who was transferred to Fotheringhay at the beginning of 1420, and whom Burton later produced before the Privy Council in London, and Raoul de Gaucourt, one of the defenders of Harfleur.

The astonishing military and political success continued. In May 1420 Henry V of England was made Regent of France by the Treaty of Troyes, which disinherited Charles VI's son, the Dauphin Charles, younger brother of the portly Louis. (Louis himself had died shortly after the challenge to a duel by the English king – perhaps out of shock, or so it was said.) The treaty was celebrated by the famous marriage alliance between Henry and Charles's daughter Katherine of Valois. Henry now held Paris and much of northern France and enjoyed the support of the Duke of

Burgundy. But the king was struck down in the prime of his life, succumbing to illness and dying at Vincennes, near Paris, on 31 August 1422.

Charles VI also died shortly afterwards, leaving Henry V's baby son – Henry VI – king of England and France, with his uncle, John, Duke of Bedford, acting as regent. However, many French aristocrats, still refusing to accept the Treaty of Troyes, instead supported Charles VI's disinherited son – Charles VII – in setting up an alternative kingdom, centred on the city of Bourges and the region around the Loire. Once again, there were two claimants to the throne, and the English would have to enforce their rights through further conquest.

For a while their fortunes prospered. Bedford was an able administrator – and he was supported by the gifted military commander, Thomas Montagu, Earl of Salisbury. The two of them won a stunning victory against the French and their allies the Scots at Verneuil on 17 August 1424. Verneuil has been rightly dubbed 'a second Agincourt'. Again, powerful pre-battle ritual and devotion to St George was used to motivate the army. The French had brought in new, heavily armoured cavalry from Milan, and these Lombard horsemen were as devastating as the cavalry at Agincourt had been useless. The bowmen could make little headway against their high-quality armour and the horsemen crashed through the entire English line. But the archers picked themselves up and joined the men-at-arms with a great shout. The revitalised army took the battle to their opponents – and won. All men who had fought in the English army – archers and men-at-arms – were rewarded with land. The wonderful sense of unity that had been born at Agincourt came to fruition at Verneuil, and together these two battles consolidated England's military reputation. Its standing army was now rightly regarded as the best in Europe.

Disaster struck four years later. The Earl of Salisbury was struck by a chance cannon ball at the siege of Orléans and died of his wounds. He was a genuine war hero and the English nation was devastated. An army under Joan of Arc subsequently relieved the city and defeated the English at Patay. Shortly afterwards Charles VII was crowned at Reims. Little by little, England lost her French possessions. By 1450 Normandy had fallen; by 1453 Gascony had gone as well – leaving Calais as the last English outpost in France.

Yet Agincourt was remembered long after enthusiasm for Henry's war in France had diminished. The king had wanted the battle to be properly commemorated. On the eve of his invasion of Normandy, in 1417, he decreed that anyone who had worn a heraldic surcoat at the battle had the right to bear a coat of arms. This royal act needs clarification. All the great lords on Henry's expedition were entitled to a coat of arms anyway, along with about 80 knights and perhaps 1,200 squires who had fought for the king. But surcoats also seem to have been distributed along the line before the battle. Henry was choosing to extend the honour to ordinary soldiers – making clear that nobility could also be won through participation in the fight. Some took up the offer, and the special clause for 'the men who, with the king, bore arms at the battle of Agincourt' recognised the bond forged between them – they were a real band of brothers.

One man determined to perpetuate the memory was the king's brother, Humphrey, Duke of Gloucester. Gloucester commissioned a life of Henry V by the Italian humanist Titus Livius, who was able to draw on Duke Humphrey's recollections of the battle. Sixty years on, in 1475, it was ordinary soldiers – now marching with Edward IV's army in northern France, and passing close to Agincourt, who paid tribute to the great battle in their letters home. In

1513 King Henry VIII, about to go to war in France himself, commissioned an English life – Titus Livius had written his in Latin – of the victor of Agincourt and sought to emulate him.

The English garrison at Calais always marked the anniversary of the battle: 'going in procession, praising God, shooting guns, with the noise and melody of trumpets and other instruments'. By the mid-Tudor period both Henry V's courage and the quality of his leadership at the battle were firmly in the collective memory. Edward Hall recalled Henry's defiant address to his troops before Agincourt: 'England shall never pay ransom, nor Frenchman triumph over me, for this day by famous death or glorious victory, I will obtain honour and fame.' And his men responded superbly to his leadership. As the popular refrain – the 'Bowman's Glory' – put it:

> *Agincourt, Agincourt!*
> *Know ye not Agincourt?*
> *Never to be forgot*
> *Or known to no men?*
> *Where English cloth yard arrows*
> *Killed the French like tame sparrows,*
> *Slain by our bowmen.*

Agincourt's story is still remembered at times of war or crisis and rightly so. The outcome was quite astonishing. Henry V was a natural leader. He understood the science of war and the language of chivalry – even if, at moments of crisis, he put necessity first. But his exceptional qualities were timeless: outstanding courage, a brilliant military instinct and remarkable empathy with his men. The best commanders make do with what they have and can conjure something extraordinary out of nothing.

But while Henry has been remembered for posterity, the man who created the winning battle plan with him, Edward, Duke of York, has largely been forgotten. York's vital role in securing the English victory was remembered throughout much of the fifteenth century, and, on the sixtieth anniversary of the clash, in 1475, Edward IV invaded France with a new army and on his march visited the battlefield of Agincourt. One of his soldiers, John Albon, dashed off a letter from the very place on 27 July 1475, saying how the king, his lords and army 'were at Agincourt this day', and speculating 'whether the French king will give him battle or not'.

And it was from Agincourt that Edward IV taunted his adversary, Louis XI of France. Edward, Duke of York had been the English king's great-uncle – and Edward kept the memory of his achievement in 1415 alive by issuing a hunting challenge to the French king: 'We shall hunt through the parts of France and there I will blow my horn and release my hounds.'

He then made a deliberate allusion to his distinguished predecessor, his hunting manual and the tactics that had won the battle, declaring emphatically: 'I am the master of game.'

In the Tudor period memory of York's achievement was lost. His political reputation was traduced and the astonishing legend was invented (without a shred of contemporary evidence) that York was fat, and because of his weight was either knocked to the ground and suffocated in his armour or suffered a heart attack. A comic caricature, he was marginalised from the battle story he had helped to create. In fact, the records of York's household show a regimen of abstinence rather than gluttony, with frequent fasting during religious festivals. And they bring out, time and again, his enthusiasm for hunting and an active lifestyle. On this 600th anniversary it is only right that he once again takes centre stage.

Henry and York had no idea where or when they would be fighting until shortly before Agincourt commenced. But their improvised use of Sts Crispin and Crispinian, and the hunting plan that accompanied it, was a stroke of genius. They stoked the fires of ordinary soldiers before the battle – the opposing French saw them as expendable, just like their hapless fellows at Soissons – and gave everyone a part to play in the clash of arms that followed. Their men responded with bravery, discipline and determination and fully deserved their astounding victory. Their voices deserve to be remembered, for Shakespeare was right:

> *This story shall the good man teach his son*
> *And Crispin Crispian shall ne'er go by,*
> *From this day to the ending of the world,*
> *But we in it shall be remembered.*

Voices from Agincourt

Thomas Basin was from a well-to-do family in the Norman town of Caudebec. A child at the time of Agincourt, he grew into a perceptive observer of human affairs, castigating the English as more devils than men and then astutely forging a career in their service, rising to become Bishop of Lisieux before jumping ship – at just the right time – when the French forces of Charles VII regained Normandy in 1449–50. At its best, Basin's writing was powerful and moving, and he certainly consulted those who had witnessed events. His account of Agincourt was short, but contained telling detail on the rout of the French infantry – the judgement of God, Basin believed, on a sinful and corrupt regime.

Jean le Meingre, Marshal Boucicaut, marshal of France and one of the premier chivalric figures of his age, whose deeds were celebrated in a biography written during his lifetime. The author of the original French battle plan for Agincourt – a course of action that was never followed, with tragic consequences – Boucicaut was taken prisoner by the English and died in captivity.

Jean de Bueil, an accomplished soldier who wrote a semifictional account of his exploits, *Le Jouvencel* (the Youth). De Bueil's father and two uncles died at Agincourt – and he wrote some brief but perceptive comments on the failure of the French infantry advance, drawn from the testimony of survivors of the battle.

Perceval de Cagny, a chronicler in the pay of the Duke of Alençon, who (unsurprisingly) always tried to portray his master in the best possible light. Alençon did not make things easy for him: fighting at Agincourt with all the finesse of a testosterone-charged bull, he abandoned his command of the second division so that he could be first to strike at the enemy, and then abandoned his retinue as well to carve a passage towards the English king, before being overwhelmed and cut down several yards short of his destination.

The English chaplain, the anonymous author of the *Gesta Henrici Quinti* (*The Deeds of Henry V*), is one of the most important sources for Agincourt. A priest attached to the royal household, he witnessed at first hand the terrible suffering of Henry V's army on the march, and watched the victory pageant in London on the expedition's return, but wisely spent most of the battle praying for a success in the relative safety of the baggage train.

Pierre de Cochon, a priest at Rouen and loyal supporter of Charles VI who briefly chronicled the bad decision making by the French that set up the disaster of Agincourt.

Edmond de Dynter, secretary and chronicler of Anthony, Duke of Brabant, who recounted in moving detail the duke's brave but mind-bogglingly stupid rush towards the battlefield, an event that made the Charge of the Light Brigade look in comparison like a model of careful military planning.

Thomas Elmham, a Canterbury monk who wrote one of the earliest accounts of the campaign (it was completed by November 1418) and was particularly interested in the ritual used by Henry V to motivate his troops.

Sir John Fastolf, first off the boats at Harfleur. It is unclear whether this Norfolk soldier fought at Agincourt or stayed in the English garrison at the Norman port, but there is no doubt that he was inspired by the battle's outcome, fighting in France for the next 20 years and then building a fine castle at Caister with the spoils. He shared his reflections on war, courage and discipline with his secretary William Worcester.

Jean Le Fèvre, a 19-year-old-herald present with the English army at the battle.

Humphrey, Duke of Gloucester, a younger brother of Henry V, whose life was saved by the king during the battle. Humphrey never forgot Agincourt, and more than 20 years later commissioned an Italian humanist, Tito Livio Frulovisi (Titus Livius), to write an account of Henry's life, drawing on his own recollections.

John Hardyng served on the Agincourt campaign in the retinue of Sir Richard Umfraville. A brave and idealistic soldier, schooled in warfare on the Scottish border, he attracted the attention of Henry V, who commissioned him to study and map the defences there. Disillusioned by the senseless death of Sir Richard's nephew, Sir Gilbert Umfraville, one of the heroes of Agincourt, at the battle of Baugé (1421), one of the most stupid military engagements conducted by the English during the entire Hundred Years War (where Henry V's brother, Thomas, Duke of Clarence, whimsically decided over supper to take on a nearby Franco-Scottish army, and rode off into the gathering twilight without proper reconnaissance and lacking most of his archers), Hardyng spent the latter part of his career as a forger of documents and falsifier of expense accounts. His notes on Agincourt are brief but contain snippets of value.

Sir Walter (later Lord) Hungerford. Hungerford's understandable if tactless request for thousands more archers before Agincourt did not get in the way of a highly successful career in the service of the Lancastrian dynasty, both before and after the battle. More than 30 years later, perhaps encouraged by the literary patronage of Humphrey, Duke of Gloucester, he commissioned an Italian humanist (whose identity is not known) to write up the events of Henry V's reign (the source is referred to by the cumbersome title of the 'Pseudo Elmham').

Jean Juvenal des Ursins, an articulate and well-informed lawyer, prolific writer and loyal servant to the French house of Valois.

Ghillebert de Lannoy, a chivalric warrior and inveterate traveller who charmed everyone he met. His reminiscences of Agincourt were brief, but he struck up a friendship with his captor Sir John Cornwall, who arranged his quick release and helped him purchase fresh military equipment. Henry V, intrigued by Lannoy's appetite for adventure, sent him on another great journey, a tour of the eastern Mediterranean and a survey of the ports of Egypt and Syria.

Enguerrand de Monstrelet, a self-styled successor to Jean Froissart, whose work lacked flair but was thorough, reasonably impartial and historically accurate.

Arthur de Richemont, a younger brother of the Duke of Brittany and a brave and able soldier who commanded a retinue at Agincourt and lost consciousness in the crush of troops fighting around Henry V's standard. After the battle he was pulled out alive from under a mound of corpses. Quickly ransomed, he enjoyed a long and distinguished military career, becoming constable of France and fighting with Joan of Arc. He never forgot the lessons of Agincourt, conducting a tour of the battlefield there in the summer of 1436. In the 1440s he initiated much-needed reforms of the French army and in 1450 he presided over the defeat of the English at Formigny, marking the end of their occupation of Normandy. His military recollections were gathered, after his death, by his household servant Guillaume Gruel.

Ruisseauville chronicler. An informed chronicler with local information on the battle.

The Monk of Saint-Denis, a remarkable writer and chronicler of the reign of Charles VI, now identified as Michel Pintouin. Always perceptive, and a careful researcher, he reconstructed two particularly dreadful events, the *Bal des Ardents* (Ball of the Burning Men), when a drunken Louis, Duke of Orléans put the torch to half the French court, and the battle of Agincourt, when his sober son Charles put the torch to most of the French nobility.

Titus Livius, the more familiar name of the Italian scholar Tito Livio Frulovisi, commissioned by Humphrey, Duke of Gloucester to write a life of Henry V.

Jean de Waurin was a 15-year-old Burgundian page present with the French army at Agincourt. He later fought in battles in his own right, and when his career as a warrior was over compiled a chivalric chronicle that borrowed heavily from Monstrelet and only enlarged upon incidents that Waurin was particularly interested in.

Thomas Walsingham, a monk of St Albans and an intelligent commentator on English political affairs. Walsingham was saddened by the country's military decline after the death of the Black Prince and delighted by Henry V's achievement at Agincourt.

Edward, Duke of York, hero of Agincourt, friend and mentor of the king. York created with his royal master the plan that won Agincourt and he died executing it. His book *The Master of Game* is the first treatise on hunting in the English language – and gives a valuable insight into how the battle was won.

Hunting Ritual and the Start of the Battle

THERE HAS, UNTIL NOW, been only one way of describing how Agincourt commenced – and our understanding of the battle is usually based on this interpretation. It runs as follows:

Henry V, after consultation with his senior captains, gave the order for the army to advance. The defensive stakes, which protected the archers' positions, were then pulled up, and the whole English army began to move across the battlefield. They continued their advance until they were at extreme bow-shot range – at between two and three hundred yards from the French army. Then the English stopped, reformed their line and the archers hammered their stakes back in. Then they put the French troops under intense arrow fire and after a short interval, first the French cavalry, and then the infantry, moved forward to attack them.

This substantial English advance on the French position was first suggested by Sir John Woodford, who did valuable research on the battlefield site in the aftermath of another famous victory – Waterloo – and mapped Agincourt in 1818. His version of events was followed by Henry V's biographer, Charles Kingsford, at the beginning of the twentieth century, and further developed by Colonel Alfred Burne in his study of the battle some 50 years later. His depiction of how Agincourt began was incorporated into all subsequent accounts.

Here is how Christopher Allmand summed it up in his 1992 biography of Henry V:

'Slowly the army advanced the better part of 700 yards, stopping some 200 yards short of the enemy, now within range of the English arrows. There the archers drove into the ground the stakes, which each had been ordered to cut some days before. It was from this second position that the English were to fight the battle. At a range of some 200 yards the English began to rain arrows upon the French.'

All the sources confirm two things. That after waiting for several hours Henry V ordered his army to advance. And that some at least of the English archers moved up to within bow range of the French position, put the enemy under fire, after which the French began their own attack.

The chronicle evidence for Agincourt – as with medieval battles in general – is sometimes contradictory, ambiguous or not easy to evaluate. But nowhere do the sources specifically indicate that the entire English army advanced to within bow range of the French. What Jean de Waurin and Enguerrand de Monstrelet do say is this:

'The English approached the French. First the archers began, with all their might, to shoot volleys of arrows against the French, for as long as they could pull the bow.'

So the assumption is, firstly, *all* the English archers approached to within bow range of the French and, secondly, that the entire battle line accompanied them. It is a plausible way of making sense of this evidence, and the ongoing shape of the battle in general. And the logic of Woodford's and Burne's interpretation of the English advance is clear. Once Henry decided to move forward, he needed to reach a position where he could dictate the battle, and setting up a new line for his army within bow range fitted the bill.

But there is a fundamental problem with this reading: knee-deep in mud, how long would it take the combined line of English men-at-arms and archers to advance – needing to keep in formation and with the men-at-arms encumbered by their armour – and set up their second line? The manoeuvre would expose them dreadfully. Professor Clifford Rogers has estimated that it would take soldiers in heavy armour 20 minutes to cover 450 yards of Agincourt's rain-soaked fields, and thus over half an hour to reach the new line – and then they would have to hammer in their stakes.

The English would be a sitting target for the French cavalry throughout this operation – giving their opponents plenty of notice of their intentions and the chance to launch their attack while the archers were without protection. Dr Matthew Strickland has acknowledged the serious problem with the accepted version:

'This was a dangerous manoeuvre, for it meant they had to abandon the defensive position on which they were so reliant and that for the moment the stakes carried by the archers would be of no protection; if the French cavalry units were to launch a sudden charge at this critical moment, all might be lost.'

Since the French had cavalry forces on the wings and, in this scenario, plenty of time to use them when the English were vulnerable, it is hard to imagine that they obligingly waited until the archers got within bow range, and then allowed them to hammer in their stakes and begin firing before launching their charge.

Henry V was, of course, on the horns of a dilemma. He wanted to get things started. But he also wanted, if at all possible, to preserve the advantages of his defensive position, on firm ground at the narrow end of the funnel – and make the French do most of the work.

The alternative scenario – in which Henry and the Duke of York used hunting ritual to provoke the French into launching their attack – helps explain a number of aspects of the battle:

1: The French cavalry units were understrength.

Monstrelet related that a group of English archers were pulled out in front of the main battle line of archers and men-at-arms. If these men – unburdened with the weight of armour – then ran quickly towards the French position and began firing (as the Ruisseauville chronicler suggests), following the tactics used at the battle of Neville's Cross in 1346, and the rest of the English army moved forward a short distance and goaded the French, who reacted quickly, the cavalry units would not have had time to gather their men and get back to full strength before the charge.

If, on the other hand, the entire English army had traversed the muddy fields, pausing to keep in alignment, there would have been ample opportunity for the French to gather all their horsemen and then charge at their opponents.

2: Sir Thomas Erpingham's signal and the hunting cry.

Shortly before the English advance, Sir Thomas Erpingham inspected the archers' position and then, riding along the line, threw his marshal's baton high in the air. After this dramatic gesture he shouted a word rendered, with minor variations, by Monstrelet, Waurin and Le Fèvre as 'Nestrocque!' If we accept the most plausible explanation of this command as '*menée* stroke' (as a number of recent studies on the longbow have done), the order to blow the 'stroke' or horn call known as the '*menée*' (the call used for hunting deer), rather than 'Knee stretch!' or 'Now strike!', commands that make little sense with the English bowmen well out of range of their opponents – we introduce hunting ritual and provocation into the opening stage of the battle.

Monstrelet was a painstaking chronicler much concerned with historical accuracy. He was describing something that he felt was significant and unusual. And the English cry that followed – the 'grand hué' – was a specific term meaning the vocal imitation of the hunting horn. Monstrelet stressed that this cry 'was a cause of great amazement to the French'.

If the English were executing a standard manoeuvre to advance, with the usual war cry to accompany it, Erpingham's signal had little point and there was nothing for the French to be amazed about – they would have seen and heard it all before. Hunting ritual provides an explanation for something Monstrelet, Waurin and Le Fèvre considered important. The use of the horn and hunting signals, and bowmen's initiative in the hunt, were of particular interest to the Duke of York in *The Master of Game*.

3: The ambush.

Both Monstrelet and Juvenal des Ursins said the English had placed an archer ambush in a hidden meadow within the Tramecourt side of the woods. Jean Le Fèvre felt compelled to investigate the story, but the soldier he spoke to denied it. However, Matthew Strickland finds it quite believable:

'There is a hint here that some regarded this as something of an underhand ruse, but there seems little reason to doubt the essential plausibility of Henry's attempt to offset the great odds against him by the use of surprise.'

If we accept the existence of the ambush, and follow the traditional account of the battle, it is unclear what this 'surprise' was supposed to achieve. It would have been suicidal for the hidden archers to spur the French into an attack while the English line was still struggling through the mud to get into its second position, less than 300 yards from the French line. But once the English line had reformed, all its bowmen would be able to hit the enemy and fire from the ambush would have little additional impact.

Monstrelet tells us that the archer ambush began firing on the French when Erpingham made his signal and the English gave their great shout. By reframing this sequence, the ploy of concealing the archers makes sense – the ambush was intended to provoke a reaction.

4: The French response.

A number of the chroniclers say that when the English began to advance, and some of their bowmen began to fire on the French, their opponents responded quickly. Thomas Walsingham believed that when the English line started to move forward the French 'considered the moment was favourable to attack'. One version of the Brut chronicle noted that when the command 'Advance banners!' was given to the English army, 'then the French came rushing down, as if to ride over our men'; another, that when the English started to advance, '*immediately* trumpets sounded, and the French came galloping down' (my italics).

Similarly, the Monk of Saint-Denis observed that, when the English started to move forward, '*at almost the same moment* the French advanced against the enemy' (my emphasis). And the anonymous chronicler of Charles VI added that when the French attacked, 'the English … had not moved from their [original] advantageous position'.

These extracts suggest that the French were quickly responding to an act of provocation rather than waiting for the entire English line to get into its new position.

5: The stakes.

If the whole English army was to advance a considerable distance, we have assumed that the stakes, which had been knocked into the ground to protect the archers, must have been pulled out again and dragged forward to the new position. But the sources are unclear on this, and difficult to interpret. Titus Livius put the fixing of stakes after the order to advance. However, the chaplain said the stakes were set into position and the advance followed later. He makes no clear reference to a repositioning of the stake wall.

And the anonymous Italian humanist commissioned by Walter, Lord Hungerford (the Pseudo-Elmham) said that they were left behind when the archers moved forward:

'The archers, *leaving behind them in the field their sharp stakes,* which they had prepared before, in case they met with the French horsemen ...' (my italics).

As the stakes clearly served an important military purpose, it would be surprising if they were abandoned. There is another possibility, that the archers employed a trick, moving out a little way from the stakes, screening them from view and then – as the French cavalry charged, dropping back behind them again. This manoeuvre would ensure the archers remained protected.

However, there is a problem with this idea that needs to be addressed head on. The chaplain related that on the morning of battle some French horsemen had discovered the position of the stake wall and warned their army of it. This seems to rule out the possibility of such a ploy being effective. Matthew Strickland has suggested a way of resolving the issue, one that also allows us to incorporate the apparently conflicting testimony of Titus Livius. If some of the archers in front of the English line had pulled up stakes, carried them on their advance and replanted them further forward when they began shooting at the French, but left the bulk of the stake wall behind them, 'The French could well have been tricked into thinking the English had abandoned all their field defences.'

Marshal Boucicaut had been the architect of the original French battle plan, which intended to use cavalry attacks to bring down the English archers – and Henry had ordered his men to carry sharpened stakes as a response to this threat. This stake wall, screened by the main body of archers, beginning their advance, set up a trap for the French horsemen, rather like the concealed nets used by huntsmen to bring down deer in the forest. Once again, York's expertise in hunting was significant, for one version of the Brut chronicle believed it was he who suggested to the king that every archer use stakes against the enemy.

6: The exhaustion of the French.

A number of sources, both French and English, said that the French men-at-arms were exhausted by crossing the battlefield, while the English remained relatively fresh. Thomas Elmham described the French as 'worn-out and exhausted'; Pierre de Fenin said they were 'much worn down'. And the anonymous chronicler of Charles VI stressed that the French 'were exhausted by their advance', whereas 'the English were fresh and unwearied, as they had not moved from their advantageous position'. Such descriptions would make little sense if the English men-at-arms, not the French, had crossed most of the muddy battlefield.

The Agincourt source material is sometimes challenging and contradictory. For example, the chaplain places the clash of the two lines of men-at-arms halfway across the battlefield (around 450 yards from the English starting position), which does not work in either the traditional interpretation or the new one that I am offering. However, on balance, I think the alternative scenario fits the evidence better. The final stage of the battle, with French exhausted and many of their men being suffocated in the crush, makes more sense with the majority of English troops still positioned near the narrow end of the funnel and their opponents increasingly constricted by the terrain as they continued to advance through the heavy mud towards them. An archer attack, a limited advance by the main body of men-at-arms and archers and ritual provocation of the enemy would achieve that.

Endnotes

Introduction

The main narrative is drawn from Barker, *Agincourt*; Curry, *Agincourt: A New History*; Mortimer, *Henry V's Year of Glory* and my own *Agincourt 1415*. Chroniclers and writers cited from Curry, *Sources and Interpretations* and Dockray, *Warrior King*. Material on the Earl of Oxford is from James Ross, 'Richard de Vere, earl of Oxford', *Oxford DNB*. All detail on Mowbray is cited with acknowledgement to Dr Rowena Archer, who kindly allowed me to use her 1984 Oxford DPhil thesis, 'The Mowbrays, Earls of Nottingham and Dukes of Norfolk, to 1432'. The original account of John Southwell, Mowbray's receiver-general, is Berkeley Castle Muniments, BCM/D/1/30. Material on Cheney is from Roskell etc (eds), *House of Commons, 1386–1422*; for Sir John Bromley's martial endeavour see Matthew Bennett, *Triumph Against the Odds*.

Chapter 1

All the main chronicle material is drawn from Curry, *Sources and Interpretations*. For Cornwall, Simon Payling, 'Sir John Cornwall, Baron Fanhope (d. 1443)', *Oxford DNB*; Barker, *Agincourt*. Details on Bourchier are from *House of Commons, 1386–1422*; and see Henry Summerson on 'John Hardyng' and 'Sir Gilbert Umfraville', *Oxford DNB*. See also Peverley, *John Hardyng's Chronicle*. For Gray, Anne Curry, 'Sir John Gray, Count of Tancarville, soldier and diplomat'; and Lannoy, David Morgan, 'Ghillebert de Lannoy (1386–1462), soldier and diplomat', *Oxford DNB*; Margaret Wade Labarge, 'Ghillebert de Lannoy: Burgundian traveller', *History Today*, 26 (1976). I have followed Allmand, *Henry V*, on the king's date of birth, supplemented by material in Carey, *Courting Disaster* (the alternative is 9 August 1387). For Edward III at Blangy see Rogers, *War Cruel and Sharp*. Brabant's dash to Agincourt is recorded in Edmond de Dynter, *Chronique des Ducs de Brabant*, Brussels (6 vols, 1854–60), vol. 3; see also Serge Boffa, 'Antoine de Bourgogne et le contingent brabançon à la bataille d'Agincourt (1415), *Revue Belge d'Histoire*, 72 (1994).

Chapter 2

Source material is from Curry, and, additionally, Walsingham, *Chronica Maiora*, Commynes, *Memoirs*. Christine de Pizan is cited in Barker, *Agincourt*. For Henry's leadership see my *Agincourt 1415* and forthcoming piece 'A Band of Brothers: Henry V as a military commander', *Medieval Warfare* (Special Agincourt edition, 2015). On risk-taking, see Jan Honig, 'Reappraising late medieval strategy: the example of the 1415 Agincourt campaign', *War in History*, 19 (2012). Ian Mortimer's *Henry V's Year of Glory* brings the king's preparations for the campaign to life. See also Gwilym Dodd, 'Henry V's establishment: service, loyalty and reward in 1413'; and Craig Taylor, 'Henry V: flower of chivalry', in *Henry V: New Interpretations*. Details on Bradmore's operation are from Strickland and Hardy, *Great Warbow*; on Morstede, Barker, *Agincourt*. For Henry's letters as Prince of Wales: Frederick Flood, 'Prince Henry of Monmouth, his letters and dispatches during the war in Wales', *Transactions of the Royal Historical Society*, 4 (1889). Further evidence of the difficulties facing the English in 1415, and the French perception that their forces were in disarray, is found in Edmond Dupont, 'Registre des recettes et dépenses de la ville de Boulogne-sur-Mer (1415), *Mémoires de la Société Académique de Boulogne-sur-Mer*, 7 (1882); Isabelle Clauzel-Delannoy, *Boulogne-sur-Mer en 1415*, giving the town reports sent to the French constable Charles d'Albret. For the context of Henry's famous pre-battle speech, immortalised by Shakespeare, but caught in its likely original form by the English chaplain on the afternoon of 24 October, see Anne Curry, 'The battle speeches of Henry V', *Reading Medieval Studies*, 34 (2008). For Hungerford: *House of Commons 1386–1422*. See also Simon Walker, 'Sir Thomas Erpingham',

Compton Reeves, 'Henry Lord FitzHugh' and John Leland, 'Thomas Lord Camoys', *Oxford DNB*. On Boucicaut see Denis Lalande (ed.), *Le Livre de Fais du Bon Messire Jehan le Meingre, dit Boucicaut, Mareschal de France* (Paris, 1985); Norman Housley, 'Le Maréchal Boucicaut à Nicopolis', *Annales de Bourgogne*, 68 (1996), and 'One man and his wars: the depiction of warfare by Marshal Boucicaut's biographer', *Journal of Medieval History*, 29 (2003), and for his battle plan, drawn up in consultation with d'Albret and de Rambures: Christopher Phillpotts, 'The French plan of battle during the Agincourt campaign', *English Historical Review*, 99 (1984). On d'Albret, 'Instructions secrètes données par Charles VI au sire d'Albret pour soulever la Guyenne contre Henri IV', *Bibliothèque de l'Ecole des Chartes*, 74 (1913).

Chapter 3

All sources cited from Curry, with the exception of de Pizan (Barker, *Agincourt*); Charny (Kaeuper, *Book of Chivalry*); Walsingham, *Chronica Maiora*; the Monk of Saint-Denis, *Chronique du Religieux*. On Henry's army the recent important research is from Anne Curry, *Agincourt: A New History*, and more specifically, Adam Chapman, 'The King's Welshmen: Welsh involvement in the expeditionary army of 1415', in *The Soldier in Later Medieval England*. The Tunstall indenture is found in Nicolas, *Agincourt*. For Rokesby, Henry Summerson, 'Sir Thomas Rokesby, soldier and administrator'; Trussell and Chaworth, *House of Commons, 1386–1422*. See also Barker, *Agincourt*, and Mercer, *The Rebirth of Chivalry*; and for the growing status of the archer, Strickland and Hardy, *Great Warbow*. For Popham: Anne Curry, 'Sir John Popham', *Oxford DNB*.

Chapter 4

For a discussion of the chroniclers see Curry, *Sources and Interpretations*, and Dockray, *Warrior King*. All chronicles cited are from Curry, *Sources*, with the exception of Brereton (ed.), *Froissart*, and Stevenson (ed), *Scalacronica*. For 'Knyghthode and Bataille' see Allmand, *Vegetius*. All discussion of Dupplin Moor and Halidon

Hill is from Strickland and Hardy, *Great Warbow*. For Sir Thomas
Dagworth see Sumption, *Trial by Fire*, and Michael C.E. Jones,
'Sir Thomas Dagworth et la guerre civile', *Annales de Bretagne*, 88
(1980). Material on the Black Prince's campaign of 1356 is from
Hewitt, *Black Prince's Expedition*; La Capelle, 1338, is from Rogers,
War Cruel and Sharp. The Orléans challenge is from Barker,
Agincourt. I owe the funnel effect at Crécy and the creation of a
killing ground to Sir Philip Preston; the tactics at Neville's Cross to
Professor Michael Prestwich. The unfolding narrative of Nicopolis
is from Housley, 'Boucicaut à Nicopolis'. For a welcome reappraisal
of Edward, Duke of York see Rosemary Horrox, 'Edward, Duke of
York', *Oxford DNB*; Barker, *Agincourt*, and Mortimer, *Henry V's
Year of Victory*. Henry's petition on behalf of York is from *Parliament
Rolls of Medieval England*. For York and Henry staying together at
Cardiff and Hanley Castle in 1409–10 see the household account
of the Duke of York: Northampts Record Office, W(A), box 4,
parcel XX, no. 4, fully transcribed in James Toomey, 'Noble house-
hold management and spiritual discipline in fifteenth-century
Worcestershire: a household account of Edward, Duke of York at
Hanley Castle, 1409–10', *Worcestershire Historical Society*, 24
(2013). They hunted together at Tewkesbury between 14 and 21
December 1409. The Prince of Wales standing as godfather to
Robert Morton's son Henry is from *House of Commons 1386–1422*.
For the hunting ritual, *The Master of Game*; supplemented by James
McNelis, 'The uncollated manuscripts of The Master of Game:
towards a new edition (University of Washington PhD thesis,
1997); Cummins, *The Hound and the Hawk*; Marvin, *Hunting
Law and Ritual*; Ryan Judkins, 'The game of the courtly hunt:
chasing and breaking deer in late medieval literature', *Journal of
English and Germanic Philology*, 112 (2013); Eric Weiskott,
'Chaucer the forester: the friar's tale, forest history and officialdom',
The Chaucer Review, 47 (2013).

Chapter 5

All chronicles cited (and additional background information from
the French side) are from Curry, *Sources and Interpretations*, with

the exception of Walsingham on Sir Hugh Calveley, from *Chronica Maiora* and the quotation from Vegetius: Milner, *Vegetius: Epitome of Military Science*. I owe the details of Courtrai to Kelly de Vries's excellent discussion in *Infantry Battles*. Social pride in armour is from Nigel Saul, *For Honour and Fame*. Sir James Douglas's obituary and Valmont (1416) are from Strickland and Hardy, *Great Warbow*. Ufford at Poitiers is from Hewitt, *Black Prince's Expedition*. For St John of Beverley I am grateful to Professor Michael Prestwich and Philip Morgan, 'The naming of battlefields in the Middle Ages', in *War and Society in Medieval and early Modern Britain*. Further information can be found in Stouck, *Medieval Saints*. Hunting material is from Cummins, *Hound and Hawk*; *The Master of Game;* McNelis, 'The uncollated manuscripts of The Master of Game'; Marvin, *Hunting Law and Ritual*; and Eva Marie Heater, 'Early hunting horn calls and their transmission: some new discoveries', *Historic Brass Society Journal*, 7 (1995).

Chapter 6

All citations are from Curry, *Sources and Interpretations*, with the exception of Milner, *Vegetius*; Nichols (ed.), *Boke of Noblesse*; Bellaguet (ed.), *Chronique du Religieux*. For a sample of John Bromyard's writing see Allmand (ed.), *Society at War*. For the Black Prince at Poitiers see Barber, *Edward Prince of Aquitaine*. Details on Auray and Cocherel are from Strickland and Hardy, *Great Warbow*; Crécy from Ayton and Preston, *Crécy*. For Bertrand du Guesclin, Michael C.E. Jones, *Letters and Orders of du Guesclin*. On the knowledge of fourteenth-century battles, and their likely influence on a commander's thinking in 1415, see Kenneth Fowler, 'News from the front: letters and despatches of the fourteenth century', in *Guerre et Société*. On literature and chivalric attitude I am indebted to Catherine Nall, *Reading and War*, and Craig Taylor, *Ideals of Knighthood*.

Chapter 7

All chroniclers cited from Curry, *Sources and Interpretations*, except broader references from Walsingham, *Chronica Maiora*.

On the *Troy Book* see Nall, *Reading and War*. For Poitiers, Barber, *Edward Prince of Aquitaine*; Mauron, Castagnaro and Othée, Strickland and Hardy, *Great Warbow*. For the ongoing battle narrative, and the vexed question of numbers on either side, Clifford Rogers, 'The battle of Agincourt', in Villalon and Kagay (eds), *The Hundred Years War*, II, has been particularly helpful. For the archer ambush and the use of deception see the recent comments of Jan Honig, 'Agincourt campaign'. The battle of Othée is described in Vaughan, *John the Fearless*. On the Dukes of Orléans, Bourbon and chivalric pride, see Champion, *Vie de Charles d'Orléans*; Tracy Adams, 'The political significance of Christine de Pizan's love poetry', *Cahiers de Recherches Médiévales et Humanistes*, 17 (2009); James Laidlaw's work on Christine de Pizan at the court of Charles VI on www.pizan.lib.ed.ac.uk/harley4431date.pdf and for Thomas Walsingham's perceptive comments on both Louis and Charles, Duke of Orléans: *Chronica Maiora*.

Chapter 8

All sources from Curry with the exception of Brereton (ed.), *Froissart*. For Neville's Cross see Rollason and Prestwich, *Neville's Cross 1346*; Crécy, Ayton and Preston, *Crécy*; hunting ritual, Cummins, *Hound and Hawk*, and Strickland and Hardy, *Great Warbow*. For recent views that 'Nestrocque' is most likely a contracted form of 'menée strake', see Loades, *Longbow*, and Soar, *Crooked Stick*. The argument on the English starting position has been refined in the light of comments by Clifford Rogers, 'Battle of Agincourt', Appendix III; see also the Appendix in this present book. For Sir Walter de Mauny, Sumption, *Trial by Battle*. Hiding the position of the stake wall by a screen of archers is from Matthew Bennett's important article, 'The development of battle tactics in the Hundred Years War', in *Arms, Armies and Fortifications*.

Chapter 9

All sources from Curry with exception of Lecestre (ed.), *Le Jouvencel*, and Nichols (ed.), *Boke of Noblesse*. Detail on Neville's

Cross I owe to Professor Prestwich; De Boissay, Barker, *Agincourt*; Crécy, to Sir Philip Preston. For armour and marching pace see Rogers, 'Battle of Agincourt'. The TV series *Battlefield Detectives* did a valuable survey of the battle in *Agincourt's Dark Secrets* (Channel 5, 2004); see particularly the work of Professor Andrew Palmer on soil composition and Dr Keith Still on crowd control. For Davy Gam, Rees Davies, 'Dafydd Gam', *Oxford DNB*; Jean de Longueval's petition is also in Curry, *Sources*.

Chapter 10

For the death of York see Kingsford, *Chronicles of London*. The casualties among his retinue are from the National Archives, E101/45/2, 19 and 47/40. The military prowess of York's soldiers is now receiving a welcome appraisal: Gary Baker, 'To Agincourt and beyond! The martial affinity of Edward duke of York', paper to be delivered at the forthcoming Agincourt 600 conference, 'War on land and sea: Agincourt in context'. Details on Dupplin Moor and Roosebeke are from Strickland and Hardy, *Great Warbow*. For Trussell and his prisoner tally: *House of Commons, 1386–1422*. On Brabant's dramatic arrival see Serge Boffa, 'Antoine de Bourgogne', and for his armour (or lack of it) Ralph Moffat, 'The importance of being harnest: armour, heraldry and recognition in the mêlée', in *Battle and Bloodshed*. For Aljubarrota, Thomas Izbicki, 'The punishment of pride: Castilian reactions to the battle of Aljubarrota', in *Medieval Iberia*. The killing of the prisoners is well discussed in general in McGlynn, *By Sword and Fire*.

Chapter 11

For this see Philip Morgan, 'The naming of battlefields in the Middle Ages', *War and Society*. And for a useful comparison with Agincourt, Kathleen Daly, 'War, history and memory in the Dauphiné in the fifteenth century: two accounts of the battle of Authon', in *Rule, Redemption and Representation*. For London, Dan Spencer, 'How did the city of London react to the news of the battle?': www.agincourt600.com. On the French sense of loss, in addition to sources drawn from Curry, see Archives Communales de Nevers, CC 20; Megan Cassidy-Welch, 'Grief and memory after the battle of Agincourt', Villalon and Kagay (eds), *The Hundred Years War*, II. For Chartier, Christopher Allmand, 'After Agincourt: women and pain', *History Today*, 62 (2012). The Saint-Sariol petition is from Cooper, *Agincourt: Myth and Reality*. On the visit to the battlefield from the citizens of Amiens, Archives Communales d'Amiens, CC 16; on the loss felt in Picardy, Archives Municipales de Saint-Quentin (1415–16). For the reaction of John the Fearless see Schnerb, *Jean Sans Peur*; Breton casualties are listed in Archives Départementales des Côtes d'Armor, lordship of Moncontour, 1 E 624, folios 23–31, noting tenements vacant at the end of 1415 because of losses at the battle. Such was the shock in Brittany that witnesses at an inquiry in 1434, nearly 20 years later, still used Agincourt ('la journée qui fut Aziencourt') as a reference point for dating events: ibid., E 1529, m. 6 (I owe these references to Professor Michael C.E. Jones).

Beyond 24 Hours

For the general outline: Barker, *Conquest*. Adam of Usk's comments are from *Chronicle of Adam of Usk, 1377–1421*. On English pride in their victory, Helen Deeming, 'The sources and origin of the "Agincourt Carol"', *Early Music*, 35 (2007); Nicola Coldstream, '"Pavilion'd in splendour": Henry V's Agincourt pageants', *Journal of the British Archaeological Association*, 165 (2012). On the fate of the French prisoners, Rémy Ambühl, 'Le sort des prisonniers d'Azincourt (1415)', *Revue du Nord*, 89 (2007). For York's tomb and memorial at Fotheringhay, Sofija Matich and Jennifer Alexander, 'Creating and recreating the Yorkist tombs at Fotheringhay Church (Northampts)', *Church Monuments*, 26 (2011). Detail on Cheney and Burton is from *House of Commons, 1386–1422*. For Baugé, John Milner, 'The battle of Baugé, March 1421: impact and memory', *History*, 91 (2006). Much of the narrative has been drawn from my *Agincourt 1415* and one of my articles: 'The battle of Verneuil (17 August 1424): towards a history of courage', *War in History*, 9 (2002). For Edward IV's hunting challenge to Louis XI see Colin Richmond, '1485 and all that, or what was going on at the battle of Bosworth', in *Richard III: Loyalty, Lordship and Law*. Abstinence and fasting in York's household is found in Toomey, 'Noble household management and spiritual discipline'. The first reference to York as a 'fatte man' occurs in John Leland's *Itinerary*, compiled in the early 1540s – there is no contemporary evidence for such an assertion: Barker, *Agincourt*. For the duke regarding courage as ennobling, an attitude he shared with Henry V, see William Salt Library, S/ Ms. 31 (29 August 1415): York granting a coat-of-arms to John Bruggeforde for his good services during the siege of Harfleur (kindly drawn to my attention by Dr Gary Baker).

Bibliography

Allmand, Christopher (ed.), *Society at War: The Experience of England and France during the Hundred Years War* (Woodbridge, 1973); *The Hundred Years War* (Cambridge, 1988); *Henry V* (London, 1992); *The De Re Militari of Vegetius: The Reception, Transmission and Legacy of a Roman Text in the Middle Ages* (Cambridge, 2011)

Ambühl, Rémy, *Prisoners of War in the Hundred Years War: Ransom Culture in the Late Middle Ages* (Cambridge, 2013)

Arn, Mary-Jo (ed.), *Charles d'Orléans in England, 1415–1440* (Woodbridge, 2000)

Autrand, Françoise, *Charles VI: Folie du Roi* (Paris, 1988)

Ayton, Andrew, and Preston, Sir Philip, *The Battle of Crécy, 1346* (Woodbridge, 2005)

Baillie-Grohman, William (ed.), *The Master of Game by Edward Duke of York* (New York, 1919)

Barber, Richard, *Edward, Prince of Wales and Aquitaine* (Woodbridge, 1978); *Edward III and the Triumph of England* (London, 2013)

Barker, Juliet, *Agincourt: The King, the Campaign, the Battle* (London, 2005); *Conquest: The English Kingdom of France in the Hundred Years War* (London, 2009)

Bellaguet, Louis (ed.), *Chronique du Religieux de Saint-Denys* (Paris, 1839)

Bennett, Matthew, *Agincourt 1415: Triumph Against the Odds* (Oxford, 1991)

Bleach, Lorna, and Borrill, Keira, *Battle and Bloodshed: The Medieval World at War* (Newcastle, 2013)

Boffa, Sergio, *Warfare in Medieval Brabant* (Woodbridge, 2004)

Burne, Alfred, *The Agincourt War* (London, 1956)

Carey, Hilary, *Courting Disaster: Astrology at the English Court in the Later Middle Ages* (New York, 1992)

Champion, Pierre, *Vie de Charles d'Orléans 1394–1465* (Paris, 1911)

Clark, Linda (ed.), *The Fifteenth Century*, VIII: *Rule, Redemption and Representation in Late Medieval England and France* (Woodbridge, 2008)

Contamine, Philippe, *War in the Middle Ages* (New York, 1984)

Contamine, Philippe, Giry-Deloison, Charles, and Keen, Maurice (eds), *Guerre et Société en France, en Angleterre et en Bourgogne* (Lille, 1991)

Cooper, Stephen, *Agincourt: Myth and Reality, 1415–2015* (Barnsley, 2014)

Cummins, John, *The Hound and the Hawk: The Art of Medieval Hunting* (London, 1988)

Curry, Anne, *The Battle of Agincourt: Sources and Interpretations* (Woodbridge, 2000); (ed.), *Henry V, Sir Thomas Erpingham and the Triumph of the English Archers* (Stroud, 2000); *Agincourt: A New History* (Stroud, 2005)

Curry, Anne, and Hughes, Michael (eds), *Arms, Armies and Fortifications in the Hundred Years War* (Woodbridge, 1994)

Davies, Rees, *The Revolt of Owain Glyn Dwr* (Oxford, 1995)

De Vries, Kelly, *Infantry Warfare in the Early Fourteenth Century* (Woodbridge, 1996)

Dockray, Keith, *Warrior King: The Life of Henry V* (Stroud, 2004)

Dodd, Gwilym (ed.), *Henry V: New Interpretations* (Woodbridge, 2013)

Dunn, Diana (ed.), *War and Society in Medieval and Early Modern Britain* (Liverpool, 2000)

Ellis, Henry (ed.), *The Chronicle of John Hardyng* (London, 1812)

Given-Wilson, Christopher (ed.), *The Chronicle of Adam of Usk, 1377–1421* (Oxford, 1997); (ed.), *The Parliament Rolls of Medieval England* (Leicester, 2005)

Goodman, Anthony, *The Wars of the Roses: The Soldiers' Experience* (Stroud, 2005)

Green, David, *The Hundred Years War: A People's History* (London, 2014)

Grummitt, David, *Henry VI* (Abingdon, 2015)

Hewitt, Herbert, *The Black Prince's Expedition of 1355–1357* (Manchester, 1958)

Hibbert, Christopher, *Agincourt* (London, 1995)

Hoskins, Peter, with Curry, Anne, *Agincourt 1415: A Tourist's Guide to the Campaign* (Barnsley, 2014)

Jones, Michael, *Agincourt 1415: A Battlefield Guide* (Barnsley, 2005)

Jones, Michael C.E. (ed.), *Memoirs of Philippe de Commynes* (London, 1972); *Letters, Orders and Musters of Bertrand du Guesclin, 1357–1380* (Woodbridge, 2004)

Jones, Robert, *Bloodied Banners: Martial Display on the Medieval Battlefield* (Woodbridge, 2010)

Kaeuper, Richard, *Chivalry and Violence in Medieval Europe* (Oxford, 1994)

Kaeuper, Richard, and Kennedy, Elspeth (eds), *The Book of Chivalry of Geoffroi de Charny* (Philadelphia, 1996)

Kagay, Donald, and Snow, Joseph (eds), *Medieval Iberia: Essays on the History and Literature of Medieval Spain* (New York, 1997)

Keegan, Sir John, *The Face of Battle* (London, 1976)

Keen, Maurice, *Chivalry* (London, 1984)

Kingsford, Charles, *Chronicles of London* (Oxford, 1905)

Lalande, Denis, *Jean II le meingre, dit Boucicaut (1366–1421)* (Geneva, 1988)

Lecestre, Léon (ed.), *Le Jouvencel par Jean de Bueil* (Paris, 1887)

Le Vavasseur, Achille (ed.), *Chronique d'Arthur de Richemont par Guillaume Gruel* (Paris, 1890)

Loades, Mike, *The Longbow* (Oxford, 2013)

Marvin, William Perry, *Hunting Law and Ritual in Medieval English Literature* (Rochester, New York, 2006)

McGlynn, Sean, *By Sword and Fire: Cruelty and Atrocity in Medieval Warfare* (London, 2008)

Mercer, Malcolm, *Henry V: The Rebirth of Chivalry* (Kew, 2004)

Milner, Nicholas, *Vegetius: Epitome of Military Science* (Liverpool, 1996)

Mortimer, Ian, *1415: Henry V's Year of Glory* (London, 2009)

Nall, Catherine, *Reading and War in Fifteenth-Century England: From Lydgate to Malory* (Cambridge, 2012)

Nicolas, Sir Harris, *History of the Battle of Agincourt* (London, 1832)

Nichols, John (ed.), *William Worcester: The Boke of Noblesse* (London, 1860)

Nuttall, Jenni, *The Creation of Lancastrian Kingship: Literature, Language and Politics in Late Medieval England* (Cambridge, 2007)

Peverley, Sarah (ed.), *John Hardyng's Chronicle: Edited from British Library Lansdowne 204* (Kalamazoo, Michigan, 2015)

Preest, David, and Clark, James (eds), *The Chronica Maiora of Thomas Walsingham (1376–1422)* (Woodbridge, 2005)

Prestwich, Michael, *Armies and Warfare in the Middle Ages: The English Experience* (London, 1999)

Poitevin, Charles (ed.), *Oeuvres de Ghillebert de Lannoy* (Louvain, 1878)

Pollard, Anthony, *Henry V* (Stroud, 2014)

Rogers, Clifford, *War Cruel and Sharp: English Strategy under Edward III, 1327–1360* (Woodbridge, 2000)

Rollason, David, and Prestwich, Michael (eds), *The Battle of Neville's Cross, 1346* (Stamford, 1998)

Roskell, John, Clark, Linda, and Rawcliffe, Carole (eds), *The History of Parliament: The House of Commons, 1386–1421* (Woodbridge, 1993)

Saul, Nigel, *For Honour and Fame: Chivalry in England, 1066–1500* (London, 2012)

Schnerb, Bertrand, *Jean Sans Peur* (Paris, 2005)

Soar, Hugh, *The Crooked Stick: A History of the Longbow* (Yardley, Pennsylvania, 2010)

Stevenson, Joseph (ed.), *Scalacronica* (Edinburgh, 1836)

Strickland, Matthew, and Hardy, Robert, *The Great Warbow* (Stroud, 2005)

Stouck, Mary-Ann (ed.), *Medieval Saints: A Reader* (Toronto, 1998)

Sumption, Jonathan, *The Hundred Years War*, Vol. I, *Trial by Battle* (London, 1999); *The Hundred Years War*, Vol. II, *Trial by Fire* (London, 2001); *The Hundred Years War*, Vol. III, *Divided Houses* (London, 2009); *The Hundred Years War*, Vol. IV, *Cursed Kings* (forthcoming).

Taylor, Craig, *Chivalry and Ideals of Knighthood in France during the Hundred Years War* (Cambridge, 2013)

Vale, Malcolm, *War and Chivalry* (Oxford, 1981)

Vaughan, Richard, *John the Fearless: The Growth of Burgundian Power* (London, 1966)

Villalon, Andrew, and Kagay, Donald, *The Hundred Years War, Part II: Different Vistas* (Leiden, 2008)

Acknowledgements

M Y IDEAS ON this famous battle have evolved over time and I would like to thank the many people who have given their support on this journey. I did my PhD thesis on the Hundred Years War at Bristol University, where James Sherborne taught me much about the logistics of medieval warfare and handling chronicle and documentary sources. When I began my research in France, Anne Curry provided valuable help over the archive collections there and subsequently gave valuable feedback on a series of articles I wrote on the war. Professor Curry's own work on Agincourt – both in assembling and translating source material – and her own ground-breaking research on the campaign and battle, form the foundation for all present studies of the battle. All who write on the subject are in her debt.

Dr Matthew Strickland generously shared his own chivalric understanding of late medieval battles. I have benefited considerably from Matthew's book, *The Great Warbow*, co-written with Robert Hardy, which forms the spine of much of my present interpretation. Professor Clifford Rogers also made an important contribution, sharing his own ideas with me, and his 2008 article on the battle forms another seminal work. And Professor Christopher Allmand discussed with me on many occasions both Henry V and Vegetius, the Roman military writer who profoundly influenced medieval battle strategy. And on matters of chivalry in general, I will always be grateful for the insights of Dr Maurice Keen.

I have led battlefield tours of Agincourt and Crécy for nearly 20 years. It was a real pleasure to have Bernard Cornwell on my first – and to discuss with him the battle and the Hundred Years War in general. And it was through tour guiding that I got to know and become friends with Sir Philip Preston. We used to present Crécy together *in situ* and then adjourn to the museum he set up for an overview of campaign and battle. My comments in the book on the creation of a killing ground in front of the Black Prince's division are all derived from the topographical and source evidence brought together by Sir Philip and Professor Andrew Ayton.

Dr Rowena Archer shared with me her ideas on the battle – particularly on the archers' protective stakes – and generously allowed me to draw upon the household accounts of John Mowbray, Earl of Norfolk, the marshal of Henry V's army, set out in her Oxford DPhil thesis. And I am also grateful to Drs David Grummitt and Malcolm Mercer for sharing their own insights about Henry V and chivalry with me and to Dr Matthew Bennett of Sandhurst for his understanding of medieval battle tactics. And it was a real pleasure to meet Juliet Barker at the Rye Conference on 25 October 2006. Juliet's exceptional books on *Agincourt* and *Conquest: The English Kingdom of France* bring the whole period alive and remind us that, whatever the dictates of military organisation and strategy, battles are fought by people.

I have enjoyed presenting my thoughts on the battle on Melvyn Bragg's *In Our Time* (on Radio 4, with Anne Curry and John Watts) and Channel 4's *Agincourt* (with Juliet Barker, Tobias Capwell and Craig Taylor), and talking to the students of Durham University history society. My ideas on the battle greatly benefited from a discussion there with Professor Michael Prestwich on medieval military leadership. And it has been a privilege to speak at the East Anglian branch of the

Battlefields Trust at Erpingham House, within walking distance of the church where that most distinguished Agincourt veteran, Sir Thomas Erpingham, constructed the great tower – spelling out his name and achievement for posterity.

I have modernised French place names with the exception of Azincourt (Agincourt) and Maisoncelle (Maisoncelles) and following convention, have also anglicised the Christian names of members of the House of Burgundy.

Research and writing on Agincourt will always continue. I am grateful to Dr Craig Taylor for his work on chivalry in late medieval France, Dr Catherine Nall for her study of reading and war in fifteenth-century England, Dr Ian Mortimer for his excellent new study of Henry V in the year 1415, Tobias Capwell, Curator of Arms and Armour at the Wallace Collection, and Bob Woosnam-Savage of the Royal Armouries, for the realities of late medieval armour, weaponry and battle wounding, Stephen Cooper for his work on the image of Agincourt through the ages and Peter Hoskins for all he has done charting the military itineraries of the Black Prince and Henry V. Other debts are acknowledged in the endnotes – and I am grateful to Geoffrey Wheeler for drawing the maps.

Finally, a big thank you to my agent, Charlie Viney, military historian Robert Kershaw, who conceived the idea for the *24 Hours* series, and Elen Jones and Ed Faulkner at WH Allen for giving me the chance to write about this extraordinary battle.

Index

('Henry' in subentries refers to Henry V of England)